高等学校工程管理专业规划教材

国际工程合同管理概论（双语）

Introduction of International Engineering Contract

李德智　刘亚臣　编著

中国建筑工业出版社

图书在版编目（CIP）数据

国际工程合同管理概论：英、汉/李德智，刘亚臣编著. —北京：中国建筑工业出版社，2019.2

高等学校工程管理专业规划教材

ISBN 978-7-112-23218-5

Ⅰ.①国… Ⅱ.①李… ②刘… Ⅲ.①对外承包-合同法-高等学校-教材-英、汉 Ⅳ.①D997.1

中国版本图书馆 CIP 数据核字（2019）第 017037 号

本书共由 12 章组成，主要包括国际建筑工程概述，建筑企业，工程合同的签约主体，招标投标，合同订立，国际工程标准合同文本，国际工程合同的主要条款，分包合同，合同变更，工程保险，索赔与反索赔和国际工程纠纷解决。

本书既可以作为高等学校工程管理专业、土木工程专业和法学专业的双语教材或教学参考书，也可用于学习工程管理专业的国际留学生"国际工程合同管理"课程用书。同时，本书可供政府建设主管部门、律师、工程咨询及监理单位、施工单位等有关工程管理人员工作和学习参考。

为更好地支持相应课程的教学，我们向采用本书作为教材的教师提供教学课件，有需要者可与出版社联系，邮箱：cabpcm@ 163.com。

* * *

责任编辑：张　晶　牟琳琳
责任校对：王　瑞

高等学校工程管理专业规划教材
国际工程合同管理概论（双语）
李德智　刘亚臣　编著

*

中国建筑工业出版社出版、发行（北京海淀三里河路 9 号）
各地新华书店、建筑书店经销
北京红光制版公司制版
北京同文印刷有限责任公司印刷

*

开本：787×1092 毫米　1/16　印张：13　字数：323 千字
2019 年 6 月第一版　　2019 年 6 月第一次印刷
定价：**32.00** 元（赠课件）
ISBN 978-7-112-23218-5
（33299）

前　　言

在国际工程实践中，合同管理是工程管理的核心。了解和掌握国际工程合同范本的内容与应用是工程管理人员的必备素质，也是工程管理的重要组成部分。目前，国际工程选择的主要合同范本大多是由美国、英国、FIDIC 组织和一些行业公司制定并推广使用的，主要包括 FIDIC，英国的 ICE，JCT，NEC 和美国的 AIA，AGC 等。

经营和管理好国际工程项目，要求工程管理人员熟练掌握国际工程合同的主体一般特征，合同的主要内容，权利义务约定中存在的主要问题，索赔程序，纠纷解决，以及合同的其他相关事项。只有深入研究和学习国际上各类具有代表性的工程合同文本，寻找其中的规律性，洞察合同条款中隐藏的深层次的含义，才能灵活运用合同中的各项约定，提高工程管理效率，保护合法权益。

本书根据国际工程实践中通用的适用于各类国际工程项目的合同文本，结合国内外在国际工程管理领域关注的问题，从国际工程合同主体、合同签订的程序、合同主要条款、分包合同，合同索赔，纠纷解决机制等方面存在的问题进行了探讨，构架了本书的基本内容。本书共由 12 章组成：第 1 章是建筑工程概述。介绍了建筑工程项目的含义，目标，种类，项目金融，工程合同等基础知识；第 2 章是建筑企业。主要探讨了承担建筑工程项目的主体的法定类型及其职责范围；第 3 章是工程合同的签约主体。主要探讨了各签约主体的法律地位以及各主体之间的法律关系；第 4 章是招标投标，主要讨论了国际工程招投标的法定程序，招标投标与要约承诺的关系，以及招标投标应注意的法律问题；第 5 章是合同订立，介绍并探讨了工程合同的订立过程中的步骤和表现形式，以及订立合同应注意的问题；第 6 章是国际工程标准合同文本，简要介绍了国际上广泛使用的 FIDIC，ICE，AIA 等合同文本的基本知识；第 7 章是国际工程合同的主要条款，分别介绍和讨论了支付条款、纠纷条款、违约赔偿金、工期条款、索赔条款和合同终止等主要条款；第 8 章是分包合同。分包商是承包商完成合同目的不可缺少的部分，分包也早已成为国际工程履行的一种常态管理方式，本章侧重探讨了承包商与分包商的法律关系与责任分担；第 9 章是合同变更。合同变更是国际工程合同中最为复杂的条款之一，本章主要介绍和探讨了国际工程变更的原因、程序和结果；第 10 章是工程保险，主要介绍工程保险的基本原则，建筑工程保险的种类及基本内容，以及雇主与承包商之间保险责任的分担；第 11 章是索赔与反索赔。索赔是国际工程合同的特有条款，也是国际工程合同管理的重要部分。本章介绍了国际工程索赔基础知识以及承包商和业主索赔的准备与程序；第 12 章是国际工程纠纷解决。这一章介绍了国际工程纠纷解决的各种形态及相关内容，着重探讨了可替代争议解决方法。

本书具有以下几个显著特点：①本书紧密结合国际工程管理的实践，对国际工程管理从合同约定的角度进行了讨论和梳理；②引用了国际工程合同标准范本 FIDIC，NEC，AIA 等合同条款对国际工程合同的原理进行了深入解读；③在写作过程中，为了适应中国学生阅读理解的需要，作者对书中缩写词和简写符号进行了解释，对疑难英语语句进行了简化。

目　　录

Chapter 1   The Construction Project Introduction

1. 1   The construction project and construction contract

1. 1. 1   What is construction project?

A project is defined, whether it is in construction or not, by the following characteristics:

(1) A defined goal or objective;

(2) Specific tasks to be performed;

(3) A defined beginning and end;

(4) Resources being consumed.

A construction project is the organized effort to construct a building or structure. In the fields of civil engineering and architecture, construction projects involve the process that consists of tangibly assembling an infrastructure or building.

Construction projects incorporate numerous mini-projects; a construction project is not a single activity. Larger scale construction projects require human multitasking; in most instances, these construction projects are managed by a project manager and supervised by a design engineer, or a construction engineer or a certified project architect which contractually authorized by the Employer.

The goal of construction project is to build something. What differentiate the construction industry from other industries is that its projects are large, built on-site, and generally unique. Time, money, labor, equipment, and, materials are all examples of the kinds of resources that are consumed by the project. Projects begin with a stated goal established by the Employer and accomplished by the project team. As the team begins to design, estimate, and plan out the project, the members learn more about the project than was known when the goal was first established. This often leads to a redefinition of the stated project goals.

In the modern world, the construction industry is the largest industry in the world. It is more of a service than a manufacturing industry. Growth in this industry in fact is an indicator of the economic conditions of a country. This is because the construction industry consumes a wide employment circle of labor. While the manufacturing industry exhibit high-quality products, timelines of service delivery, reasonable cost of service, and low failure rates, the construction industry, on the other hand, is generally the opposite, most projects exhibit cost overruns, time extensions, and conflicts among parties.

In general, the construction industry is more challenging than other industries due to its unique nature: every project is one-of a kind; many conflicting parties are involved; projects are constrained by time, money and quality; and high risk.

1.1.2 What is a construction contract?

A construction contract, for the purposes of this book, is a contract under which one party (commonly called the Contractor) agrees for valuable consideration to undertake to carry out works for another party (commonly called the Employer) involving design (where applicable), fabrication, erection, alteration, repair or demolition of structures and/or installations on a site. It covers a whole range of contracts i. e. from a simple oral agreement to repair a house roof to a mega highway contract. Such contracts are usually termed "building contracts" when they relate to infrastructure, systems and equipment installations. The distinction between these terms is of no legal significance, and indeed construction contracts as a class are regarded by China law, not as a separate category of contracts but a part of the general law of contract. In most cases, the parties to a construction contract are the Employer and the Contractor. However, in actual practice, in all likelihood, a construction project frequently involves a large number of participants who are contractually interlinked by a matrix of contractual arrangements. The roles of such contributors are discussed below.

International contract law concerns the legal rules relating to cross-border agreements. One key element of international contract law includes the provision that the parties' nationality does not play any role when applying the law, thereby placing all parties on an equal playing field. Rules of the contracts are interpreted by what a reasonable person would consider fair and appropriate given the circumstances. International contract law is a branch of private international law, which relates to the cross-border dealings of individuals or companies. This differs from public international law, which concerns the interaction between governments and other state agencies.

A contract is a legally enforceable agreement between two or more parties that creates a legal obligation between them. The rules related to contracts can vary substantially among different types of legal systems. In common law jurisdictions, for example, the participants in a contract are typically allowed a very wide scope concerning the terms of the agreement. In civil law jurisdictions, however, established legal principles are often applied to individual contracts. The most basic element of any contract is the mutual agreement between two parties to participate in an arrangement. Common law jurisdictions typically require consideration in a contract, meaning that both sides receive something of value as part of the contract. In civil law countries, however, consideration is not considered as a necessary component.

Historically, merchants developed their own sort of international contract law. Traders wanting to deal differences in language, culture and laws developed their own code for international dealings. These rules have evolved into the good faith of today's contract laws.

Large international construction projects often have a range of major contractors, sub-contractors and consultants in different parts of the world and working based on different legal theories and understandings. This can lead to confusion in the understanding, interpretation and execution of the construction contract, which can result in significant disruption to the construction project.

1. 2   The Project Goal and Scope

1. 2. 1   Project Goal

To achieve construction project goal, the Contractor or project manager must know what the employer want him to accomplish. Implementing a winning strategy starts with a scoreboard showing the targets the employer want him to hit. The Project manager must update it regularly and communicate results to every team member on an ongoing basis. At the completion of your projects, review and analyze the results of the works done to determine what could have improved.

1. 2. 2   Project scope

The documentation of a project's scope explains the boundaries of the project, establishes responsibilities for each team member and sets up procedures for how completed work will be verified and approved. The documentation may be referred to as a scope statement, statement of work or terms of reference. During the project, this documentation helps the project team remain focused and on task.

The scope statement also provides the project team leader or facilitator with guidelines for making decisions about change requests during the project. It is natural for parts of a large project to change along the way, so the better the project has been scoped at the beginning, the better the project team will be able to manage change. When documenting a project's scope, stakeholders should be as specific as possible in order to avoid scope creep, a situation in which one or more parts of a project ends up requiring more work, time or effort because of poor planning or miscommunication.

Effective scope management requires good communication to ensure that everyone on the team understands the scope of the project and agrees upon exactly how the project's goal will be met. As part of project scope management, the team leader should solicit approvals and sign-offs from the various stakeholders as the project proceeds, ensuring that the finished project, as proposed, meets everyone's needs.

1. 3   Construction categories

The field of construction is as diversified as the uses and forms of the many types of structures it produces. However, construction is commonly divided into four main categories, although there is some overlap among these divisions and certain projects do not fit neatly into any one of them.

1.3.1 Residential Housing Construction

Residential housing construction includes single-family houses, multi-family dwellings, and high-rise apartments. During the development and construction of such projects, the developers or sponsors who are familiar with the construction industry usually serve as Employers and take charge, making necessary contractual agreements for design and construction, and arranging the financing and sale of the completed structures. Residential housing designs are usually performed by architects and engineers, and the construction executed by builders who hire subcontractors for the structural, mechanical, electrical and other specialty work. An exception to this pattern is for single-family houses which may be designed by the builders as well.

The residential housing market is heavily affected by general economic conditions, tax laws, and the monetary and fiscal policies of the government. Often, a slight increase in total demand will cause a substantial investment in construction, since many housing projects can be started at different locations by different individuals and developers at the same time. Because of the relative ease of entry, at least at the lower end of the market, many new builders are attracted to the residential housing construction. Hence, this market is highly competitive, with potentially high risks as well as high rewards.

1.3.2 Institutional and Commercial Building Construction

Institutional and commercial building construction encompasses a great variety of project types and sizes, such as schools and universities, medical clinics and hospitals, recreational facilities and sports stadiums, retail chain stores and large shopping centers. The Employers of such buildings may or may not be familiar with construction industry practices, but they usually are able to select competent professional consultants and arrange the financing of the constructed facilities themselves.

1.3.3 Specialized Industrial Construction

Specialized industrial construction usually involves very large scale projects with a high degree of technological complexity, such as oil refineries, steel mills, chemical processing plants and coal-fired or nuclear power plants. The Employers usually are deeply involved in the development of a project, and prefer to work with designers-builders such that the total time for the completion of the project can be shortened. They also want to pick a team of designers and builders with whom the Employer has developed good working relations over the years.

Although the initiation of such projects is also affected by the state of the economy, long range demand forecasting is the most important factor since such projects are capital intensive and require considerable amount of planning and construction time. Governmental regulation such as the rulings of the Environmental Protection Agency and the Nuclear Regulatory Commission in the United States and other countries can also profoundly influence decisions on these projects.

1. 3. 4   Infrastructure and Heavy Construction

Infrastructure and heavy construction includes projects such as highways, mass transit systems, tunnels, bridges, pipelines, drainage systems and sewage treatment plants. Most of these projects are publicly owned and therefore financed either through bonds or taxes. This category of construction is characterized by a high degree of mechanization, which has gradually replaced some labor intensive operations.

The engineers and builders engaged in infrastructure construction are usually highly specialized since each segment of the market requires different types of skills. However, demands for different segments of infrastructure and heavy construction may shift with saturation in some segments. For example, as the available highway construction projects are declining, some heavy construction contractors quickly move their work force and equipment into the field of mining where jobs are available.

1. 4   Project Finance

Project finance is the financing of long-term infrastructure, industrial projects in which project debt and equity used to finance the project are paid back from the cash flow generated by the project. Project financing is a loan structure that relies primarily on the project's cash flow for repayment, with the project's assets, rights and interests held as secondary security or collateral. Project finance is especially attractive to the private sector because companies can fund major projects off balance sheet.

1. 4. 1   By Employer

The Employer makes the necessary financial arrangements for the construction of most construction projects. This normally requires obtaining the funding from some external source. In the case of public Employers, the necessary capital may be obtained via tax revenues, appropriations, or bonds. A large corporate firm may obtain the funds by the issurance of its own securities, such as bonds. For the average private Employer, funding is normally sought from one of several possible loan sources-banks, savings and loan associations, insurance companies, real estate, or government agencies.

Where construction funding is obtained by commercial loans, the Employer must typically arrange two kinds of financing (1) short-term, to pay the construction costs, and (2) a long term mortgage. The short term financing involves a construction loan and provides funds for land purchase and project construction. The construction loan usually extends only over the construction period and is granted by a lending institution with the expectation that it will be repaid at the completion of construction by some other loan such as the mortgage financing. The mortgage loan usually applies for an appreciable period such as 10 to 30 years.

When the construction loan has been approved, the lender sets up a "draw" schedule, which specifies the rate at which the lender will make payments to the contractor during the construction period. Typically, the short term construction loan is paid off by the mortgage lender when the construction is completed.

1.4.2   By Builder-vendor

A builder - vendor is a business entity that designs, builds and finances the construction of structures for sale to the general public. The most common example of such structures is tract housing, for which the builder-vendor acquires land and builds the housing units. This is a form of speculative construction, whereby the builder vendor act as their own prime contractors, build dwelling units on their own accounts, and employ sales forces to market their products. Hence, the ultimate Employer incurs no financial obligation until the structure is finished and a decision to buy is made.

In much construction of this type, the builder-vendor constructs for an unknown Employer. Most builder vendors function more as construction brokers than contractors per se, choosing to subcontract all or most of the actual construction work. The usual construction contract between Employer and prime contractor is not present in such cases because the builder-vendor occupies both roles. The source of business for the builder vendor is entirely self-generated, as opposed to that of the professional contractor that obtains its work in the open construction marketplace.

1.4.3   By Developer

A developer acquires financing for an Employer's project in two different ways. A comparatively recent development in the construction of large buildings for business corporations and public agencies is the concept of design finance. In this case, the Employer teams up with a developer firm that provides the Employer with a project design and a source of financing for the construction process. The procedure minimizes or eliminates altogether the initial capital investment of the Employer. Developers are invited to submit proposals to the Employer for the design and funding of a defined new structure. A contract is then negotiated with the developer of the Employer's choice. After the detailed design is completed, a construction contractor is selected and the structure is erected.

The second procedure used by developers is currently being applied to the design and construction of a wide range of commercial structures. Here, the developer not only arranges the project design and financing for the Employer but is also responsible for the construction process. Upon the completion of the project under either of the two procedures just discussed, the developer sells or leases the completed structure to the Employer.

1.5   Construction Contract Types

Although there are many different types of construction contracts, they can be divided into two large groups. One group includes those contracts for which the Employer selects a contractor based on competitive bidding, and the other includes those in which the Employer negotiates a contract directly with a contractor of the Employer's choosing. Many public construction contracts, as well as much private work, fall in the first category. Competitive bids contracts are customarily prepared on a fixed price basis and consist of two types, lump-sum and unit price. With a lump-sum contract, the cost amount is a fixed sum that covers all aspects of the work described by the contract documents. The unit price contract, the second of the two types, is drawn based on estimated quantities of specified work items and a unit price for each item. There are also a cost plus fee contract arrangement, whereby the Employer agrees to reimburse the contractor for the full a-mount of the construction cost and pay a stipulated fee for the contractor's services.

1. 5. 1   The Lump sum contract

A lump-sum contract is normally used in the construction industry to reduce design and contract administration costs. It is called a lump-sum because the contractor is re-quired to submit a total and global price instead of bidding on individual items. A lump-sum contract is the most recognized agreement form on simple and small projects and pro-jects with a well-defined scope or construction projects where the risk of different site con-ditions is minimal.

(1) Lump-Sum Contract Basics

A lump-sum contract or a stipulated sum contract will require that the supplier agrees to provide specified services for a stipulated or fixed price. In a lump-sum contract, the employer has essentially assigned all the risk to the contractor, who in turn can be expec-ted to ask for a higher markup in order to take care of unforeseen contingencies.

(2) When to Use This Type of Contract

A lump-sum contract is a great contract agreement to be used if the requested work is well-defined and construction drawings are completed. The lump-sum agreement will re-duce employer risk, and the contractor has greater control over profit expectations. It is also a preferred choice when stable soil conditions, complete pre-construction studies, and assessments are completed and the contractor has analyzed those documents.

(3) Lump-Sum Contract Advantages

A lump-sum contract offers the following advantages: (a) Low risk to the employer; (b) Fixed construction cost; (c) Minimize change orders; (d) employer supervision is reduced when compared to Time and Material Contract; (e) The contractor will try to complete the project faster; (f) Accepted widely as a contracting method; (g) Bidding a-nalysis and selection process is relatively easy; (h) The contractor will maximize its pro-duction and performance.

(4) Lump-Sum Contract Disadvantages

Although lump-sum contracts are the standard and preferred option for all contrac-tors, it might also have some limitations: (a) It presents the highest risk to the contrac-tor; (b) Changes are difficult to quantify; (c) The employer might reject change order requests; (d) The project needs to be designed completely before the commencement of activities; (e) The construction progress could take longer than other contracting alternatives; (f) The contractor will select its own means and methods; (g) Higher contract prices that could cover unforeseen conditions.

1.5.2   The unit price contract

A unit-price contract is based on estimated quantities of the defined items of work and costs per unit amount of each of these work items. The Employer or architect-engineer compiles the estimated quantities, and the unit costs are those bid by the contractor for carrying out the stipulated work in accordance with the contract documents. However the total sum of money paid to the contractor for each work item remains an indeterminable factor until completion of the project, because payment is made to the contractor based on units of work actually done and measured in the field. Therefore, the Employer does not know the exact ultimate cost of the construction until the completion of the project. In addition, the Employer often must support, either directly or through the architect – engineer, a field force for the measurement and determination of the true quantities of work accomplished.

The contractor is obligated to perform the quantities of work actually required in the field at the quoted unit prices, whether they are greater or less that the architect-engineer's estimates. This obligation is subject to any contract provision for redetermination of unit prices when substantial quantity deviations occur. This form of contract has the same requirement for contractor performance, regardless of the difficulties and problems encountered, as described in the previous section for lump-sum contracts.

Unit-price contracts offer the advantages of open competition on projects involving quantities of work that can not be accurately forecast at the time of bidding or negotiation. Examples of such work include the driving of piles and the excavating of foundations. A price per linear foot of pile or per cubic yard of excavation allows a reasonable variation in the driven length of the individual piles or the actual quantity of excavation because of job conditions that can not be determined precisely before actual construction operations. However, drawings and specifications that are complete enough for the contractor to access the overall magnitude of the project and the general nature and complexity of the work must be available for bidding.

1.5.3   Cost Plus contracts

Cost-plus contracts are normally negotiated between the Employer and the contractor. Most cost-plus contracts are open ended in the sense that the total construction cost to the Employer cannot be known until completion of the project. When the drawings and specifications are not complete at the time of contract negotiation, the Employer and contractor negotiate what is commonly called a scope contract. Based on preliminary drawings and outline specifications, the contract arrives at a project target estimate. The contract provides that the original contract documents will be subsequently amplified within the original intent of the preliminary drawings and specifications. When negotiating contracts of the cost-plus type, the contractor and the Employer must pay particular attention to four important considerations:

(1) A definite and mutually agreeable subcontract-letting procedure should be arranged. Both parties generally prefer competitively bid subcontracts when they are feasible.

(2) There must be a clearly understood agreement concerning the determination and payment of the contractor's fee. Fees may be determined in many different ways. Involved here is not only the amount of the fee, but also the method by which it will be paid to the contractor during the life of the contract. A statement concerning any variation of fee with changes in the work should be included.

(3) A common understanding regarding the accounting methods to be followed is essential. Many problems and controversies can be avoided by working out in advance the details of record keeping, purchasing, and the reimbursement procedure. Some Employer-clients have need of accurate and detailed cost information for tax, insurance purposes. Employer requirements of this type, made known at the beginning of the contract, enable the contractor to better serve the Employer.

☞ 疑难词句 ☜

1. However, in actual practice, in all likelihood, a construction project frequently involves a large number of participants who are contractually interlinked by a matrix of contractual arrangements. 然而，在实践中，在所有可能的情况下，一个建设项目往往涉及大量的参与者，这些参与者是由合同安排的矩阵下相互关联的。

2. Field crew and team leaders 现场团队和团队负责人

3. Employee retention 员工留任

4. On-the-job skills 在职技巧

5. Take a back seat 处于次要地位

6. Get down to 开始认真考虑

7. Deliverables and parameters 交付成果和参数

8. Scope creep 范围蔓延

9. Sign-offs 签署同意，签收

10. Pinning down 确定，使受约束

11. High-rise apartments 高层公寓

12. Recreational facilities 娱乐设施

13. Because of the relative ease of entry, at least at the lower end of the market, many new builders are attracted to the residential housing construction. 由于市场准入相对容易，至少在低端市场，许多新的建筑商被住宅建筑项目所吸引。

14. Mass transit systems 公共交通系统

15. Off balance sheet 资产负债表外，不上资产负债表的

16. Companies can fund major projects off balance sheet. 公司可以在资产负债表外为主要项目提供资金。

17. Tract housing 成片住宅建设

18. The ultimate Employer 最终所有者

19. Teams up with 与……合作，协作

20. The major differences between the various types of cost plus fee contracts lie in the provisions regarding the compensation of the contractor. 不同类型的成本加费用合同的主要区别在于承包商的赔偿条款。

21. Linear foot 纵尺，英尺

22. Cubic yard 立方码

23. The amount of overhead calculated under a lump-sum contract will vary from builder to builder，but it will be based on their risk assessment study and labor expertise. 根据一份总价合同计算的费用总额将因建造者不同而异，但它将基于风险评估研究和工作技能。

24. General overhead 一般间接费用

25. be tied to these target figures 受这些目标指数的约束

☞ **中文综述** ☜

1.1　国际工程与国际工程合同

1.1.1　国际工程的含义

国际工程一般包含以下几个因素：

（1）有明确的目标或范围；

（2）可执行的具体任务；

（3）确定的开始和结束日期；

（4）资源消耗；

（5）工程主体分属于不同国家或地区。

国际工程是一种综合性的国际经济合作形式，是国际技术贸易和国际劳务合作的具体表现。它是指个人或企业，在国际市场上通过投标、接受委托或其他途径承揽国际组织、外国政府或私人雇主的工程建设项目、物资采购及其他方面的承包业务，是一种涉及资金、技术、设备、劳务等多方面内容的综合性国际经济合作形式。它既包括一国对外工程公司已经承包施工的海外工程（Overseas Projects），也包括一国境内的国际性公开招标和管理的国内工程项目（Domestic Projects）。

国际工程一般有以下几个特点：

（1）国际工程分为国内和国外两个市场

国际工程既包括一国公司去海外参与投资或承包的各项工程，也包括国际组织和外国的公司在国内投资和实施的工程。

（2）国际工程包括咨询和承包两个领域❶

一是国际工程咨询：国际工程咨询活动贯穿于工程项目决策和实施过程，一般可以包

---

❶ 何伯森，《国际工程合同与合同管理（第二版）》，北京：中国建筑工业出版社，2010：2.

括：项目前期阶段的咨询业务、项目准备阶段的咨询、项目实施阶段的咨询、项目运营阶段的咨询。二是国际工程承包：国际工程承包：是指个人或企业，在国际承包市场上通过投标、接受委托或其他途径承揽国际组织、外国政府或私人雇主的工程建设项目、物资采购及其他方面的承包业务，是一种涉及资金、技术、设备、劳务等多方面内容的综合性国际经济合作形式。

（3）国际工程项目内容和程序复杂

国际工程涉及面广，程序复杂。例如，国际工程合同不仅在技术上涉及勘探、设计、建筑、施工、安装等，在经济上涉及商品贸易、资金信贷、技术转让、招标与投标、项目管理等，同时在法律上，国际工程合同既要遵循国际惯例，又要熟悉东道国法律、法规、税收政策等。

（4）国际工程营建时间长、投资大，风险高

国际工程项目，从招标投标到工程完成，需要经过很长的时间，一般在 1～5 年，有的项目期限更长；项目投资一般也在几百万美元以上，甚至高达几十亿美元。

（5）国际工程受政府政策影响较大

很多国际工程是涉及国计民生的国家投资建设的工程项目，例如铁路，高速公路，给水排水工程，环境工程等，这就需要政府政策的支持和特许，例如很多国际工程进行的前提条件是政府许可发放，减免税收政策出台等。

（6）国际工程履约具有连续性

国际工程承包履约具有渐进性和连续性，施工过程就是履约过程。在整个施工期间，合同各方依据合同约定履行自己的义务。合同验收合格后，承包商根据约定和当地法律的规定需要在一定时间内继续对建筑工程承担一定的质量责任。

1.1.2　国际工程合同的含义

国际工程合同就是国际工程的各参与方之间权利义务的约定。合同是双方或多方设立的法律上可执行的协议，合同内容涉及的权利的享有和义务的履行对合同各方有法律约束力。在普通法国家，合同各方在合同条款约定上有更广泛的空间，对违反约定的后果有更多的应对措施，对价（Consideration）被认定为合同的重要组成部分；而在大陆法系国家，颁布的成文法适用于个体合同，法官按照成文法或司法解释对合同纠纷进行处理，法官的自由裁量权受到限制，对价（Consideration）不被认定为合同的组成部分。

我国属于大陆法系国家，《合同法》第二百六十九条规定，建设工程合同是承包人进行工程建设，发包人支付价款的合同。住房和城乡建设部、国家工商行政管理总局制定的《建设工程施工合同（示范文本）》GF-2017-0201（以下简称《示范文本》）1.1.1.1 条规定："合同是指根据法律规定和合同当事人约定具有约束力的文件，构成合同的文件包括合同协议书、中标通知书（如果有）、投标函及其附录（如果有）、专用合同条款及其附件、通用合同条款、技术标准和要求、图纸、已标价工程量清单或预算书以及其他合同文件。"在实践中，"承包人"是指在建设工程合同中负责勘察、设计、施工任务的一方当事人；"发包人（雇主）"是指在建设工程合同中委托承包人进行勘察、设计、施工任务的建设单位。在建设工程合同中，承包人的最主要义务是勘察、设计、施工等工作；发包人的最主要义务是向承包人支付相应的价款。

不同国家的政府、商业组织、公司或个体之间达成的关于一方进行工程建设，另一方

支付价款并接收建成工程的建设合同被视为国际工程合同。国际工程合同因合同主体来自于不同的国家,协议的达成与履行大多受建筑标的所在国法律管辖,也可以由合同各方选择适用的法律。因此,即使合同各方的国籍不同,但在选择的法律面前一律平等,并受其约束。

1.2　国际工程的目标与范围

1.2.1　国际工程的目标

工程目标是工程项目所要达到的结果。工程实施的过程就是追求工程目标的过程。明确建设工程的目标对于投资人、承包商以及工程各方参与者都是至关重要的。建设工程的目标的实现过程作为一种沟通方式,使得所有工程利益相关者及项目管理成员明确各自的职责,在权利的实现程序,纠纷解决方式等众多事项上达成统一。

为了实现工程目标,承包商需要采取各种措施,包括但不限于选择经验丰富的项目经理和最佳项目管理组合进驻现场,认真研读工程合同和工程设计要求;组织分包商的招标投标活动,并根据主合同精神签订分包合同;明确工程施工中的各方权利义务,工程程序;对相关岗位员工进行培训。

1.2.2　国际工程项目范围

工程项目范围就是指把工程项目的主要交付成果划分为更小的、更容易管理的组成部分。工程项目范围以合同界定为依据,了解工程项目范围对于实现工程目标非常重要。高效的现场施工管理建立在有效的沟通上,这样可以确保工作团队每名员工了解工作范围,以及实现的手段。作为工程范围管理的一份,项目经理也应积极与雇主人员,工程师,以及其他相关者对工程完工部分进行的积极沟通,取得书面统一意见,为工程最终验收做准备。

1.3　国际工程分类

国际工程项目分类较为复杂,根据不同的标准,分类有所不同。各项分类亦有交叉,有重叠。按照自然属性,可分为建筑工程、土木工程和机电工程三类,涵盖房屋建筑工程、铁路工程、海洋石油工程、航天与航空工程、电子与通信工程和广播电影电视工程等。按照建设性质,可以分为新建工程、扩建工程、改建工程、迁建工程、恢复工程。按照投资作用,工程建设项目可分为生产性建设项目和非生产性建设工程。按照建设工程项目投资效益,可分为竞争性项目、基础性项目和公益性工程。综上各项分类,对建筑工程项目的自然属性,建设性质,投资作用,项目效益等进行统一归纳总结,下述四个类别基本涵盖建筑工程项目的所有类别。

1.3.1　居住类房屋建设

居住类房屋建设包含独体别墅,联体别处,高层或超高层公寓和低层公寓等。在这类建设项目发展过程中,开发商一般比较熟悉建筑市场,充当雇主角色,对工程设计、建设直接通过合同进行合理安排。通过招标投标,雇主选择设计师对建设项目进行设计,选择有实力和经验的承包商对项目进行建设。

1.3.2　机构和商业建设工程

机构和商业建设工程包含的工程项目类及其广泛,例如大学建设工程,医院建设工程，娱乐设施，体育场馆，商业广场，仓库，厂房等。在这类建筑工程中，投资方可能熟悉或者并不熟悉建筑工程管理，但是他们一般会挑选胜任的职业工程师对项目进行管理，聘任职业的金融咨询师完成项目的融资工作。

1.3.3 专业的工业建设工程

专业的工业建设工程通常包括有高技术内涵的大型建设项目，例如石油天然气工程、海洋石油工程、火电工程、水电工程、核工业工程等。在这类工程项目中，投资人或雇主一般深涉工程建设，在建设过程中积极地就项目技术问题、设计问题等与承包商进行沟通。

1.3.4 基础设施和重大建设工程

基础设施主要包括交通运输，机场，港口，桥梁，通信，水利及城市供排水供气，供电设施和提供无形产品或服务于科教文卫等部门所需的固定资产，它是一切企业、单位和居民生产经营工作和生活的共同的物质基础，是城市主体设施正常运行的保证。基础工程和重大建设工程项目一般由政府或 PPP 公私联营方式投资建设。这类项目专业性强，承接工程的承包商也都是在某个领域具有特殊技能的行业专家。

1.4 国际工程项目融资

1.4.1 国际工程项目融资含义

国际工程项目融资（Project Financing）是指国际贷款人向特定的工程项目提供协议融资，对于该项目所产生的现金流量享有偿付请求权，并以该项目资产作为附属担保的融资类型。国际工程项目融资的信用结构有三项要点：首先，国际贷款人的债权实现依赖于拟建工程项目未来可用于偿债的现金流量，即其偿债资金来源并不限于正常的项目税后利润；其次，国际项目融资要求以建设项目的资产权利作为项目运营和偿债的安全保证，它不同于以资产价值为抵押的普通担保；最后，国际项目融资通常需创造足以防范或分散各种项目风险的多重信用保障结构，包括借款人提供的有限担保、承包人提供的项目完工担保、项目关系人提供的现金流量缺额担保、项目产品用户提供的长期销售协议及政府机构提供的政府担保或承诺等。

国际工程项目融资一般以特定的建设项目为融资对象。同时，国际贷款人的债权实现依赖于拟建项目未来的现金流量以及该现金流量中可以合法用来偿债的净现值。正是基于这一特征，国际项目融资的贷款人在决定贷款前必须对项目未来的现金流量做出可靠的预测，并且须通过复杂的合同安排确保该现金流量将主要用于偿债。为了确保到期贷款偿付，国际项目融资通常以项目资产作为附属担保，但根据不同国家法律的许可，又可通过借款人或项目主办人提供有限信用担保。正因如此，国际工程项目融资具有融资额大、风险高、周期长、融资成本相对高的特点。

1.4.2 国际项目融资的参与者

每个国际工程项目的开发，都是一个多方参与的过程。就国际工程项目融资而言，主要有以下几个参与主体。

（1）项目发起人（Proiect Sponsors）。项目发起人是项目的实际投资者和真正主办人，可以是单独一家开发企业，也可由多个投资者组成联合体。

（2）项目公司（Proiect Company），即项目建设管理人。通常，项目公司由项目发起人出资，专门为该项目成立一个单一目的，具有独立法人资格的项目公司，作为借款人对外融资，参与项目投资和项目管理，并直接承担项目的债务责任和风险。

（3）贷款银行（Lending Bank）。贷款银行可以是单独一家金融机构，也可以是多家金融机构的联合体，这主要由贷款规模和项目风险等决定。在由多个金融机构联合提供融资时，往往需要设立一个经理银行（Manager）来管理贷款事务，其他为参与银行。

（4）产品购买者或设施使用者（Buyers or Users），即项目产品的销售对象。

（5）工程承包商（Contractors）。通常，承包商通过与项目公司签订承包合同，负责项目的设计和建设工作，并承担延期误工和工程质量不合格的风险。承包商的资金情况、工程技术能力及经营纪录，会影响贷款银行对项目建设期风险的判断。

（6）担保受托方（Security Trustee）。由于贷款银行主要以项目公司的资产及项目未来收益作为还款保证，因此为防止项目公司违约或转移资产，贷款银行一般都要求项目公司将其资产及收益账户交由一个具有信托资格的机构保管，这家机构被称为担保受托方。担保受托方一般由境内商业银行独家或境内、外商业银行联合担任。

（7）项目管理公司。是指项目建成后，负责项目经营管理的公司。项目管理公司的专业水平和经营业绩，可以在很大程度上影响贷款银行对项目经营期风险的判断。

（8）项目融资顾问，律师和税收顾问等。

1.5　国际工程合同的主要形式

国际工程合同是工程项目主体之间就权利义务达成的合意。其一般可以分为雇主或投资人通过招标投标选择承包商；或者雇主非经过招标投标程序，与自主选择的承包商签订协议。很多公共建筑项目采用公开招标的形式，雇主与中标的承包商签订协议。在实践中，国际工程合同一般分为以下几种形式。

1.5.1　总价合同

所谓总价合同，是指根据合同规定的工程施工内容和有关条件，雇主应付给承包商的款额是一个规定的金额，即明确的总价。总价合同也称作总价包干合同，即根据施工招标时的要求和条件，当施工内容和有关条件不发生变化时，雇主付给承包商的价款总额就不发生变化。总价合同又分固定总价合同和变动总价合同两种。

1. 固定总价合同

固定总价合同适用于以下情况：①工程量小、工期短、施工过程中环境因素变化小，工程条件稳定并合理；②工程设计详细，图纸完整、清楚，工程任务和范围明确；③工程结构和技术简单，风险小；④投标期相对宽裕，承包商可以有充足的时间详细考察现场、复核工程量，分析招标文件，拟定施工计划。

2. 变动总价合同

变动总价合同又称为可调总价合同，合同价格是以图纸及规定、规范为基础，按照时价进行计算。它是一种相对固定的价格，在合同执行过程中，由于通货膨胀等原因而使工程所使用的工、料成本增加时，可以按照合同约定对合同总价进行相应的调整。

1.5.2　单价合同

单价合同是承包人在投标时，按招标投标文件就分部分项工程所列出的工程量表确定各分项工程费用的合同类型。这类合同的适用范围比较宽，其风险可以得到合理的分摊，并且能鼓励承包商通过提高工效等手段节约成本，提高利润。这类合同能够成立的关键在于双方对单价和工程量技术方法的确认。在合同履行中需要注意的问题则是双方对实际工程量计量的确认。当施工发包的工程内容和工程量尚不能十分明确、具体地予以规定时，则可以采用单价合同（Unit Price Contract）形式，即根据计划工程内容和估算工程量，在合同中明确每项工程内容的单位价格（如每米、每平方米或者每立方米的价格），实际支付时则根据每一个子项的实际完成工程量乘以该子项的合同单价计算该项工作的应付工程款。

单价合同的特点是单价优先，例如 FIDIC 红皮书中，雇主给出的工程量清单表中的数字是参考数字，而实际工程款则按实际完成的工程量和合同中确定的单价计算。虽然在投标报价、评标以及签订合同中，人们常常注重总价格，但在工程款结算中单价优先，对于投标书中明显的数字计算错误，雇主有权先作修改再评标，当总价和单价的计算结果不一致时，以单价为准调整。由于单价合同允许随工程量变化而调整工程总价，雇主和承包商都不存在工程量方面的风险，因此对合同双方都比较公平。

采用单价合同对雇主的不足之处是，雇主需要安排专门人员来核实已经完成的工程量，需要在施工过程中花费不少精力。另外，用于计算应付工程款的实际工程量可能超过预测的工程量，即实际投资容易超过计划投资，对投资控制不利。单价合同又分为固定单价合同和变动单价合同。

1.5.3 成本加酬金合同

成本加酬金合同也称为成本补偿合同，这是与固定总价合同正好相反的合同类型，工程施工的最终合同价格将按照工程的实际成本再加上一定的酬金进行计算。在合同签订时，工程实际成本往往不能确定，只能确定酬金的取值比例或者计算原则。采用这种合同，承包商不承担任何价格变化或工程量变化的风险，这些风险主要由雇主承担，对雇主的投资控制很不利。而承包商则往往缺乏控制成本的积极性，常常不仅不愿意控制成本，甚至还会期望提高成本以提高自己的经济效益。所以，应该尽量避免采用这种合同。成本加酬金合同通常用于如下情况：

（1）工程特别复杂，工程技术、结构方案不能预先确定，或者尽管可以确定工程技术和结构方案，但是不可能进行竞争性的招标活动并以总价合同或单价合同的形式确定承包商的工程项目；

（2）时间紧迫，如抢险、救灾工程，来不及进行项目详细的计划和商谈。

Questions

1. How do you understand construction contract and international construction contract?

2. Describe the difference between the lump sum contract and a unit price contract?

3. Please discuss four main categories of construction industry?

Chapter 2   Construction Enterprises

The traditional forms of business ownership used by construction contractors are the individual proprietorship, the partnership and the corporation. Selection of the proper type depends on many considerations and is a matter deserving careful study. Each of business organization has its own legal, tax and financial implications that must be investigated and understood. Each type of organization has advantages and disadvantages and must be carefully evaluated in light of the individual context. The advice of a lawyer and a tax specialist is desirable when setting up a new business or when changing the form of a going concern.

2.1   The individual Proprietorship

The simplest business entity is the individual Proprietorship, also called sole ownership. It is the easiest and least expensive procedure for establishing and administering a business and enjoys a maximum degree of freedom from governmental regulations. No legal procedures are needed to going to business as a sole owner, with the exception of obtaining the required insurance, registration with appropriate tax authorities, and possible licensing as a contractor. The owner has the choice of operating under his or her own name or under a company name, in some jurisdictions a company name must be registered with a designated public authority.

The proprietor owns and operates the business, provides the capital, and furnishes all the necessary equipment and property. As the sole manager of the enterprise, the owner can make any and all decisions unilaterally and can act immediately. Title to property used in the business may be held in the name of the proprietor or in the name of the firm, if they differ. All business transactions and contracts are made in the owner's name. This mode of doing business offers many advantages, such as possible tax savings, simplicity of organization, and freedom of action.

As an individual proprietor, however, the owner is personally liable for all debts, obligations, and responsibilities of the business. This unlimited liability extends to personal assets even though they may not be directly involved in the business. Although management is immediate and direct, the owner alone must shoulder all of the burdens and responsibilities that accompany this function. A proprietorship has no continuity in the event of the death of the owner, unless there is a direction in the proprietor's will that the executor continue the business until it can be taken over by the person to whom the business is bequeathed. In the case of sickness or absence of the proprietor, the business may suffer severely unless there is a competent person available to take over. Entrepreneurs who form proprietorships can raise money for business purpose only through personal contribution, borrowing, or the sale of company assets. The owner must pay income taxes at normal individual rates on the full earnings of the business, whether or not such profits are actually withdrawn. Such earnings are added to income from other sources, and tax is computed on the whole.

2. 2   The general partnership

A general partnership is an unincorporated association of two or more persons who, as co-owners, carry on a business for mutual profit. The principal benefits to be gained by such a merger are the concentration of assets and personal credit, equipment, facilities, and individual talents into a company course of action. The pooling of financial resources results in the increased bonding capacity of the business, offering the possibility of a great scope and volume of construction operations than would be possible for the partners individually. Each general partner customarily makes a contribution of capital and shares in the management of business. Profits or losses are usually allocated in the same proportion as the distribution of ownership. If no such agreement is made in the articles of partnership, however, each partner receives an equal share of the profits or bears an equal share of the losses, regardless of the amount invested.

For most purposes a partnership is not recognized by the law as being an entity separate from the partners. For example, a partnership pays no income tax, although it must file an information return, but partners must pay annual income taxes at the normal individual rates on their salaries and on their allocated shares of the partnership profits.

A partner's share of the profits in a partnership can be assigned. However, an individual partner cannot sell or mortgage partnership assets. Nor can a partner sell, assign, or mortgage an interest in a functioning partnership without the consent of the other partners. Partners act as fiduciaries and, commensurately, have an obligation to act in good faith toward one another.

2. 2. 1   Establishing a Partnership

Laws regarding partnership are not completely standardized, although most states (USA) have adopted the Uniform Partnership Act. It is customary and advisable to draw up written articles of partnership. It is usual that articles of partnership, signed by the parties concerned, certain complete and explicit statements concerning the rights, responsibilities, and obligations of each partner. Although, such articles must be individually tailored for each specific case, the following list indicates the kinds of provisions typically included in partnership agreements. They are ①names and addresses of partners; ②business name of the partnership; ③name of the business, with any international thereof; ④ location of the business; ⑤date on which business operation will commence; ⑥contribution of each partnership in the front of capital, equipment, property, contracts, good will, service, and the like. ⑦division of responsibilities and duties between partners; ⑧any statement requiring partners full time attention to partnership affaires; ⑨division of ownership as it affects allocation of profits and losses; ⑩voting strength of each partner; ⑪ drawing accounts or salaries of the partners; ⑫any restriction of management authority of individual partner; ⑬specification of need for majority or unanimous decision on management questions; ⑭payment of expenses incurred by a partner in carrying out partnership duties; ⑮rental or other remuneration for use of a partner's own property or for personal services; ⑯arbitration of disputes between partners; ⑰record keeping and inventories; ⑱ right of each partner to full access to books and audits; ⑲rights and responsibilities of the individual partners upon dissolution; ⑳procedure in the event of an incapacitating disability of a partner. ; ㉑extraordinary power of surviving partners, such as option to purchase the interest of a deceased or withdrawing partner; ㉒provision for final accounting of business in the event of death, retirement, or incapacity of any partner; ㉓provision that an executor or spouse of a deceased partner continue as partner; ㉔termination date of the agreement, if any.

2.2.2 Liability of a general partner

The liability of a general partner for the debts of the partnership is based on two legal principles. First, each general partner is an agent of the partnership and can bind the other partners in the normal course of business without express authority. Second, partners are individually liable to creditors for the debts of the partnership.

As agency exists when one party, called the principal, authorizes another, called the agent, to act for the former in certain types of business or commercial transactions. An agency relationship exists by agreement, and an agent can be appointed by the principal to do any act the principal might lawfully do. The principal is liable for all contracts made by the agent while the agent is acting within the scope of his actual or apparent authority. The principal is also responsible for non-willful torts (civil wrongs) the agent commits in the furtherance of the principal's business. The general agent is one empowered to transact all of the business of his principal. Each full member of a partnership is a general agent of the partnership and has complete authority to make binding commitments, enter into contracts, and otherwise act for the other partners within the scope of the business. This is subject, of course, to any limitations set forth in the partnership agreement.

2.2.3 Dissolution of a partnership

One of the major weakness of the partnership form of business organization is it automatic dissolution upon the death of one of the partners. However, this weakness can be circumvented by making provision in the partnership agreement that the business will continue and that the supervising partners will purchase the decedent's interest. Dissolution may also be precipitated by bankruptcy. Dissolution is not a termination of the partnership but simply a restriction of the authority of the partners to those activities necessary for the conclusion of the business. It has no effect on the debts and obligations of the enterprise. Voluntary dissolution is often accomplished by a written agreement between the partners. This agreement provides that the partners will undertake to complete all contracts in progress, settle company affairs, and pay all partnership obligations from the proceeds and assets of the business.

In the settlement of the partnership debts, outside creditors enjoy a position of first priority. If partnership assets are insufficient to satisfy the outgoing obligations, the partners must been satisfied, partnership assets are used to repay any loans or advances that were made by partners above and beyond their capital contributions. If additional assets remain, these are treated as profits and are distributed accordingly. When construction contracts involving considerable time for their completion are involved, the clearing of partnership account is often subject to substantial delay pending payment of all debts, receipt of all accounts receivable, and discharge of all contract obligations of the partnership.

2. 3   The Limited Partnership

A general partner is a recognized member of the firm, is active in its management, and has unlimited liability to its creditors. In contrast, a limited partner is one who contributes cash or property to the business and commensurately shares in the profits and losses, but provides no services and has no voice or vote in matters of management. Unlike general partners, limited partners are liable for partnership debts only to the amount of their investments in the partnership. This is true, however, only as long as their names are not used as part of firm name and they do not participate in the management. Limited partners can be held fully liable if the true nature of their participation in the partnership has been withheld from creditors. The interest of a limited partner is assignable.

Under Partnership Enterprise Law (China), a limited partnership may be formed by two or more persons, at least one of whom must be a general partner. A contract is drawn up between the partners that clearly define their individual duties and financial obligations. In addition, a limited partnership certificate must be signed and filed with a designated public office. The operation of a limited partnership, as well as its establishment, must be in strict accordance with the laws of the state in which it is formed. The partnership is not automatically dissolved by the death of a limited partner, as in the case of a general partner.

2. 4   The Corporation

A corporation is an entity created by state law that is composed of one or more individuals united into one body under a special or corporate name, corporations have certain privileges and duties, enjoy the right of perpetual succession, and are regarded by the law as being separate and distinct from their owners. A corporation is authorized to do business, own and convey real and personal property, enter into contracts, and issue debts in its own name and on its own responsibility. It sues and is sued in its corporate name. the principal advantages of this form of business organization are the limited liability of its owners, and the corporation itself perpetual life of the company, the ease of raising capital, the easy provision for multiple ownership, and the economic benefit that owners pay taxes only on profits (dividends) actually received. In a corporation, unlike a partnership, the owners can also be employees.

A corporation is formed under state law by a prescribed number of shareholders filing a certificate of articles of incorporation with the appropriate governmental department. The corporation comes into being upon receipt of its corporate charter from the state of domicile. The powers of a corporation are limited to those enumerated in its charter and to those that are reasonably necessary to implement its declared purpose. The provisions of the corporate charter are usually made very broad so that the new corporation will be authorized to do many things that may become necessary or desirable in future years. These powers include the drawing up of bylaws pertaining to the day to day conduct of business. Acts of the corporation are governed and controlled by its articles of incorporation, its bylaws, and state law.

2.4.1　Shareholders

The ownership of a corporation in exercised through shares of stock that entitle the owners thereof to a portion of the business profits and the net assets on liquidation. This does not mean the shareholders own the corporate assets, because the corporation itself holds legal title to its own property. However, each share of stock does represent a share in the ownership of the corporation. Under the Company law of China, a single individual can own all the stock of a corporation, and the courts recognize a clear distinction between the individual and its corporation.

Stock ownership entitles the owner to participate and vote in annual meetings. These meetings are mandated by law and are to be scheduled each year. They are open to all shareholders. Shareholders do not participate in the day-to-day active management of a company unless they are corporate officers, managers or other employees who happen to own stock. Each year, a company produces an annual report detailing the financial condition of the company. The report lists the company's top managers and their compensation. The report also lists the top shareholders and summarizes corporate sales, earnings and important company events that occurred during the year, such as acquisitions. An annual report will also relate the company's plans for the future.

Shareholders can take legal action against a company's management or board if they believe the management has committed wrongful acts that could harm the corporation, or to prevent the management from acting in violation of the corporate charter. Small shareholders can bring up issues that concern them at annual shareholder meetings, nominate their own board candidates and solicit other stockholders' proxy votes. Some activists acquire small stakes in a company for the sole purpose of attending shareholder meetings to advance their agendas.

2.4.2 Corporate Directors and officers

The voting shareholders elect a board of directors that exercises general control over the business, determines the overall policies of the corporation. The directors must conduct the firm's affairs in accordance with its bylaws and are ultimately responsible to the stockholders. Directors have no authority to act individually for the corporation and are not agents of the corporation or of the shareholders. Their powers must be exercised only through the majority actions of the board. Directors occupy the position of fiduciaries and are required to serve the corporation's interests with prudence and reasonable care.

The president, vice president, secretary, and treasure are the corporate officers, normally appointed by the board of directors, who carry out the everyday administrative and management functions. The officers are empowered to act as agents for the corporation. The president is authorized to function for the firm in any proper way, including making contracts, whereas the lesser officers generally have more limited authority. Officers also serve in the capacity of fiduciaries and may be held personally liable for corporation losses caused by their neglect or misconduct.

2.5 The foreign corporations in China

A business corporation is created under the laws of a specific state and within that state is known as a domestic corporation, even though the investors are foreign registered corporations. The state of incorporation may be chosen not on the basis of location of work done by the company, but rather because of favorable corporation laws. The incorporated contractor that wishes to extend its operations beyond the borders of its state of incorporation must apply for and receive certification to do business as a corporation within each additional state.

2.5.1 The Wholly Foreign Owned Enterprise (WFOE)

The Wholly Foreign Owned Enterprise (WFOE) is a limited liability company wholly owned by the foreign investor (s). In China, WFOE is originally conceived for encouraged manufacturing activities that were either export orientated or introduced advanced technology. However, with China's entry into the WTO, these conditions were gradually abolished and the WFOE is increasingly being used for service providers such as a variety of consulting and management services, software development and trading as well.

The registered capital of a Wholly Foreign Owned Enterprise (WFOE) should be subscribed and contributed solely by the foreign investor (s). A WFOE does not include branches established in China by foreign enterprises and other foreign economic organizations. The Chinese Laws on WFOE do not have a clear definition of the term of " branches" . The term of " branches" should include both the branch companies engaged in operational activities and representative offices, which are generally not engaged in direct business activities. Therefore, branches and representative offices set up by foreign enterprises are not WFOE.

2.5.2　The Joint Venture

A joint venture (JV) is a form of foreign invested enterprise (FIE) that is created through a partnership between foreign and Chinese investors, who together share the profits, losses and management of the JV. As a foreign investor, there are two major reasons to create a JV, ①when entering a certain industry requires a local partner according to the restrictions outlined in the PRC Foreign Investment Industrial Guidance Catalogue, ② when a local partner is able to offer tangible benefits such as well established distribution channels, government relationships or significant knowledge of the local market.

There are two forms of Joint Venture partnerships between foreign and Chinese firms. The first of these is the EJV or Equity Joint Venture with limited liability and in which the foreign partner invests no less than 25% of the registered capital of the new entity. The second type of joint venture is the CJV or Cooperative Joint Venture, which itself has two versions, limited and unlimited liability, where the former does not require a new entity to be formed and where both parties both assume unlimited liability.

Joint-Ventures in China can either take an Equity Joint-Venture (EJV) structure or a Contractual Joint-Venture (CJV) structure. Equity Joint-Venture consists in a new company funded by two or more partners. Liabilities and profits are proportionate to the amount of money they have invested in the first place. The initial investment can take many different forms: pure cash, staff, factories, lands or even intellectual property or trademark.

Contractual Joint-Venture is a much more flexible structure, but this flexibility goes along with much more challenges. It basically reposes on a unique contract, regulating the whole relationship between the foreign and the Chinese partner. Liabilities and profits are distributed according to it, not according to equity shares. A CJV doesn't even need to be an independent structure but can just be a contract regulating relationships between two partners.

☞ 疑难词句 ☜

1. Executor 遗嘱执行人

2. Bonding capacity 胶合能力、结合能力

3. Tax withholding 预扣税款

4. Be bequeathed 遗赠、将……遗赠给

5. A competent person 称职人选

6. Drawing accounts 提存账户、预支佣金

7. Ruling out statutory requirements 除了法律上的规定

8. Civil wrongs 民事不法行为

9. Circumvent 避免、规避

10. Precipitate 促成

11. Promissory notes 本票、期票

12. Ratably 可估价地

13. Declared dividends 已经公告的分配股利

14. Preemptive right 股票优先购买权

15. To subscribe new stock issues 认购新股

16. In the furtherance of the principal's business 为了促进委托人的业务

17. Limited partners can be held fully liable if the true nature of their participation in the partnership has been withheld from creditors 只有当债权人掌握了其参与合伙管理的事实，有限合伙人才承担无限责任

18. Exert some control over 施加影响

19. Perpetual succession 永久存续

20. Limited partners can be held fully liable if the true nature of their participation in the partnership has been withheld from creditors. 如果有限合伙人参与合伙企业的真实性质不为债权人所知，则有限合伙人可负全责。

☞ 中文综述 ☜

在我国，承包商的传统企业形式是个体企业、合伙企业、全民企业、集体企业和公司企业。由于多年来我国对国有和集体所有制企业的公司制改造的不懈努力，加之我国相关法律法规对建筑资质等级的要求，目前承包商采纳的企业形式以公司制企业为主。对企业形式的选择的考虑因素有很多，每种企业形式有其优缺点，并有其自己的法律，税务和金融上的含义。

2.1 个人独资企业

个人独资企业是较为简单的企业组织形式，也是单独所有权企业。它的设立程序简单，费用低廉，规模小，因此个人独资企业较少地受到政府规章制度的关注。在美国，个人独资企业设立一般不需要法定程序，取而代之的是个人独资企业需要购买相关的保险，到当地税务机构进行登记，取得作为承包商的许可。在我国，个人独资企业设立要遵守《个人独资企业法》。《个人独资企业法》第八条规定："设立个人独资企业应当具备下列条件：（一）投资人为一个自然人；（二）有合法的企业名称；（三）有投资人申报的出资；（四）有固定的生产经营场所和必要的生产经营条件；（五）有必要的从业人员。"

根据我国相关法律规定，个人独资企业可以从事建筑或与建筑相关的产业，但是由于个人独资企业规模小，资金和技术有限，只能申请资质等级较低的许可。例如根据《建筑业企业资质管理规定》（中华人民共和国住房和城乡建设部令第 22 号）第八条规定："企业可以申请一项或多项建筑业企业资质"。第十一条规定："下列建筑业企业资质，由企业工商注册所在地设区的市人民政府住房和城乡建设主管部门许可：（一）施工总承包资质序列三级资质（不含铁路、通信工程施工总承包三级资质）；（二）专业承包资质序列三级

资质（不含铁路方面专业承包资质）及预拌混凝土、模板脚手架专业承包资质；（三）施工劳务资质；（四）燃气燃烧器具安装、维修企业资质。"

2.2 合 伙 企 业

合伙企业分为普通合伙与有限合伙。普通合伙是依法设立、由各合伙人订立合伙协议，共同出资、合伙经营、共享收益、共担风险，并对合伙企业债务承担无限连带责任的营利性组织。根据这一概念，合伙有如下特征：第一，合伙协议是合伙成立的前提条件，也是合伙存在的基础。与公司相比较，合伙有更紧密的人合性；第二，合伙人必须共同出资。所谓共同出资，就是各合伙人为了共同经营的需要，各自将自己拥有的资金、实物、技术、劳务等生产要素组合起来。合伙人的出资数额可以是均等的，也可以是不均等的。出资种类不限，既可以是实物形态的，如房屋、资金、设备、工具等；也可以是无形财产，如劳务、技术以及信誉。合伙出资构成合伙财产，各合伙人对合伙财产享有平等使用权，且合伙人的经营权利不因出资多少而不同。第三，合伙由合伙人合伙经营。合伙是一种共同经营、共同劳动的关系，在共同出资的前提下，各合伙人均应直接以自己的行为参与合伙经营，这是合伙在经营方式上的重要特征；第四，合伙人分享合伙利益，并对合伙债务负连带责任。合伙的利益分配方式依合伙协议执行，一般按出资比例划分，合伙期间如出现意外事故等风险，其所受损失由合伙人共同负担。合伙的对外债务由合伙人连带承担，即对合伙经营所欠之债，债权人可向任一合伙人追偿，而受追偿的合伙人不能拒绝，包括不得以自己的份额为由进行抗辩。

有限合伙是指一名以上普通合伙人与一名以上有限合伙人所组成的合伙，是介于合伙与有限责任公司之间的一种企业形式。与普通合伙相比较，有限合伙有如下特点和优势：第一，有限合伙中，普通合伙人执行合伙事务，有限合伙人不执行合伙事务，对外不代表有限合伙企业；第二，合伙中的普通合伙人对合伙企业承担无限责任，有限合伙人以其认缴的出资额为限承担有限责任；第三，有限合伙人可以按照合伙协议的约定向合伙人以外的人转让其在有限合伙企业中的财产份额，但应当提前三十日通知其他合伙人。有限合伙人退伙后，对基于其退伙前的原因发生的有限合伙企业债务，以其退伙时从有限合伙企业中取回的财产承担责任。

正因有限合伙的上述特征，使有限合伙具备其他企业组织形式不具备的优势：首先，有限合伙中的有限合伙人对合伙债务承担有限责任，有利于极大调动投资者的投资热情。其次，有限合伙有利于实现投资者与创业者的最佳组合，做到有钱的出钱，有力的出力。其三，从为投资者节约纳税的角度着眼，投资者采取有限合伙有利于避免双层征税。美国、德国等国家的税法均对公司和股东分别征税，公司要缴纳公司所得税，股东取得股利后还要缴纳个人所得税；而很多国家的税法只对从有限合伙取得投资回报的合伙人征收个人所得税，对合伙所得不征税。其四，有限合伙的经营活动比公司的经营活动更具有保密性。凡是公司，都要满足起码的信息披露制度要求，即公示要求。上市公司遵守的信息披露要求比起其他类型的公司来说更加严格。而根据《合伙企业法》的规定，合伙企业应当遵守的信息披露要求要比公司宽松得多，而且此种要求仅以满足合伙企业债权人和政府监管机构为限。有限合伙的这种保密性，对于有限合伙中的有限合伙人和普通合伙人当然具有吸引力。

根据《合伙企业法》和《建筑业企业资质管理规定》（中华人民共和国住房和城乡建设部令第 22 号）规定，普通合伙和有限合伙企业在取得建筑资质后也可以从事建筑商事活动。但是，从目前建筑市场企业组织形式分布看，与个人独资企业一样，合伙企业由于受企业规模限制，也只能取得资质较低的建筑许可，从事简单的建筑活动。

2.3 公 司

公司是指股东依照《公司法》的规定，以出资方式设立，股东以其认缴的出资额或认购的股份为限对公司承担责任，公司以其全部财产对公司债务承担责任的企业法人。公司有如下几个特征：第一，公司是依法成立的企业法人。与一般的法人组织不同，公司的设立具有特定的条件和程序。例如我国《公司法》第六条规定："设立公司，应当依法向公司登记机关申请设立登记。符合本法规定的设立条件的，由公司登记机关分别登记为有限责任公司或者股份有限公司；不符合本法规定的设立条件的，不得登记为有限责任公司或者股份有限公司。法律、行政法规规定设立公司必须报经批准的，应当在公司登记前依法办理批准手续。"只有满足这些条件和程序，公司才能成立。这体现了公司法的强制性要求。违反公司法对公司设立及行为的强制性要求，公司将不能成立或将受到法律的严惩；第二，公司有自己的章程。公司章程是指就公司组织及运行规范、对公司性质、宗旨、经营范围、组织机构、活动方式、权利义务分配等内容进行记载的基本文件。我国《公司法》规定："设立公司必须依法制定公司章程。公司章程对公司、股东、董事、监事、高级管理人员具有约束力。"从这一规定可以看出，章程是公司必备的重要法律文件，其效力范围不仅适用于公司股东，而且对于将来成立的公司以及公司的董事、监事、高级管理人员也具有约束力。国家有宪法，公司有章程，章程对于公司的作用有如宪法对于国家的作用；第三，公司拥有独立的财产。这种独立财产既是公司赖以进行业务经营的物质条件和经营条件，也是其承担财产义务和责任的物质保证。公司的财产主要由股东出资构成，公司的盈利积累或其他途径也是公司财产的来源。虽然公司财产主要是由股东出资构成，但一经出资给公司，所有权即归公司享有，而股东只享有股权。我国《公司法》第三条也明确规定，公司"有独立的法人财产，享有法人财产权"。同时公司拥有独立的财产还意味着公司能够履行适当的义务，可以承担与其独立财产相匹配的责任。因此说，公司拥有独立的财产，也就具有了对外承担责任的独立性。公司财产责任的独立性，保障了投资者的安全，因而大大地增强了公司在吸引资本方面的作用；第四，公司设有独立的组织机构。公司设有独立的组织机构是公司与合伙等非法人组织机构的确主要区别。公司的确组织机构主要包括股东会、董事会、经理和监事会；第五，公司有限责任。所谓公司有限责任是指公司以其所有财产对其债务承担责任，股东以其出资额为限对公司债务承担责任。有限责任公司的股东只以其认购的出资额为限对公司负债，对超过其出资额范围的公司债务不承担责任，公司的债权人不得直接向股东主张债权或请求清偿。公司以其全部财产对外承担责任，如果公司所有财产不能承担公司债务，公司也不得主张由股东来清偿。有限责任制度的存在在责任承担机制方面使公司与合伙、无限责任公司等其他经济组织形式严格区分开来，它是公司最重要最基本的特征；第六，公司股份的自由转让。股份自由转让制度，是现代公司制度最为成功的表现之一。正是凭着充分而有效的股份自由转让制度，新老投资者不断更替，资本市场不断拓展，公司运营所需资本源源不断地得到补充与供应，以资本为基础追求商业财富增长的现代市场经济才得以充满生机和活力。但股份的自由转让不是无限制的自由，而是满足一定条件下的自由转让。在这方面，有限责任公司股东股份或出资的转让要受到一定程序性限制。股份有限公司的股份可以自由转让、公司章程不得禁止当事人之间的股份转让；第七，公司永久存续。在英美法系国家和地区，公司具有法人人格，不仅意味着公司能够以自己的名义享有权利、履行义务并承担相应的法律责任，而且还意味着公司可以永久存续。在包括我国在内的大陆法系国家和地区，尽管大多未就公司的存续年限作出明确的限制性规定，但一般要求在公司章程中确定一个公司经营期限，从而使公司的存在期间具有了一定限制。公司的法人地位在经过确定的年限或完成了指明的商事活动时，并不自动终止，章程也不必周期性地更新。当然，永久存在并不意味着公司不能终止其存在，但是在执行有效的解散程序之前，公司作为法人可以继续存在下去。

根据《公司法》和《建筑业企业资质管理规定》（中华人民共和国住房和城乡建设部令第 22 号）规定，公司在取得建筑资质后可以从事建筑商事活动。从目前建筑市场企业组织形式分布看，公司是建筑承包市场的主要竞争者。

2.4　全民与集体所有制企业

全民所有制工业企业（以下简称"企业"）是依法自主经营、自负盈亏、独立核算的社会主义商品生产的经营单位。企业的财产属于全民所有，国家依照所有权和经营权分离的原则授予企业经营管理。企业对国家授予其经营管理的财产享有占有、使用和依法处分的权利。

全民所有制企业依法取得法人资格，以国家授予其经营管理的财产承担民事责任。

集体所有制企业是指以生产资料的劳动群众集体所有制为基础的、独立的商品经济组织。集体所有制企业分为城镇集体所有制企业和乡村集体所有制企业。城镇集体所有制企业，按照《城镇企业条例》规定，是指财产属于劳动群众集体所有，实行共同劳动。在分配方式上以按劳分配为主体的社会主义经济组织。它包括城镇的各种行业、各种组织形式的集体所有制企业。乡村集体所有制企业，按照《乡村企业条例》规定，是指由乡（含镇）村（含村民小组）农民集体举办的企业。实际上就是泛称乡镇集体企业，它包括除农业生产合作社、农村供销合作社、农村信用合作社以外的所有由乡村农民集体举办的企业。乡村集体所有制企业，依其性质，为我国社会主义公有制经济的组成部分。

2.5　外商投资建筑业企业在中国

根据我国相关法律规定，外商投资建筑企业，在取得我国建筑资质证书后，可以在中国境内从事建筑产业。

根据建设部、对外贸易经济合作部《外商投资建筑业企业管理规定》（部令第 113 号）、建设部、商务部《〈外商投资建筑业企业管理规定〉的补充规定》（部令第 121 号）、建设部《关于印发〈建设部关于外商投资建筑业企业管理规定中有关资质管理的实施办法〉的通知》（建市［2003］73 号）、《关于做好在中国境内承包工程的外国企业资质管理有关工作的通知》（建市［2003］193 号）等文件规定，对外商投资建筑业企业的管理主要包括：

1. 关于外商投资建筑业企业的申请与审批

（1）外商投资建筑业企业，是指根据中国法律、法规的规定，在中华人民共和国境内投资设立的外资建筑业企业、中外合资经营建筑业企业以及中外合作经营建筑业企业。

（2）设立外商投资建筑业企业，并从事建筑活动，应当依法取得国务院商务行政主管部门颁发的外商投资企业批准证书，在国家工商行政管理总局或者其授权的地方工商行政管理局注册登记，并取得建设行政主管部门颁发的建筑业企业资质证书。

（3）省商务行政主管部门在授权范围内负责外商投资建筑业企业设立的管理工作；省建设行政主管部门负责本行政区域内外商投资建筑业企业资质的管理工作。

（4）外商投资建筑业企业设立与资质的申请与审批，实行分级、分类管理。

申请设立施工总承包序列特级和一级、专业承包序列一级资质外商投资建筑业企业的，其设立由国务院商务行政主管部门审批，其资质由国务院建设行政主管部门审批；申请设立施工总承包序列和专业承包序列二级及二级以下、劳务分包序列资质的，其设立由省政府商务行政主管部门审批，其资质由省政府建设行政主管部门审批。

2. 关于外商投资建筑业企业资质的过渡问题

根据《外商投资建筑业企业管理规定》，外国企业必须取得建筑业企业资质证书后方可在中国境内承包工程。该管理规定第六条规定：外商投资建筑业企业设立与资质的申请和审批，实行分级、分类管理。申请设立施工总承包序列特级和一级、专业承包序列一级资质外商投资建筑业企业的，其设立由国务院对外贸易经济行政主管部门审批，其资质由国务院建设行政主管部门审批；申请设立施工总承包序列和专业承包序列二级及二级以下、劳务分包序列资质的，其设立由省、自治区、直辖市人民政府对外贸易经济行政主管部门审批，其资质由省、自治区、直辖市人民政府建设行政主管部门审批。中外合资经营建筑业企业、中外合作经营建筑业企业的中方投资者为中央管理企业的，其设立由国务院对外贸易经济行政主管部门审批，其资质由国务院建设行政主管部门审批。

3. 外国企业申请办理《资质证》，须向审查机关提交下列文件和资料：

（1）企业法人代表签署的在中国境内承包工程申请书；

（2）企业原注册国主管机关出具的企业营业证书（正本或复印件）；

（3）企业近三年的资产负债表；原注册国或其他国会计事务所或银行、金融机构出具的企业资信证明；

（4）企业近五年承包过的有代表性工程的名称、规模、地点以及发包方对工期、质量、服务的评价资料；

（5）企业派驻中国境内从事承包工程活动的负责人和主要技术负责人的简历以及技术人员名单；

（6）企业拟在中国境内从事承包工程活动的专业和地域范围；

（7）企业在中国境内承包工程活动办事机构的地点。

4. 外商建筑企业只允许在其资质等级许可的范围内承包下列工程：

（1）全部由外国投资、外国赠款、外国投资及赠款建设的工程；

（2）有国际金融机构资助并通过根据贷款条款进行的国际招标授予的建设项目；

（3）外资等于或者超过50%的中外联合建设项目，以及外资少于50%但因技术困难而不能由中国建筑企业独立实施，经省、自治区、直辖市人民政府建设行政主管部门批准的中外联合建设项目；

（4）由中国投资，但因技术困难而不能由中国建筑企业独立实施的建设项目，经省、自治区、直辖市人民政府建设行政主管部门批准，可以由中外建筑企业联合承揽。

Questions

1. What are the basic advantages of ①sole proprietorship；②a partnership and ③a corporation.

2. The form of business ownership impacts the taxes，liability and finance of a construction company. Describe how these vary between a partnership and a corporation.

3. Large international construction projects are often done by Joint venture enterprise. What are the advantages and disadvantages of this type of organization?

Chapter 3　The Contract Parties

3. 1　Participants in a construction contract

A construction contract is made between two parties only "the Employer" and "the Contractor". Their roles are defined in the contract. However, because there is a need for day-to-day supervision of civil engineering construction, the two parties may agree that a third person should carry out such duties. This third person can have varying powers under the contract and this is reflected in his designation. It is defined in FIDIC as Engineer and in AIA as Architect.

The employer, referred to as 'the purchaser' in some conditions of contract, initiates the process of acquiring the works. He sets down what he requires and specifies this in the tender documents, which he issues to firms of contractors to seek their offers to carry out the works. His obligations include ensuring that the works are legally acceptable and practical, and that the site for them is freely available. He may also need to arrange that associated needs, such as the supply of power, drainage and the like which he is providing, are available. If any dispute remains unresolved under the contract, the employer must decide what action to take; either to negotiate some settlement or, perhaps, take the dispute to negotiation, arbitration or the courts.

The contractor takes on the obligation to construct the works. In his offer to the employer he puts himself forward as being able to build the works to the requirements set out in the tender documents. In order to do this he will have studied the documents and any geotechnical or other information provided or otherwise available, visited the site and checked the availability of such labour, plant and materials as may be needed. Once his offer is accepted and the contract is formed the contractor takes on the obligation of doing all and anything needed to complete the works in accordance with the contract, regardless of difficulties he may encounter. He is responsible for all work done by his sub-contractors and suppliers, and any design work the contract requires him to undertake.

The Architect/Engineer designated in the traditional form of contract under the ICE or FIDIC conditions described in Sections 4. 2 (a) and 4. 3, has a role independent of the employer and the contractor. He is not a party to the contract; but he is named in it with duties determined by the parties. Although he is appointed (and paid) by the employer, he has to supervise the construction of the works as an independent person, making sure they accord with the specified requirements. He also acts as an independent valuer of what should be paid to the contractor, and as a decider of issues arising in the course of construction.

The engineer will normally be an experienced and qualified professional whose knowledge and standing should be sufficient to assure both employer and contractor that the decisions he makes are likely to be satisfactory, and given independently and impartially.

3. 1. 1 The Employer

The employer, as well as called owner in the USA construction field, which it means the person named as employer in the Appendix to Tender and the legal successors in title to this person under the Red Book 1999 FIDIC, in another words, the Employer is the public or private instigating party for whose purpose the construction project is designed and built. Public employers range from agencies of the central government, through province, city and municipal entities, to a multiplicity of local boards, commissions, and authorities. Public projects are paid for by appropriations, bonds, tax levies, or other forms of financing and are built to meet some defined public need. Public employers must proceed in accordance with applicable statutes and administrative directives pertaining to the advertising for bids, bidding procedures, construction contracts, contract administration, and other matters relating to the design and construction process.

The key public employers for the UK construction industry are:

(1) Central government department, who are responsible for their own programme of construction on projects.

(2) Local authorities, who are responsible for the provision of housing, school, libraries, swimming pool, halls, sports centers and the like.

(3) Some health authorities, which are responsible for hospital buildings.

(4) Public corporations (e. g. British Rail and Air Transport boards), who are responsible for the provision of buildings and other construction products for their own use.

Private employer may be individuals, partnerships, corporations or various combinations thereof. Most private employers have structures built for their own use: business, habitation, pleasure, or otherwise. However, some private employers do not intend to become the end users. The completed structure is to be sold, leased or rent to others.

The private sector employers for the construction industry are many and may be classified as follows:

(1) Multi-national companies (e. g. Ford, Huawei, Mcdonald's, ICI and Esso) who construct factories, production plants, offices and distribution depots for their own use.

(2) National companies (e. g. Tesco, Sainsbury's and Woolworth's) who construct buildings for their own use in warehousing and retail.

(3) Local property development companies, who construct offices, factories, shops and houses speculatively for hire, lease or sale.

(4) Private employers, who construct new buildings, or extent, refurbish or repair the existing building for own occupation, letting, leasing or sale.

3. 1. 2　The contractor

The contractor, also known as the prime contractor or general contractor, is the business firm that is in contract with the employer for the construction of the project, either in its entirety or for some specialized portion thereof. The contractor is the party that brings together all of the diverse elements and inputs of the construction process into a single, coordinated efforts.

The essential function of the contractor is close management control of construction. Ordinarily, this contractor is in complete and sole charge of the field operations, including the procurement and provision of necessary construction materials and equipment. The chief contribution of the contractor to the construction process is the ability to marshal and allocate the resource of labor, equipment, and materials to the project in order to achieve completion at maximum efficiency of time and cost. A construction project presents the contractor with many difficult management problems. The skill with which these problems are met determines, in large measure, how favorably the contractor's efforts serve its own interests as well as those of the project employer.

3. 1. 3　Architect/Engineer

Traditionally, the design function in the construction process is the responsibility of an Engineer/Architect who is a professionally qualified person whose role is to interpret the client's project requirements into a specific design or scheme. Design is taken to include appearance composition, proportion, structure, function and economy of product, but in addition the Engineer/Architect performs the function of obtaining planning permission for the scheme. In most times, too, the Engineer/Architect supervises and organizes the entire construction process, starting with consulting with the client and ending with commissioning. As an established practice, the Engineer/Architect plays the leading role in the construction process. He or she collects, coordinates, controls and disseminates project information to all project participants. As a project team supervisor, the Engineer/Architect performs various functions in all stages of construction process, which includes:

(1) Ascertaining, interpreting and formulating the client's requirement into an understandable project brief.

(2) Designing a building to meet the client's requirement and constraints imposed by such factors as statutory obligations, technical feasibility, environmental standards, site conditions and cost.

(3) Bringing together a team of construction professionals such as the quantity surveyor, structural engineer and service engineer to give expert guidance on specific points of the client's construction project.

(4) Assessing client's cost limit and timescale, and specifying the type and grade of materials/components for use on the construction project.

(5) Preparing production information for pricing and construction and inviting tenders from building contractors.

(6) Supervising the construction on site, constantly keeping client informed of the project's progress and issuing production instructions as and when required.

(7) Keeping the client informed of the status of the project's cost and advising on when payment should be made or withheld.

(8) Advising on the conduct of the project generally and resolving all contractual disputes between client and the building contractor.

(9) Issuing the certificate of completion, the certificate of making good defects and the final certificate for payment.

Generally, the Engineer/Architect acts as an agent for all purposes relating to designing, obtaining tenders for and superintending the construction work for whish he or she has been commissioned. To be able to perform above function efficiently, the Engineer/Architect must process, among other things, the attributes of foresight, an understanding of construction materials, communicating and coordinating abilities, essential design skills and an ability to design within a set budget.

In Red book (1999), FIDIC define the Engineer as the person appointed by the Employer to act as the Engineer for the purposes of the Contract and named in the Appendix to Tender, or other person appointed from time to time by the Employer and noted to the Contractor under Sub-Clause 3.4. Under the FIDIC conditions (1999), the engineer has significant role in the process of construction contract administration. In general he can act as agent of the employer. But his role is not restricted to agency relationships. At the same time he is acting as independent arbitrator in the relations between the employer and the contractor.

The position of the engineer is also defined same as well in China "Construction Contract for Construction Projects". (GF-2013-0201).

3.1.4   The subcontractor

Building construction is a common example of how the contractor-subcontractor relationship works. Before offering the bid or before contract negotiations begin, the contractor normally asks the subcontractors to estimate the price they will charge to do their part of the work. Thus, the contractor will collect information from electricians, plumbers, dry wall installers, and a host of other subcontractors. Once construction begins, the contractor coordinates the construction schedule, making sure the subcontractors are at the building site when needed so that the project remains on schedule. The sequencing of construction and the supervision of the work that the subcontractors perform are key roles for the contractor.

Subcontractors sign contracts with the contractor that typically incorporates the agreement between the contractor and the employer. A subcontractor who fails to complete work on time or whose work is not acceptable under the general contract may be required to pay damages if the project is delayed because of these problems.

A subcontractor's biggest concern is getting paid promptly for the work and materials provided to the project. The contractor is under an obligation to pay the subcontractors any sums due unless the contract states otherwise. Some contracts state that the subcontractors will not be paid until the contractor is paid by the employer. If the employer refuses to pay the contractor for work a subcontractor has performed, the subcontractor has the right to file a mechanic's lien against the property for the cost of the unpaid work.

3. 2　Rights and responsibilities of the Employer

Under the FIDIC Conditions of Contract, the developer (Employer) of a project will have taken a number of specific actions before reaching the stage where he is involved in the role of employer. He will already have received professional advice and have taken a number of decisions in connection with the following:

(1) The choice of professional advisers for the planning, engineering and other aspects of the construction project;

(2) The most suitable contractual arrangements for the employment of these professional advisers;

(3) The design of the project, the site, assessment of budget costs, choice of financial arrangements and any services which must be obtained to permit construction to start on site;

(4) The most appropriate procurement and contractual arrangements for the purpose of constructing the project;

(5) The criteria to be adopted for selecting the contractor who will be responsible for construction of the project;

(6) The most appropriate arrangements for the day-to-day control over the quality of the construction and final completion of the project;

(7) The manner in which any legislative or governmental approvals are to be obtained;

(8) The relevant information required in respect of the various clauses of the conditions of contract chosen to govern the construction of the works.

3. 3　The rights and responsibilities of the Contractor

3. 3. 1　Introduction

Generally, a building contractor is supposed to supervise, inspect, and direct a construction project from start to finish regardless of the project scope. The contractor is expected to apply the relevant skills and expertise to ensure success during the project development process as specified by the contract documents. In a typical building and construction project, all the three main parties — that is the project employer, the building engineer, and the building contractor — involved in the project have specific roles and responsibilities, which are all crucial to the achievement of project success. The building contractor ensures that the entire project complies with all the specifications as outlined in the contract documents.

3.3.2   The contractor's obligations during the tendering stage

Prior to submitting the bid, the contractor shall be deemed to have:

(1) inspected the site and its surroundings;

(2) inspected any information available in connection with the site;

(3) received and interpreted data on hydrological and sub-surface conditions obtained by or on behalf of the employer;

(4) satisfied himself (so far as is practicable, within financial and time constraints) as to:

a. the form and nature of the site, including the sub-surface conditions;

b. the hydrological and climatic conditions;

c. the extent and nature of work and materials necessary for the execution and completion of the works and the remedying of any defects in these works, the means of access to the site and the accommodation he may require;

(5) obtained, in general, all necessary information as to risks, contingencies and all other circumstances which may influence or affect his tender;

(6) based his tender on the data made available by the employer and on his own inspection and examination; and

(7) satisfied himself as to the correctness and sufficiency of his tender to cover all his obligations and all matters for the proper execution and completion of the works and the remedying of any defects therein.

3.3.3   The contractor's obligations during the construction stage up to substantial completion

The letter of acceptance, as the formal acceptance by the employer of the tender, forms the contract between the employer and the contractor. In some jurisdictions, the date of the contract is the date of receipt of this letter whilst in others it is the date of transmission. Within the specified period of time, the engineer should issue to the contractor the notice to commence the works.

The time lag between the issue of the letter of acceptance and the notice to commence is an important period during which many activities should take place. For the employer, this period should be utilized to ensure that possession of the site and access to it can take place and that all the necessary legal and financial matters are processed. For the contractor, this period should be utilized in initiating mobilization formalities; finalizing commitments with suppliers and sub-contractors; finalizing arrangements for securities and insurances; arranging the work programme; and finalizing estimates of cash flow requirements and details of the breakdown of lump sum items.

3.3.4   Contractor's obligations after substantial completion of the works

After substantial completion, the contractor has the obligation to complete the works and execute any outstanding work and remedy defects. According to the clauses of FIDIC, the contractor's obligations after substantial completion of the works are:

(1) Site clearance: the contractor, upon the issue of the taking-over certificate, is required to clear away and leave clean that part of the site to which such taking-over certificate relates. He is, however, permitted to retain on site certain items which are required by him for the purpose of fulfilling his obligations during the defects liability period.

(2) Defects: if any defect, shrinkage or other fault appears, the contractor is required, if instructed by the engineer, to search under the directions of the engineer for the cause. The contractor is also required to remedy any defects and faults for which he is found to be liable.

(3) Statement of completion: The contractor should submit a detailed statement at completion within 84 days after the issue of the taking-over certificate in respect of the whole of the works.

(4) Draft of final statement: The contractor, within 56 days after the issue of the defects liability certificate, should submit to the engineer, for his consideration, a draft final statement with supporting documents.

(5) Further information: In the event that the engineer disagrees with or cannot verify any part of the draft final statement, the contractor should submit such further information as the engineer may reasonably require. He should also prepare and submit the final statement.

3.4   The role of the Engineer

It is evident from the FIDIC clauses that the role of the engineer is central to the construction contract. Indeed, the engineer has many, sometimes what appear to be conflicting roles.

The concept of engaging a consulting engineer for any of the tasks detailed stems from the idea that when a promoter initiates a construction project he is faced with a multiplicity of technical, commercial and legal considerations with which he is not familiar, or at least in which he is not an expert. In civil engineering construction, in order to transform the promoter's ideas into reality, the traditional method, and also the method adopted by FIDIC, has been to engage the services of a consulting engineer to carry out the following functions:

(1) To complete a skillful design of the project sought by the promoter. Such design includes, but is not limited to, the preparation of drawings which should express and communicate the details of every aspect of the project to be constructed; to draft a specification of the materials to be used and of the standard of the workmanship to be achieved; and to prepare the bill of quantities;

(2) To prepare all documents necessary for obtaining a competitive price for carrying

out the work by a competent contractor and to advise the promoter on the tenders received and on the selection of the contractor;

(3) Once work starts on the project, to supervise or to inspect the work carried out by the contractor in order to ensure conformity with the design requirements; and

(4) To administer the contract, to deal with situations as they arise, to certify and to act as an adjudicator of disputes.

In New Zealand, the engineer is a person appointed under clause 6 of NZS 3910: 2013❶. The engineer must be suitably qualified and a natural person (rather than a company or firm). He or she is appointed by the principal and has two key functions: agent for the principal; and an impartial quasi-judicial decision maker.

☞ **疑难词句** ☜

1. To abide by 遵守，承担后果

2. The repercussions of breaking the pact 破坏约定的影响

3. Have evolved into 发展成为

4. Quality assurance system 质量保证体系

5. Most employers relegate by contract the design of their projects to professional architect-engineer firms 大多数雇主将设计任务通过协议提交给设计公司来完成

6. To marshal and allocate the resource of labor, equipment, and materials to the project in order to achieve completion at maximum efficiency of time and cost 管理和分配项目上的人力资源、设备和材料，以实现时间和成本上的最大效率。

7. A mechanic's lien 设备留置

8. A local authority may enter into contracts inclusive of construction contracts necessary for the discharge of any of its functions 地方政府可以签订合同，包括必要的建筑合同，来履行它的职责

9. Standing orders 现行命令

10. Save for particular requirements 作为特殊的要求

11. Ostensible authority 名义代理权

12. Parole 口头，诺言

13. Falling within 属于，适合于

14. Performance Security 履约担保

15. Advance payment 预付款

16. Mobilization（项目）启动

17. Emanate from 源自于，出自

---

❶ NZS 3910: 2013 means Conditions of contract for building and civil engineering construction, published on 1 October 2013. It is the first revision in 10 years of the form of contract most commonly used for building and civil engineering construction contracts in New Zealand. Although a limited revision, this edition includes significant changes and improvements in the content and presentation of this well-known document that will affect all users.

18. To facilitate 帮助，促进

19. Project cycle 项目周期

20. Hydrological and sub-surface conditions 水文和地表下条件

21. Finalizing 最后确定

22. Be fleshed out 具体化

☞ 中文综述 ☜

3.1 国际工程合同的主要参与者

国际工程合同的参与者即是与工程利益相关的个人、企业、组织或政府。这些参与者之间通过合同链接的形式形成紧密的，半紧密的和松散的合作关系。在这个合作链条中，处于核心地位的参与者是雇主与承包商以及雇主与承包商在履行合同义务过程中不可或缺的分包商和工程师。除此之外，国际工程合同的参与者还包括供应商，职业设计公司，政府，律师，会计师，金融机构，消费者等等。国际工程合同参与者应具有民事权利能力和民事行为能力，能够享有合同权利、并有能力承担合同义务。根据 FIDIC 新红皮书的规定，工程施工合同包括以下主要参与者：

3.1.1 雇主

雇主（the Employer 或 the Owner）也称为发包人或发包方，是指工程项目的所有者和拥有者以及其财产的合法继承人。雇主在美国大多称之为"the Owner"或者"Building Owner"，具有对其工程使用的土地和对地上建筑物拥有所有权的含义，而在其他英语国家的建筑工程领域被称为"the Employer"，具有"雇主"的含义。在标准合同格式中，如 FIDIC、NEC、JCT、ICE 等，雇主均被称为"the Employer"。具有雇主主体资格的，可以是私人、合伙、公司，也可以是政府部门。私人雇主一般是建造住宅工程的所有者，在土木工程建设领域，绝大多数雇主是公司和政府部门。

3.1.2 承包商

按照 FIDIC 合同 1987 年第 4 版第 1.1（a）（ii）款的规定，承包商（the Contractor）的定义如下："承包商指其投标已为雇主接受的当事人以及取得此当事人资格的合法继承人，但除非雇主同意，不指此当事人的任何受让人。"FIDIC 合同 1999 年版第 1.1.2.3 款规定承包商的定义是："承包商是指已为雇主接受的投标信中指明作为承包商的当事人及其财产上的合法继承人。"

简而言之，承包商是指与雇主签订工程合同，负责实施、完成和维护工程项目的当事人。该定义有助于区别分包商和工程师，特别是分包商、供货商的含义。承包商的主要义务就是在合同规定的时间内实施和完成他所签约的工程，如工程有缺陷，有义务在缺陷责任期内修补任何缺陷。

3.1.3 工程师

工程师（the Engineer），又称监理工程师或咨询工程师，是指由雇主聘任代表雇主对承包商实施的工程项目质量、进度、工艺和成本等进行监督管理的人。在 FIDIC 合同范本中，称监理工程师或咨询工程师为"工程师"。FIDIC 合同 1999 版第 1.1.2.4 款规定工程师的定义是："工程师指雇主为合同目的而指定作为工程师并在招标附录中保持这一

称谓的人员；或者雇主根据第 3.4 条随时指定的并通知承包商的任何其他人员。"工程师不属于雇主和承包商之间合同关系的一方，按照建筑和土木工程业界惯例，雇主和工程师之间将签订咨询服务合同，明确雇主和工程师的权利和义务及其权利的限制。这种雇主与工程师之间委托合同关系中确定的权利义务的相关内容对承包商具有一定的约束力。

3.1.4   分包商

分包（Subcontracting）是指（主）承包商（以下称"主包商"）将部分工程交由他人实施和完成的行为。在分包合同关系中，分包商只是承揽、实施和完成承包商交给他的部分工程，而主合同中对雇主的全部责任和义务仍由承包商承担。分包合同成立的前提是以雇主与承包商签订的主合同为前提条件，没有这个前提，分包就不能成立。

3.2   雇主、工程师、承包商之间基础法律关系

3.2.1   雇主和承包商的法律关系

雇主和承包商之间是互为权利义务主体的、互相监督的合同法律关系。合同是一种民事法律行为，其基本特征之一便是行为主体的法律地位完全平等。在合同中，合同双方的责任和利益是互为前提条件的，雇主的主要义务是提供施工的外部条件及支付工程款，这是承包商享有的权利，承包商的主要义务是按合同规定的工期及质量要求对工程项目进行施工、竣工及修复其缺陷，这是雇主享有的权利。

在施工过程中，雇主一般不直接与承包商接触，雇主是通过工程师来下达指令、行使权利、管理工程的。但是，作为施工合同的主体，必然由雇主和承包商行使最终权利。当双方发生争端时，工程师可以调解，调解不成而履行仲裁和诉讼程序时，工程师的意见只具有一般参考价值。

作为合作者，雇主和承包商在各自利益方面又是对立的两方。雇主希望少花钱多办事，而承包商既要完成项目，又要争取最大效益。承包商的行为会对雇主构成风险，雇主的处事也会威胁承包商的利益，双方利益冲突的结果就导致索赔和反索赔行为的产生。如果雇主违约，承包商可以降低施工速度或中止工程，提出索赔，乃至撤销合同。如果承包商违约，雇主可授权其他人去完成工作，如果承包商未能履约，雇主可以终止合同。

3.2.2   雇主和工程师的法律关系

雇主和工程师之间是合同法律关系，确切地说是一种委托关系。雇主聘用工程师代他进行工程管理。工程师的任务和职权是由雇主与承包商之间签订的施工合同及雇主与工程师签订的监理服务合同两种文件确定的。工程师在行使监理权利时，是雇主的代理人，应维护雇主的利益。工程师的良好服务，能为雇主带来巨大利益。如工程师对承包商完成的工程量进行严格的计量和审核、控制变更工程和额外工程费用、处理索赔事宜等工作，能直接降低工程成本；工程师促使承包商按时或提前完工，能使工程项目早日产生效益；工程师严格控制质量，能使工程的未来维护费用、运行费用降低；工程师提出的改进建议能节省投资等。

3.2.3   承包商与工程师的法律关系

承包商与工程师之间没有合同，因而不存在合同法律关系。但在工程实施中，承包商要时时与工程师打交道，因为工程师是雇主的代理人，雇主是通过工程师来管理工程的。承包商必须接受和遵从工程师的指示，工程师在行使权利时，须经雇主事先批准。承包商

无权核实工程师是否已获得此类批准。根据 FIDIC 合同 2.1 款可以理解：如果承包商按工程师指示施工增加了费用，那么即使工程师无权对该项工作下达命令，承包商也有权得到该项工作的付款。尽管承包商可能不同意工程师颁发的某项指示，但根据 FIDIC 合同 13.1 条，他必须执行该指示。

在工程实践中，不经承包商同意，雇主不得更换工程师。因为在 FIDIC 合同中，工程师有很大的权利，具有特殊的作用。所以工程师的信誉、工作能力、公正性等，已是承包商投标报价必须考虑的重要因素之一。

3.3 雇主的主要权利与义务

3.3.1 雇主的主要权利

1. 任命工程师的权利

任命工程师是雇主的基本权利。在施工合同中，工程师不是合同的主体，但是雇主为了确保工程的质量与管理，其需要在项目开始运作时指定工程师完成一些前合同工作，例如工程设计等工作。在传统工程承包模式中，设计和监督工程项目的实施往往都是由一个咨询工程师或一家咨询公司进行的。在 FIDIC 合同中，咨询工程师被称为"工程师"。然而，由于工程师在 FIDIC 项目管理中的巨大作用，雇主不得不考虑对工程师的权利进行限制，即在工程师行使权利时需要雇主的授权，雇主需要在与工程师的合同中明确工程师的权利范围，这些限制也必须清晰地体现在 FIDIC 合同里，以使所有投标人在报价或投标前了解这种限制。

2. 发布指示的权利

为了使工程按期完工，雇主有权向承包商发布指示、任命、计划和细节。如需要，雇主、雇主代表或者其代理人，如建筑师或工程师必须在适当的时间内向承包商发出指示，以使承包商能够履行合同义务。如果合同没有明示规定发布指示的时间，则雇主应在合理的时间内发出指示。合理时间取决于合同的明示规定或具体情况，但并不单独取决于承包商的方便和金钱利益。

3. 指定分包商或供货商的权利

分包商和供货商是完成整体建设施工合同不可分割的组成部分，分包商、供货商与承包商直接签订分包合同或供货合同，但是在某些条件下，雇主可以直接指定分包商或供货商，要求承包商与某分包商或供货商签订某一项目的分包合同。

3.3.2 雇主的主要义务

1. 提供现场占有权的义务

对于现场占有权（Possession of Site）的表述，不同的施工合同使用了各种不同的术语，例如"占有"（Possession）、"使用"（Use）、"进入"（Access）或者"占据"（Occupation）等。在 FIDIC 合同 1987 年第 4 版第 42.1 款和第 42.2 款和 1999 年版新红皮书、新黄皮书和银皮书第 2.1 款中使用了"进入"（Access）和"占有"（Possession）的专业术语。

FIDIC 合同 1987 年第 4 版和 1999 年版系列合同并没有对"占有"和"进入"给出定义解释。一般而言，"现场占有权"和"进入现场"（Access to Site）的含义、范围及其因此产生的风险分配取决于合同的明示条款的规定和默示条款的内容。

2. 安排资金和支付义务

红皮书（1999）第 2.4 款对雇主的资金安排进行了明示规定如下："在收到承包商的任何要求后的 28 天内，雇主应提交其已做的并将予以保持的资金安排的合理证据，以便雇主有能力按照第 14 条［合同价格和付款］的规定，支付合同价格（按当时估算）。如雇主拟对其资金安排做出任何重要的变更，应将有关变更细节通知承包商。"

支付或许诺支付是雇主的一项最重要的义务。在施工合同中，施工合同的对价是承包商实施工程项目，而雇主为此支付工程价款。施工合同的性质不同，支付方式也有所不同。

3. 披露信息的义务

1999 年版 FIDIC 新红皮书、新黄皮书和银皮书中的多个条款对雇主披露信息的义务作了明示规定，主要包括：

（1）文件的照管和提供。

（2）雇主的资金安排。资金安排确保工程项目建设的顺利进行，任何资金安排的变动，对于承包商都有着重大的影响。因此，融资安排的任何变更需要进行信息披露，使相关利益者及时掌握。

（3）雇主的索赔。雇主对其他合同主体提出的索赔，应披露索赔细节。

（4）工程师的替换。更换工程师的细节需要披露。

（5）现场数据。主要内包括地质、水文、环境等数据的披露。

（6）完成扫尾工作和修补。主要包括缺陷通知期内缺陷信息的披露。

（7）修补缺陷的费用。主要包括非承包商自费负责的缺陷，未能修补缺陷的日期信息披露。

（8）雇主终止。雇主有终止合同的权利，但对终止的原因应进行披露。

（9）知识产权和工业产权。对侵犯知识产权和工业产权进行披露。

（10）不可抗力的通知。对不可抗力事件的具体情况进行披露，对饮不可抗力实践引发的终止合同进行披露。

（11）取得争议裁决委员会的决定。对不满争议裁决委员会的决定进行披露。

4. 合作义务

1999 年版 FIDIC 新红皮书第 4.6 款对承包商的"合作"作了规定，承包商应根据合同规定或工程师的指示，为可能被雇佣在现场或其附近从事未包括在合同中工程的下列人员提供适当的条件：

（1）雇主人员；

（2）雇主雇佣的任何其他承包商，和

（3）任何合法设立的公共当局的人员。

5. 按照合同规定提供设备和免费材料的义务

1999 年版新红皮书第 4.20 款"雇主设备和免费供应的材料"规定了雇主应按照合同规定提供设备和免费材料的义务："雇主应准备雇主设备（如有），供承包商根据规范规定的细节、安排和价格，在工程施工中使用。"

3.4 承包商的主要权利与义务

3.4.1 承包商的主要权利

1. 索赔权利

FIDIC 新红皮书 20.1 规定：如果承包商认为，根据本条件任何条款或与合同有关的其他文件，他有权得到竣工时间的任何延长期和（或）任何追加付款，承包商应向工程师发出通知，说明引起索赔的事件或情况。

2. 额外费用不承担权

FIDIC 红皮书（1987）《应用指南》第 36.4 款规定："工程师可能要求承包商进行规范规定以外的检验。如果检验不能表明承包商的工作有缺陷，那么承包商不承担检验费用。"

3. 指定分包商不接受权

红皮书（1999）5.2 条规定了承包商对指定分包商的不接受权，其中一个重要的理由是，如果承包商有理由相信，该分包商没有足够的能力、资源或财力。

4. 雇主风险和特殊风险不承担权

红皮书（1999）第 20.4 款对雇主风险规定了明确的定义，而且豁免了雇主的责任。

5. 终止合同权

FIDIC 新版红皮书 16.2 条规定：如出现工程师未能在收到报表和证明文件后 56 天内发出有关的付款证书，雇主实质上未能根据合同规定履行其义务等情况，承包商应有权终止合同。

6. 暂停工作的权利

FIDIC 新版红皮书 16.1 条规定：如果工程师未能按照第 14.6 款［期中付款证书的颁发］的规定确认发证，或雇主未能遵守第 2.4 款［雇主的资金安排］或第 14.7 款［付款］的规定，承包商可在不少于 21 天前通知雇主，暂停工作（或放慢工作速度），除非直到承包商根据情况和通知中所述，收到了付款证书、合理的证明或付款为止。

7. 进入现场的权利

在 FIDIC 合同和附录中，相关进入现场的文件为承包商进入现场提供方便，如果合同和附录中没有相关文件，雇主有义务根据项目要求为承包商进入和占有现场提供方便。在这种情况下，慎重的承包商项目现场移交文件，在人和情况下，全部或部分移交不能迟于中标通知书发出的 42 天内。

8. 特定情况下的单独验收和竣工检验权

FIDIC《电气与机械工程合同条件》第 28.2 款规定："如果工程师没有在承包商要求之后指定检验时间，或未在指定时间和地点参加检验，承包商应有权在工程师不在场的情况下着手进行检验。该检验应被视为是在工程师在场的情况下进行的，并且检验结果应被认为是准确的。"

9. 警告权

FIDIC 新红皮书第 1.8 款规定："如果一方发现为实施工程准备的文件中有技术性错误或缺陷，应迅速将该错误或缺陷通知另一方。"1999 版黄皮书和银皮书第 1.8 款也规定了相同的内容。

3.4.2　承包商的主要义务

1. 实施和完成工程项目的义务

实施和完成工程项目的义务是承包商的一项最基本的、最重要的义务。1987 年第 4 版 FIDIC 红皮书第 8.1 款"承包商的一般责任"规定:"承包商应按照合同的各项规定,以应有的谨慎和努力(在合同规定的范围内)对工程进行设计、施工和竣工,并修补其中的任何缺陷。承包商应为该工程的设计、施工和竣工以及为修补其任何缺陷而提供所需的不管是临时性的还是永久性的全部工程的监督、劳务、材料、工程设备以及其他物品,只要提供上述物品的必要性在合同内已有规定或可以从合同中合理地推论得出。"

2. 质量义务

在施工合同中,承包商的质量义务有明示的质量义务,即承包商实施的工程应符合合同文件的要求。在 1999 年版新红皮书中,工程质量应符合设计文件、规范的要求。同时,承包商有默示的质量义务。在施工合同中,默示质量义务包括设计、材料、工艺、建筑师或工程师的满意。

3. 进度义务

FIDIC 新红皮书、新黄皮书和银皮书第 8.2 款规定:"承包商应在工程或区段工程(如有)的竣工时间内,完成整个工程和每个区段工程(视情况而定)。"在 FIDIC 合同中,投标附录必须写明工期和竣工日期,但承包商可根据第 8.4 款"竣工时间的延长"的规定要求给予工期延长。在延长工期后,承包商应在延长后的工期内完成工程项目。

4. 合作义务

在施工合同中,承包商的合同义务包括:

(1) 及时提供报表、文件、索赔通知

(2) 向建筑师/工程师提交质量保证体系文件

(3) 提交进度计划、图纸、规范和其他文件

(4) 避免干扰

(5) 现场保安

(6) 安全保障

(7) 环境保护

(8) 健康保护

1999 年版 FIDIC 新红皮书、新黄皮书和银皮书第 4.6 款规定了合作义务。如前所述,本款规定的不是雇主和承包商如何合作的问题,而是规定承包商如何与其他承包商、雇主人员和公共当局人员合作的事项。

5. 提供保证、保障和保险的义务

FIDIC 新红皮书中,承包商也承担了提供保证、保障和保险的义务,主要包括:

(1) 承包商应在收到中标函后 28 天内向雇主提交履约担保,并向工程师送一份副本。履约担保应由雇主批准的国家(或其他司法管辖区)内的实体提供,并采用专用条件所附格式或雇主批准的其他格式。

承包商应确保履约担保直到其完成工程的施工、竣工及修补完任何缺陷前持续有效和可执行。如果在履约担保的条款中规定了其期满日期,而承包商在该期满日期前 28 天尚无权拿到履约证书,承包商应将履约担保的有效期延长至工程竣工和修补完任何缺陷时

为止。

（2）承包商应保障和保持使雇主、雇主人员以及他们各自的代理人免受索赔以及损害赔偿费，损失和开支（包括法律费用和开支）带来的损害。

（3）对于每种类型的保险，"应投保方"是指对办理并保持相关条款中规定的保险负有责任的一方。

当承包商是应投保方时，应按照雇主批准的条件向保险人办理每项保险。这些条件应与双方在中标函颁布日期前协商同意的任何条件相一致。这一条件协议的地位应优先于本条各项规定。当雇主是应投保方时，应按照与专用条件所附的详细内容相一致的条件，向保险人办理每项保险。

3.5 工程师的主要权利义务

根据 FIDIC 合同条款的规定，工程师的权利义务主要表现在以下几个方面：

3.5.1 工程师的主要权利

1. 施工监理权利

工程师工作应该贯穿工程建设项目的始终，包括投资决策阶段、设计阶段、招投标阶段、施工阶段及保修阶段。在建筑和土木工程施工阶段，工程师的一项最重要的任务就是施工监理的权利。工程师受雇主委托对土木工程项目实施监理，其目的是为了保证工程项目能够按照合同的规定和要求进行施工。工程师承担项目监理的范围和程度取决于雇主和工程师之间签订的咨询服务合同的约定内容以及工程项目的性质。工程师必须对工程项目进行合理的监督。

2. 发布指示的权利

在建筑和土木工程施工合同中，工程师在工程项目中处于核心地位。他必须时时或每天发布指示，监督参与工程项目的众多人员，完成工程项目的实施任务。所有的施工合同以及标准合同格式都对工程师发布指示的义务作了明示规定。在 FIDIC 合同中，许多条款都规定了工程师发布指示的明示权利。

3. 作出决定的权利

FIDIC 新红皮书中规定了工程师作出决定的权利，这是工程师的一项权利，但同时也是工程师的一项义务。这些权利包括了工程建设管理中的各个方面。工程师在作出决定时，应考虑工程师应考虑的所有有关情况，根据合同规定作出公正的决定。同时，工程师在作出决定时，不能修改合同的规定，不能解除任何一方当事人的合同义务、责任。尽管工程师的决定对双方当事人具有一定的约束力，但工程师的决定不能产生新的责任和义务。

4. 作出变更的权利

1987 年第 4 版 FIDIC 红皮书第 51.1 款"变更"规定："如果工程师认为有必要对工程或其中的任何部分的形式、质量或数量作出任何变更，为此目的或出于任何其他理由，工程师认为上述变更适当时，他有权指示承包商进行而承包商也应进行下述工作。"

1999 年版 FIDIC 新红皮书第 13.1 款规定："在颁发工程接收证书前的任何时间，工程师可通过签发指示或要求承包商提交建议书的方式作出变更。"

3.5.2 工程师的主要义务

1. 设计和提供图纸的义务

FIDIC 新红皮书的规定，工程师负有向承包商提供图纸的义务。如果工程师未能在承包商要求的时间内提供图纸，并且发生了承包商没有图纸、无法施工的情况，承包商可根据第 1.9 款的规定发出通知，提出工期延长和费用索赔要求。另一方面，承包商也应让工程师有充分的时间准备图纸。在 FIDIC 黄皮书中，工程师没有设计义务，设计的义务由承包商来完成。

2. 通知与被通知义务

1999 年版红皮书中工程师的通知与被通知义务主要包括：一方合同当事人向另一方合同当事人发出的通知，应抄送给工程师；雇主向承包商发出的通知，应抄送给工程师；承包商向雇主发出的通知，应抄送给工程师；工程师向承包商和雇主发出的通知；工程师向承包商发出的通知，应抄送给雇主；承包商向工程师发出的通知；合同双方当事人向争议裁决委员会每一个成员发出的通知；争议裁决委员会成员向双方当事人发出的通知。

3. 检查义务

FIDIC 新红皮书第 7.3 款"检查"规定了检查的内容、范围、时间要求和费用问题。工程师检查工程的目的是为了避免工程缺陷的发生，本条的规定反映了施工行业质量控制体系的要求。在实践中，工程师和承包商可以建立检查工程的时间和内容的特定通知程序，可通过周或月度进度报告或工地例会确定工程师的检查时间和内容。

4. 计量义务

1999 年版第 12.1 款"需计量的工程"规定了计量程序，工程师决定需要对部分工程进行测量并通知承包商，承包商应参加测量工作并协助工程师进行测量，如果承包商未能参加计量工作，应认为工程师的计量结果是准确的。

Questions

1. Discuss the major players that make up the construction industry?

2. Why do subcontractors occupy such an important place in the construction process?

3. What are rights and liabilities of Engineer in construction contract?

Chapter 4　Construction Tendering

4.1　Construction tendering

A tender can be said as an offer to do work or supply goods at a fixed price. Initiating step of a tendering process in which qualified contractors are invited to submit sealed bids for construction or for supply of specific and clearly defined goods or services during a specified timeframe. The tender process is designed to ensure that the work to be done for client/employer is given out in a fair way. For example in China, there are a number of policies known as procurement policies which guide government on how to make decisions on which bid to accept. Although price is very important in the decision on which bid to accept, it is not the only factor to be taken into account.

Once client/employer accepts a bid, it is binding on both parties. This means that the person or company that won the tender has to provide the goods or services in the manner agreed to and at the price offered, and client/government must pay the agreed price at the agreed time. In other words, once accepted, a acceptance letter issued by client/employer is a binding contract.

4.2　Types of tendering

When talk about tendering, it is involved some kind of complicated process and procedure. Before any tendering process can be done, professional team and employer must make sure all necessary tender documents have been prepared, checked and approved. The source of the funding also must have been identified and the project financing put in place. The procedures for subsequent stages should have been established with the express consent of the employer to ensure the tendering process will go smoothly.

What types of tendering applied depended on nature of contract, complexity of the construction, expertise needed and several other reasons. But usually for the government project, it is suggested to make open tender to ensure the procurement and works to be done in fairly manner without prejudice.

4.2.1　Open tendering

Open tendering allows anyone to submit a tender to supply the goods or services that are required. Generally, an advert will be placed giving notice that the contract is being tendered, offering an equal opportunity to any organisation to submit a bid.

On larger projects, there may then be a pre-qualification process that produces a short-list of suitable suppliers from the respondents expressing interest in the contract. This short list will then be invited to prepare tenders. The selection of a short list can include pre-qualification questionnaires and interviews. This sort of pre-qualification process is not the same as selective tendering. Selective tendering only allows suppliers invited from a pre-selected list to take part in the tender process.

The advantages and disadvantages of open tender are stated below:

(1) It allows any interested contractor to tender. Therefore it gives opportunity for an unknown contractor to compete for the work.

(2) The tender list can be long as too many contractors bidding for one job.

(3) Allowing the tender list to be made without bias. Client will obtain the bargain possible. No favoritism in selecting contractors.

(4) Uneconomic use of source.

(5) Ensuring good competition.

(6) Public accountability may be questioned if the lowest offer is not accepted.

(7) Traditional method of tendering, familiar to all sector of the engineering and construction industry.

(8) Does not attract reputable and established contractor unless they are forced to, due to lack of work.

4.2.2　Selective tendering

Selective tendering is the one alternatives developed to address the limitations of the open tendering procedure. In this method, a short list of contractor is drawn up and they are invited to submit tenders. The purpose of the elective tendering are to improve the quality of the bids received, to ensure that contractors with the necessary experience and competence are given the opportunity to submit the necessary bids, due to urgency work involved, for specific reasons of the employer, e. g. security reasons in government projects, Etc. and to make the tendering procedure more manageable and less a burden on the parties involved. Such list may be prepared through recommendation from the Client's professional adviser whom have knowledge of the Contractors undertaking the work in the past or advertisement through the newspaper (pre-qualification).

The advantages and disadvantages of the selective tendering are stated below.

(1) Only the competent contractors were invited to tender;

(2) Reduces the availability of work for other contractors especially new contractors.

(3) It reduced the cost of tendering, tender price may invariably higher than would have been in open tendering.

(4) Greater chance of collusion.

(5) Tendering period longer because it involved two distinct stages.

(6) Favoritism's may occur in the short listing.

4. 2. 3　Negotiated tendering

Negotiated tendering is extensively used in the engineering and construction industry commencing from tendering till dispute resolutions, i. e. under the styles of pre-contract negotiations and post contract negotiations. Usually with single contractor but may be up to three contractors.

Negotiation process involves are as follows:

(1) Identification by the employer of a suitable contractor to negotiate with.

(2) The contractor can be selected either from the employer's own list of preferences or on the advice of the professional team.

(3) The contractor being apprised of the work scope.

4. 3　Single stage and two stage tendering process

Tender procedures will vary depending on the nature of the goods or services that are being procured, but very broadly they can be classified as either single stage or two stages.

4. 3. 1　Single stage tendering

Single-stage tendering is the more traditional route, used when all the information necessary to calculate a realistic price is available when tendering commences: An invitation to bid is issued to prospective suppliers. The invitation to bid will include information describing the goods or services required in sufficient detail to enable prospective suppliers to prepare an accurate tender.

Tenders are prepared and provided by prospective suppliers (this may involve questions and answers and a mid-tender interview to clarify the client's requirements). Submitted documents are then assessed and compared (this may involve further interviews). The preferred bidder is selected and negotiations opened. Subject to the outcome of those negotiations the preferred bidder may then be appointed.

4. 3. 2　Two stage tendering

Two-stage tendering is used to allow the early appointment of a contractor, prior to the completion of all the information required to enable them to offer a fixed price. In the first stage, a limited appointment is agreed allowing the contractor to begin work and in the second stage a fixed price is negotiated for the contract.

It can be used simply to appoint the main contractor early, or more commonly as a mechanism for early appointment of a specialist contractor. A two-stage tender process may also be adopted on a design and build project where the employer's requirementsare not sufficiently well developed for the contractor to be able to calculate a realistic price. In this case, the contractor will tender a fee for designing the building along with a schedule of rates that can be used to establish the construction price for the second stage tender.

The first-stage appointment might be made on the basis of a bespoke agreement, a consultancy agreement or a pre-construction services agreement (PCSA), with an appendix setting out all tender items to be applied to the construction contract, with a clause that makes it clear there is no obligation to proceed to the construction contract, and in such circumstances the pre-construction fee would be full and final settlement of the contractor's costs.

In theory, the early involvement of the contractor should improve the build ability and cost-certainty of the design as well as creating a better integrated project team and reducing the likelihood of disputes. Ideally the second-stage negotiation is simply a mathematical exercise using the pricing criteria agreed in the first stage agreement. In reality however, there will be some items not previously considered, around which negotiations will ensue. In the case of sub-contractors, the second stage construction contract is negotiated by the main contractor subject to the approval of the design team.

4.4　Conventional tender procedure

4.4.1　Invitation to tender

An invitation to tender may follow the completion of a pre-qualification questionnaire (PQQ) in response to an advert posted by the Employer and perhaps a pre-tender interview. The purpose of a pre-qualification questionnaire and pre-tender interview is to enable the Employer to produce a short list of suppliers that are likely to be most appropriate for their particular project who will then be invited to tender. This helps reduce inefficiency and wasted effort in the tender process.

Ideally, tender documents should be broken down into a series of packages (even if there will only be one main contract) each with its own design drawings and specifications suitable to be issued by the main contractor to potential sub-contractors. This makes the tender easier to price for the contractor and easier to compare with other bidders for the Employer. It is important when this is done to ensure that the interfaces between packages are properly identified and clearly allocated to one package or another. Having too many packages increases the number of interfaces and so the potential problems. The cost plan (pre-tender estimate) should also be re-assembled package by package to allow easy appraisal of tenders received.

4.4.2　Clarification

Mid-tender interviews may be arranged to allow clarification of matters that might otherwise lead to an inaccurate tender being submitted, they can also give the Employer insights into potential problems or opportunities in the project as it is described by the tender documentation.

Responses to queries raised during the tender process can lead to clarification or amendment of the tender documentation which may also result in an extension of the tender period. It is better to allow sufficient time during the tender process to investigate opportunities and clarify problems, as the resulting tenders will then be better prepared and will be likely to save time and money later.

It is important that any clarification, additional information or changes to the tender documents are circulated to all of the tenderers to ensure a level playing field. Such information must be treated as confidential.

4.4.3　Submission

In response to an invitation to tender, invited bidders will submit their bid, which will include their price for supplying the goods or services along with proposals for how the Employers requirements will be satisfied if these have been requested. The precise content of tenders will vary considerably depending on procurement route, however they might include:

(1) A bid return slip, with details of the contract, return address, bid checklist etc.

(2) A completed bid pricing document (or contract sum analysis on design and build projects).

(3) Schedules of rates.

(4) An initial construction phase plan.

(5) Any design proposals or method statements that have been requested.

(6) Programme.

(7) Procedures to be adopted such as procurement procedures, cost management procedures etc.

(8) Demonstration of capability, for example design capability, systems used etc.

(9) Key project personnel.

(10) Management organization.

(11) Plant and labour resources and availability.

(12) Prior experience.

(13) References.

4.4.4　Settlement

Once bids have been received, negotiations might proceed with two preferred tenderers prior to selection of the successful one. They are an opportunity to agree or clarifying any matters regarding the pricing and quality of the proposed works, conditions of contract and programme. This is the last chance the Employer and consultant team will have to negotiate with bidders while they are still subject to the pressures of competition.

Tender negotiations may involve:

(1) Bidder qualifications to the proposed contract conditions.

(2) Anomalies or clarification in the tender pricing document.

(3) Alternative offers to the design or specification.

(4) Resolution of provisional sums.

4.5   Contractors acknowledgement in bidding

4.5.1   Pre-contractual stage

Active lobbying may pay off when the contractor is able to influence the specifications, the procurement procedure that will be used, the contractor selection criteria and more particularly, the contract model that will be applied by a public institution. The contract model should be in line with the allocation of risks and responsibilities of the parties involved.

Contractors should have a thorough knowledge of the public tendering procedures that are used most, i. e. the open procedure and the restricted procedure. It is important to acknowledge the minimum response times that are allowed according to these procedures. This is a specific task for the contractor's tender manager.

Contractors should be keen on the principles that need to be followed by public institutions. Once the tender process has started no changes in scope and requirements can be made unless approved by all market partners. Contractors should keep an eye on the level playing field, which needs to be created by public institutions. All contractors should receive the same information at the same time. No single contractor may be put in an advantageous position by the public institution.

4.5.2   Contractual stage

In order to be pre-selected, contractors need to meet the information needs of the public institution as communicated in its tender documents. The contractor needs to abide by the specified response times. Being five minutes overdue in delivery will mean that all your work will be put aside. Bids should reflect all technical, quality, maintenance and commercial requirements as communicated in the tender documents. Not meeting these requirements will mean that your offer will be put aside.

Most public tendering procedures do not allow for negotiation after the bidding. As this happens all the time, the contractor could enforce its negotiation position by keeping a detailed diary of their discussions with the prospective Employer. This information may be used to put the Employer under pressure, when necessary. If the contractor did not get the job, he should review the process. Based upon his detailed dairies and reports, he should assess the weaknesses of the Employer's procedure and assess whether a case could be brought to court for compensation.

4.5.3   Post-contractual stage

When the contract is signed, the contractor can mobilize for the start-up of the work. This should be done only after all permits have been gained. Any scope change or change of technical requirements and specifications should be checked and the cost consequences identified and agreed before implementing them. Contractors should have frequent face-to-face meetings with the Employer and/or its engineering representative, given the often fast-changing political landscape and Employer environment. Contractors need to take care of a flawless tracing and tracking of all their activities and those of their subcontractors and suppliers in order to be able to mitigate and/or share the burden of claims, when issued by the Employer. Contractors should keep an eye on the roles and responsibilities of the Employer, given the scope of the contract that was signed. In the case of an EPC contract, the Employer should demonstrate a hands-off attitude and not interfere in the contractor's design and project execution. If this happens, the contractor should stipulate its role, and point out consequences for the Employer.

4.6 China tendering

4.6.1 Brief History of China's Tendering System

In September 1984, the State Council (SC) of China promulgated a document related to construction industry reform requiring that the tendering system be used for allocating construction work. Since then, the tendering system has become increasingly popular in China. The MOC also issued a decree " Administrative Measures for Bidding and Submission of Tendering for Construction Projects" on November 6, 1992, which is the first state level regulation related to the tendering system.

Foreign contractors were not formally permitted to bid for construction works in China, except those approved under some special situations, until 1994 when the MOC issued a decree "Temporary Provisions for Foreign Contractors to be Qualified for Undertaking Construction Works in China", which became effective on July 1, 1994.

To further regulate the project procurement and administration activities, and to minimize related corruption, the Chinese government began drafting the national Tendering Law in 1994, which was formally promulgated on August 30, 1999 and scheduled to come into effect on January 1, 2000. As the first state-level law related to tendering, the national Tendering Law is one of the milestone laws in China that will help shift China's economic system from a planned to market-oriented one.

4.6.2 Scope of Tendering

The following construction projects in the territory of the People's Republic of China, including surveying and prospecting, design, engineering and supervision of such projects as well as the procurement of major equipment and materials related to the construction of such projects, must be subject to tenders:

(1) projects such as large-scale infrastructure facilities and public utilities involving the social and public interests and public safety;

(2) projects which are, completely or partly, invested by the State-owned funds or funded through State financing; and

(3) projects using loans or aid funds from international organizations or foreign governments.

The specific scope and standards on the scale of the projects listed in the preceding paragraph shall be worked out by the department of the State Council for development planning, jointly with relevant departments of the State Council, and be reported to the State Council for approval.

If laws or the State Council have the provisions on the scope of other projects which must be subject to tenders, such provisions shall govern.

4.6.3   Types of Tendering

Tenders include public tenders and invitational tenders.

(1) A public tender means that a tenderer, in the form of tender announcement, invites unspecified legal persons or other unspecified organizations to submit their bids.

(2) An invitational tender means that a tenderer, in the form of invitation for submission of bid, invites specified legal persons or other specified organizations to submit their bids.

4.6.4   Bid Opening

Bid opening shall be started openly at the same time of the deadline for submission of bid documents set in the tender documents; and the place of opening bids shall be the place predetermined in the tender documents. Bid opening shall be presided over by the tenderer, and all bidders shall be invited to join.

When opening bids, the bidders or the representatives selected by them shall check the sealing of bid documents, and the sealing may also be checked and notarized by the notary organization commissioned by the tenderer; after being checked and verified, the working personnel shall open them in public, announce the names of bidders, bid price quotations and other main contents of bid documents.

All bid documents received by the tenderer prior to the deadline for submission set in the tender documents shall be opened and announced in public when opening bids. Records on the bid opening shall be made and shall be placed on files for future reference.

4.6.5   Bid Assessment

Bid assessment shall be the responsibility of the bid assessment committee established according to law by the tenderer.

If a project must be subject to tender according to law, the bid assessment committee shall be composed of the representative of the tenderer and experts in the related technological and economic fields, and the number of committee members shall be an odd number at or above five, of the members, experts in technological and economic fields may not be less than two-thirds of the total members.

The bid assessment committee shall assess and compare all bid documents in accordance with the bid assessment standards and methods set in the tender documents and; if there is a base bid price, shall take it as reference. After finishing the assessment, the bid assessment committee shall give a written report thereon to the tenderer and recommend the qualified candidate winning bidders.

The tenderer shall, pursuant to the written report on bid assessment given by the bid assessment committee, determine the winning bidder from among the candidate winning bidders recommended by the bid assessment committee. The tenderer may also authorize the bid assessment committee to directly determine the winning bidder.

4. 6. 6　Winning Bidder

The bid of a winning bidder shall satisfy any of the following requirements:

(1) to be able to satisfy the maximum various comprehensive assessment standards set in the tender documents; or

(2) to be able to satisfy the substantial requirements set in the tender documents and to have the lowest bid price quotation upon assessment, with the exception of the bid price quotation which is below cost.

4. 6. 7　Projects That Foreigners Can Bid For

According to the Tendering Law, the qualified foreign developers/contractors are allowed to bid for the following projects:

(1) Projects directly invested by foreigners (organisations, governments, individuals, etc).

(2) Projects financed with loan made entirely by foreign financial institutions that require open competitive bidding.

(3) Projects financed by a joint venture between Chinese and foreign investors, when the local contractors cannot execute the works on their own for technological reasons.

(4) Projects invested by local entities, when the local contractors for some reasons are incapable of executing on their own. However, when bidding for projects under this category, the foreigners are required to form a joint venture with local contractors subject to the approval of the central or provincial construction administrative authority.

(5) All infrastructure projects adopted build-operate-transfer (BOT) scheme. From the end of 1996, BOT project will be awarded to foreign developer only after open competitive tendering, while previously it was awarded through direct negotiations.

In addition, the Chinese government strongly encourages local key contractors to form joint ventures with foreign contractors to bid for any kind of international and local projects. The government is due to issue details on the related incentives.

4. 6. 8　Pre-qualification of Foreign Developers

The pre-qualification of foreign developers depends greatly on the project. Foreign developers have to follow the requirements to apply for the pre-qualifications. Usually, for pre-qualification, documents are required to show the foreign developers':

(1) Past experiences of similar projects;

(2) Financial strength;

(3) Business licenses obtained in China and home country;

(4) Qualifications and experiences of key technical and managerial personnel;

(5) Completed applications forms;

（6）Financial and other support from home country, e. g. export credit, especially for mega-projects.

A point worth noting is that the pre-qualification obtained by foreign developers is project-oriented, i. e. prequalification obtained for one project is only valid for that project. In other words, a foreign developer has to apply for a new pre-qualification for every new project, unlike a foreign contractor who can carry out a few different projects by virtue of one Qualification Certificate, as long as the projects fall within an areathat is covered by the Certificate.

☞ 疑难词句 ☜

1. Tender 招标投标

2. Tender out 招标

3. Bid 投标，出价

4. Limited tenders 限制性投标

5. Explicit milestones and deadlines 明确的时间表和截止日期

6. Pre-qualification 资格预审

7. Track record 业绩记录

8. Level playing field 公平竞争环境

9. Break it down to labour, plant and material costs 分解为人工、设备和材料成本

10. Broken down into a series of packages 分解成系列文件包

11. Bid solicitation 招标

12. A flat rate 统一收费率

13. Renege or revoke 否认或撤回

14. Pre-qualification questionnaire 资格预审问卷

15. Demonstration of capability 能力证明

16. Anomalies or clarification in the tender pricing document 招标价格文件的异常与说明

17. Active lobbying may pay off when the contractor is able to influence the specifications, the procurement procedure that will be used, the contractor selection criteria and more particularly, the contract model that will be applied by a public institution 积极地游说可能会帮助承包商影响项目规格，采购程序、承包商选择标准，特别是公共机构可能使用的合同模型

18. On the level 诚实的，老实的

19. Rating schedules 产量表

20. Be put aside 放置一边，暂不考虑

21. Mobilize for the work 组织工作（开工）

22. Hands-off attitude 不干预态度

23. First pilot project 试点项目

24. Winning bidder 中标人

25. The abolition of national quotas and restrictions in public procurement 政府采购中国家配额与限制的废除

26. Outsourcing of public services 公共设施的外部采购

27. For pecuniary interest 为了金钱上的利益

☞ **中文综述** ☜

4.1　招标投标概述

工程项目招标投标是一种国际上普遍运用的、有组织的市场交易行为。招标是指招标人（雇主）发出招标公告或投标邀请书，说明招标的工程、货物、服务的范围、标段划分、数量、投标人的资格要求等，邀请特定或不特定的投标人在规定的时间、地点按照一定的程序进行投标的行为。

在国际工程实践中，招标和投标是国际工程合同达成必经的两个阶段。招标指的是雇主对拟发包工程的内容标明，它主要包括项目概况、数量、质量要求，以及采用的图纸和规范、标准等，以招引或邀请某些愿意承包并符合投标资格的承包者对承包工程进行投标，通过比价而达成交易的一种经济活动。投标是与招标相对应的概念，它是指投标人应招标人的邀请或投标人满足招标人最低资质要求而主动申请，按照招标的要求和条件，在规定的时间内向招标人投标，争取中标的行为。实践中，中标的投标人成为承包商。国际工程招标投标使得承包商与工程师开始接触，在这个阶段，工程师代理雇主对承包商的工作进行监督和管理（FIDIC 条件下）。投标也是承包商和雇主接触的第一阶段，只有中标的承包商才有可能就所投标的工程与雇主达成协议。

近年来，随着海外经营业务规模的迅速拓展，中国公司海外工程所面临的市场环境的复杂性和风险的不可预见性大大增加，与此相对应的海外经营面临的法律风险日益增加。因此，必须提高对经营过程中法律风险的认识和敏感性，了解海外工程适用的国际惯例和当地法律环境，总结经验教训，在签约前的投标阶段，加强投标风险的审查，以便及早识别并控制、规避与防范招标投标风险，防患于未然。

4.2　招标投标的种类

当讨论投标时，它涉及一系列复杂的过程和程序。在投标程序完成之前，招标投标专业团队，雇主必须确保所有必要的招标文件已经准备妥当，并经过检查和批准。项目资金的来源也必须确认或者项目融资正在进行。后续阶段程序经雇主的明示同意已经建立，以确保招标投标程序的顺利进行。

雇主在选择招标投标类型时主要取决于合同的性质，工程的复杂性，所需要的专业技能和一些其他原因。但是，在世界范围内，政府工程项目往往使用公开招标的方法，以确保政府采购和工程建设公平而没有偏见。目前，招标投标主要类型包括公开招标，选择性招标和谈判招标。

4.2.1　公开招标

我国《招标投标法》第十六条规定：招标人采用公开招标方式的，应当发布招标公告。依法必须进行招标的项目的招标公告，应当通过国家指定的报刊、信息网络或者其他媒介发布。招标公告应当载明招标人的名称和地址、招标项目的性质、数量、实施地点和时间以及获取招标文件的办法等事项。

公开招标的优点在于能够在最大限度内选择投标商，竞争性更强，择优率更高，同时也可以在较大程度上避免招标活动中的贿标行为，因此，国际上政府采购通常采用这种方式。但是，公开招标由于投标人众多，一般耗时较长，需花费的成本也较大，对于采购标的较小的招标来说，不宜采用公开招标的方式；另外还有些专业性较强的项目，由于有资格承接的潜在投标人较少，或者需要在较短时间内完成采购任务等，最好也采用邀请招标的方式。

4.2.2　选择投标或邀请招标

选择性招标是解决公开招标程序的局限性的一种选择。它也称邀请招标或有限竞争性招标，即由招标单位按照邀请招标流程选择一定数目的企业，向其发出投标邀请书，邀请他们参加招标竞争。一般都选择 3～10 个之间参加者较为适宜，当然要视具体的招标项目的规模大小而定。选择性招标的目的是提高投标报价的质量，以确保有经验和实力的承包商在招标投标中胜出，也使招标投标程序易于管理，减轻招标方和投标方的负担。备选投标人名单可由专业顾问推荐，他们对这些潜在的承包商在过去的工作或在报纸上的广告（资格预审）有了解。选择性招标可以通过对承包商行业了解的专业咨询师的推荐来完成或者通过传媒广告来完成。

与公开招标方式相比，选择性招标的特点主要有：一是发布信息的方式为招标人或者雇主直接向被选择的承包商发出投标邀请函，不需要发布招标公告；二是招标人或者雇主在一定范围内邀请承包商参加投标；三是竞争范围有限，招标人或者雇主只要向三家以上承包商发出邀请标书即可；四是招标时间大大缩短，招标费用也相对较低；五是公开程度与公开招标相比较，不如公开招标。

4.2.3　议标或谈判招标

议标或谈判招标由雇主直接与选定的承包方就发包项目进行协商的招标方式。目前，我国实践中特别是在建筑领域里有一种使用较多的采购方法，被称为"议标"，实质上即为谈判性采购，是采购人和被采购人之间通过一对一谈判而最终达到采购目的的一种采购方式，不具有公开性和竞争性，因而不属于招标投标法所称的招标投标采购方式。

从实践上看，公开招标和邀请招标的采购方式要求对报价及技术性条款不得谈判，议标则允许就报价等进行一对一的谈判。因此，有些项目比如一些小型建设项目采用议标方式目标明确，省时省力，比较灵活。在我国，《招标投标法》根据招标的基本特性和我国实践中存在的问题，未将议标作为一种招标方式予以规定。因此，议标不是一种法定招标方式。依照《招标投标法》的规定，凡属《招标投标法》第三条规定必须招标的项目以及按照《招标投标法》第二条规定自愿采用招标方式进行采购的项目，都不得采用议标的方式。

4.3　一阶段和双阶段招标投标程序❶

4.3.1　一阶段招标投标程序

一阶段招标投标程序又分为一阶段一步法招标程序、一阶段两步法招标程序：

1. 一阶段一步法招标程序

---

❶ 凌文．常用招标程序浅析［J］．企业技术开发中旬刊，2014（12）．

一阶段一步法招标程序是目前绝大多数工程项目采用的招标程序，即在投标截止时间前投标人将技术投标文件、商务投标文件和投标报价一并提交，开标时同时开启所有投标文件。开标后，评标委员会即进入评标流程，通过初评、详评、澄清、价格调整和打分（若有），最终选出中标候选人。由于该招标程序过程简单、清晰，被广泛适用于货物、工程和服务招标中。

2. 一阶段两步法招标程序

一阶段两步法招标程序即在投标截止时间前投标人将技术投标文件、商务投标文件和投标报价一并提交，开标时只开启技术投标文件和商务投标文件，投标报价由监督组或招标代理机构保存。开标后，评标委员会先对技术投标文件和商务投标文件进行评审，根据评标专家的阅标情况，可以要求投标人对技术和商务投标文件澄清、补充和修正，并根据技术投标文件修正的内容提供补充报价。在技术评审和商务评审结束后，评标委员会确定递交补充报价的时间和宣布投标报价的时间。投标报价开启后，一并唱出投标报价和补充报价。

4.3.2 两阶段招标程序

《招标投标法实施条例》第三十条明确规定，对技术复杂或者无法精确拟定技术规格的项目，招标人可以分两阶段进行招标。第一阶段，潜在投标人按照招标公告或者投标邀请书的要求提交不带报价的技术建议书，这一阶段主要是招标人与投标人反复磋商，通过评审、商讨和论证，采用一个或几个已经提交的建议书，或者综合所有提交的建议书研究确定一套新的技术方案，以此作为技术标准和要求编制完整的招标文件。第二阶段，招标人编制完成招标文件后，向第一阶段递交技术建议书的投标人发投标邀请书，或发布招标公告接受未参与第一阶段提交技术建议书的潜在投标人参与投标。

两阶段招标程序主要针对以总承包方式采购的大型复杂设备、技术难度大的特殊复杂工程和技术发展快捷，难以事先确定技术方案的信息通信领域项目。在这些项目的招标采购过程中，存在着诸如对市场技术不熟悉，难以编制技术规范书；虽然了解市场情况，但存在多种相近的可接受技术方案；存在多种技术方案，各方案均有利弊等问题。通过两阶段的招标程序，可以通过投标人的力量，确保招标人以最优的方案完成招标采购。

4.4 传统招标投标程序

招标投标最显著的特点就是招标投标活动具有严格规范的程序。按照《招标投标法》的规定，一个完整的招标投标程序，必须包括招标、投标、开标、评标、中标和签订合同六大环节。

4.4.1 招标

招标是指招标人按照国家有关规定履行项目审批手续、落实资金来源后，依法发布招标公告或投标邀请书，编制并发售招标文件等。根据项目特点和实际需要，有些招标项目还要委托招标代理机构协助完成。

4.4.2 投标

投标是指投标人根据招标文件要求，编制并提交投标文件，响应招标活动。投标人参与竞争并进行一次性投标报价是在投标环节完成的。在投标截止时间结束后，招标人不能接受新的投标，投标人也不得再更改投标报价及其他实质性内容。

4.4.3　开标

开标是招标人按照招标文件确定的时间和地点，邀请所有投标人到场，当众开启投标人提交的投标文件，宣布投标人名称、投标报价及投标文件中其他重要内容。开标最基本要求和特点是公开，保障所有投标人的知情权，这也是维护各方合法权益的基本条件。

4.4.4　评标

招标人依法组建评标委员会，依据招标文件规定和要求，对投标文件进行审查和比较，确定中标候选人。评标是审查确定中标人的必经程序。对于依法必须招标的项目招标人必须根据评标委员会提出的书面评标报告和推荐的中标候选人确定中标人。

4.4.5　中标

中标，也称定标，即招标人从评标委员会推荐的中标候选人中确定中标人，并向中标人发出中标通知书，并同时将中标结果通知所有未中标的投标人。

4.4.6　签订书面合同

中标通知书发出后，招标人和中标人应当按照招标文件和中标人的投标文件在规定时间内，协商订立书面合同。

4.5　国际招标投标中注意的问题

近年来，随着海外工程承包业务规模的迅速拓展，中国公司承接海外工程所面临的市场环境的复杂性和风险的不可预见性大大增加，与此相应的法律风险也日益增加。因此，必须了解海外工程适用的国际惯例和当地法律环境，总结经验教训，在签约前的投标阶段，加强投标风险的审查，以便及早识别并控制、规避与防范投标风险，防患于未然。

（1）组建经验丰富的招标投标工作组。在这个阶段，积极地沟通可能产生意想不到的结果，这使得承包商在工程技术参数、采购程序方面得到雇主的认可，同时对于承包商选择标准，使用的标准合同文本亦产生一定的影响。但是，在进行积极地沟通时，注意不要侵犯当地政府规章制度，项目所在国的法律，例如不要违背反贿赂，反不正当竞争等相关法律。因此，在投标准备阶段，组织一支招标投标经验丰富的队伍就至关重要。

（2）审查项目资金来源。资金来源是建设工程能否顺利进行的关键。首先要考察项目资金是否属世行、亚行或其他国际组织贷款项目？如果是世行、亚行或其他国际组织贷款项目，投标人可以大胆参加，通常此类项目工程款的回收是有保障的。同时也要考察，项目资金是否由项目所在国政府出资？如果是项目所在国政府出资，则要充分考虑该政府的经济状况、偿还信誉和能力等方面，从而决定是否参加该项目。

（3）合约的性质和特殊条款。当拿到标书后，要明确标书规定的合约性质：是单价合约，还是总价合约；是有条件的合约，还是条件待定合约。另外，在国际工程招标中，通常采用 FIDIC 条款作为合约的基本条款。雇主会根据实际情况，针对不同的项目，制订特殊条款。

（4）审查中标文件与合同文件一致性是避免开工后纠纷的重要的工作。同时，充分的时间可以使承包商充分评审招标文件和接下来的合同文件，避免不准确定义和合同条款不一致引起的纠纷。

（5）投标前应确保雇主对项目资金有合理的来源和充分的安排。有的项目投标人没有认真了解雇主的资信和项目资金状况，就盲目投标。合同签署后，发现雇主其实没有足够的项目资金，导致项目无法正常开工或者中间停工。

（6）投标前应当对当地建筑规范进行了解

有的项目投标时只处于概念设计或方案设计阶段，设计深度不够，诸多设计参数都没有确定，承包商对项目所在国建筑规范不了解，无法编制详细的工程量清单，项目存在较大的潜在风险。因此，建议承包商在投标前与工程师和雇主进行信函沟通，要求提供足够深度的图纸，投标前对当地建筑规范进行必要的了解，特别是图纸设计深度不够的项目。

（7）注意价格与支付条款

合同价格与支付条款对于承包商来讲是合同最重要的条款之一，承包商承包工程的最主要目的就是拿到合理的合同价格，取得及时的付款；而雇主为了确保工程期限和质量，一般会通过合同价格和支付条件限制承包商。

（8）合同纠纷解决方式是否合理

纠纷解决条款在合同评审时经常被忽略，该条款也是承包商最容易向雇主让步的条款之一，因为承包商一般觉得合同关于纠纷解决方式的规定只是摆设。但是，一旦发生纠纷，如果纠纷解决方式不合理，承包商会面临无法克服的法律障碍。

Questions

1. Discuss the traditional process of construction tendering?

2. Please introduce your country's Tendering System?

3. What acknowledgements the Contractors should have in Bidding?

Chapter 5   Signing the Contract

5.1   How to properly sign a contract so it will be enforceable

Most people think that actually signing a contract is a mere formality. However, it is important not to let your guard down at this point. Whether you properly sign the contract may make the difference between a smooth business transaction or a messy court fight. The following steps should be followed when signing any contract:

1. Make sure the contract to be signed is the contract agreed to sign

If the contract has gone through a number of rounds of negotiations or revisions, don't just assume that the copy put in front of you to sign is what you think it is. Before you sign it, be absolutely sure that you fully know and understand the terms of the document. Under Michigan law (USA), you are generally bound by a contract that you sign even if you have no knowledge of its contents. Unless you can prove that the other party engaged in fraud or other wrongdoing in preparing the contract or inducing you to sign it, you will be required to abide by it.

2. Date the contract

The date a contract was signed can become an important issue if you get into a contract dispute with the other party. For example, a contractor could claim that a one-year service agreement was signed 10 years ago and has long since expired. Without a date listed on the contract, you can't prove otherwise.

3. Make sure both parties sign the contract

There is absolutely no better way of proving that a party intended to be bound by a contract then by whipping it out and displaying their signature on the document. If it is possible that the parties to a contract will not sign it at the same time, you might consider adding a section in the contract providing that the contract will not be legally binding unless it is signed by both parties.

The parties do not necessarily have to sign the same copy of the contract in order for it to be binding. If the parties do sign different copies of the contract, they must agree that each of their signature pages together constitute a complete executed agreement. That's why contracts often contain a provision stating that " the parties may execute this contract in counterparts, each of which is deemed an original and all of which constitute only one agreement. "

4. Make sure any last minute changes to the contract are initialed

The best course of action is to have any changes included in the signature version of the contract. This will help ensure there are no misunderstandings as to what the parties intended to sign. However, if it is not possible to have a contract revised and reprinted before it is signed, make sure that any changes made to the contract by hand are initialed by each party to the contract.

5. The parties must sign the contract in their correct capacity

If an entity is a party to a contract, it is imperative that the signature block properly identifies the party signing on behalf of that entity. Why is this so important? Because signing correctly on behalf of an entity will prevent any later claims that the person signing the contract is personally liable for the entity's contractual obligations.

6. Keep an Original Signed Copy of the Contract in Your Files

Each party should get an original signed copy of the contract for their files. That means if there are two parties to the contract, two identical contracts must be signed. One original copy of the contract should go to you, and one original copy should go to the other party.

5. 2   Finding agreement in practice

English law generally adopts an objective theory of contract formation, the governing criterion being the reasonable expectations of honest sensible business persons. The formulaic approach to finding agreement through offer and acceptance is not always possible. Contracts may come into existence, not as a result of offer and acceptance, but during and as a result of performance.

The courts will often takea pragmatic approach and find a contract even though it is difficult or impossible to analyse the transaction in terms of offer and acceptance-because for example protracted negotiations make it difficult to 'fit' the respective communications between the parties into a strict offer / acceptance analysis. Therefore, performance or consideration are important elements in finding a effective agreement in practice.

5. 3   Offer

5. 3. 1   What is an offer

(1) An 'offer' is an expression of willingness by one person (the offeror) to contact with another (the offeree) on the terms stated in the offer

(2) It is necessary to show that the offeror has an intention to be legally bound by what is being promised-not merely a genuine intention to do what is being promised.

(3) The offer must be capable of acceptance by the offeree.

5. 3. 2   The relationship between the offeror and the offeree

It is the offeree who has the ultimate power to bring a contract into existence - an offer has no contractual force until it has been accepted.

"What kind of act creates a power of acceptance and is therefore an offer? It must be an expression of will or intention. It must be an act that leads the offeree reasonably to conclude that a power to create a contract is conferred. This applies to the content of the power as well as to the fact of its existence. "❶

5. 3. 3   Invitations to treat

In Andrew Burrows' words, an invitation to treat is "... an expression of willingness to negotiate. A person making an invitation to treat does not intend to be bound as soon as it is accepted by the person to whom the statement is addressed. "

A contract is a legally binding voluntary agreement that is formed when one person makes an offer, and the other accepts it. There may be some preliminary discussion before an offer is formally made.

"The transmission of such a price-list does not amount to an offer to supply an unlimited quantity of the wine described at the price named, so that as soon as an order is given there is a binding contract to supply that quantity. If it were so, the merchant might find himself involved in any number of contractual obligations to supply wine of a particular description which he would be quite unable to carry out, his stock of wine of that description being necessarily limited. "❷

There is no absolute rule that communications of a particular kind such as newspaper advertisements are (or are not) offers. Whether an offer has been made is judged objectively-what matters is how a reasonable person in the position of the person to whom it was made would interpret the communication.

5. 3. 4   Commercial Advertisment is not a offer

It seems to me that in order to arrive at a right conclusion we must read this advertisement in its plain meaning, as the public would understand it. It was intended to be issued to the public and to be read by the public. How would an ordinary person reading this document construe it? It was intended unquestionably to have some effect, and I think the effect which it was intended to have, was to make people use the smoke ball, because the suggestions and allegations which it contains are directed immediately to the use of the smoke ball as distinct from the purchase of it. It did not follow that the smoke ball was to be purchased from the defendants directly, or even from agents of theirs directly. The intention was that the circulation of the smoke ball should be promoted, and that the use of it should be increased⋯ And it seems to me that the way in which the public would read it would be this, that if anybody, after the advertisement was published, used three times daily for two weeks the carbolic smoke ball, and then caught cold, he would be entitled to

---

❶   Leonard v Pepsico Inc 88 F. Supp. 2d 116 (1999) at 127.

❷   See Grainger & Son v Gough [1896] AC 325 at 334 per Lord Herschell.

the reward⋯**❶**

5.3.5 How long does an offer last?

(1) The general rule is that an offer continues to be available for acceptance⋯

(a) until the time (if any) specified.

(b) unless the offer is revoked by the offeror in the meantime.

(c) provided that the offeree has not already rejected the offer.

(2) An offer might come to an end because of

(a) Prior revocation

An offer may be revoked (withdrawn) by the offeror at any time before acceptance.

(b) Lapse of time

Where time is stipulated the offer lapses on expiry of the specified period. Where no time is stated the offer must be accepted within a reasonable time.

(c) Failure of a condition

If an offer is subject to a particular 'contingency' or 'requirement' being satisfied, the offer terminates if that requirement is not satisfied-for example, making an offer subject to finance; a builder's report or a satisfactory AA report.

(d) Death

The general rule is that an offer terminates on the death of either the offeror or the offeree. However, it is possible that the offeror's estate may be bound if the offeree performs an act of acceptance in ignorance of the offeror's death-would only be possible where the offer is of a promise which is independent of the offeror's personality.

(e) Prior rejection

An offer is terminated if the offeree rejects it. A counter-offer has the same effect as a rejection. An enquiry or a request for further information does not constitute a rejection or a counter-offer. **❷**

5.4 The acceptance

5.4.1 Legal significance of acceptance

(1) The acceptance of the offer brings the contract into existence.

(2) As a general proposition, all terms in the contract are agreed at that point.

(3) Both parties are legally bound by what they have agreed.

(4) Failure to perform an obligation flowing from a legally binding promise gives the innocent party a right to damages (and possibly other remedies).

5.4.2 Requirements of acceptance

(1) Acceptance takes place when there is compliance with the requirements stated in

---

❶ Carlill v Carbolic Smoke Ball Co 〔1893〕 1QB 256 at 266-268.

❷ See Stevenson v McLean (1880) 5 QBD 346 at 350 which is an English contract law case concerning the rules on communication of acceptance by telegraph. Its approach contrasts to the postal rule.

the offer.

(2) Only the person to whom the offer was made may accept the offer.

(3) The offeree can only accept an offer if he/she knows about it.

(4) Unless the offer states otherwise, acceptance must be unequivocal; and Communicated to the offeree.

5.4.3　Unequivocal acceptance

(1) It must be clear that the offer is being accepted.

(2) Any unequivocal indication by words or conduct that the offer is being accepted will suffice.

(3) There must be complete and unconditional compliance with the requirements stated in the offer -ie the acceptance must 'match' the offer.

(4) Any deviation from the offer is not acceptance even where it may be legallyinconsequential.

(5) With a counter-offer (see above) the offeree does not accept the terms proposed by the offeror but instead puts forward different terms for the proposed contract.

5.4.4　Acceptance must be communicated

(1) It is not sufficient for the offeree merely to decide to accept the offer.

(2) The general rule is that acceptance is not effective unless and until it is communicated to the offeror.

(3) Communication need not be by the offeree personally.

(4) The offeror can specify the manner of acceptance.

5.4.5　Acceptance inferred from conduct

What the court is trying to do in most cases is to determine whether there is an appearance of mutual agreement; would the reasonable bystander consider the offeree to have assented to the terms proposed by the offeror.

Sometimes conduct may demonstrate an acceptance even though there have been no express words indicating agreement[1].

5.4.6　Electronic communications

Electronic communications such as email, text and SMS messages are virtually instantaneous. The preferred view therefore is that there is no rationale for departing from the general rule that there must be a communication of acceptance-ie no contract comes into existence until the offeror actually receives the acceptance.

This approach is consistent with the Contract and Commercial Law Act 2017 (New Zealand) Part 4 Electronic Transactions (formerly the Electronic Transactions Act 2002). The Act provides default rules which govern the status and effect of electronic communications in the absence of any contrary agreement by the parties.

Section 214 Time of receipt:

---

[1]　See Brogden v Metropolitan Railway Co Ltd (1877) 2 App Cas 666.

An electronic communication is taken to be received,

(1) in the case of an addressee who has designated an information system for the purpose of receiving electronic communications, at the time the electronic communication enters that information system; or

(2) in any other case, at the time the electronic communication comes to the attention of the addressee.

Section 217 Time of communication of acceptance of offer:

For the purpose of the formation of a contract, an acceptance by electronic communication of an offer is taken to be communicated to the offeror at the time determined by section 214 to be the time of receipt for that electronic communication.

5. 5　Consideration

5. 5. 1　What is consideration

Consideration is the main requirement for enforceability of a contract at common law. The doctrine of consideration represents the idea of bargain and mutual obligations - the essence of the doctrine is that only promises which have been "purchased" should be enforced as a contract. Gratuitous promises are not binding as contracts-although they may be enforced as a deed❶ or on some other basis. Consideration is provided by the 'promisee'-ie the person to whom the promise is made, and who seeks to enforce it, must show that she provided something of 'value' for that promise. No action for damages for breach of contract is available unless the promise alleged to have been breached is supported by consideration.

5. 5. 2　Benefit-detriment and bargain theory of consideration

1. Benefit-detriment theory

The question is: What constitutes good consideration in the eyes of the law? The early cases defined consideration in terms of benefit and/or detriment. The classic formulation of the definition was provided in *Currie v Misa*❷: "A valuable consideration, in the eyes of the law, may consist either in some right, interest, profit, or benefit accruing to the one party, or some forebearance, detriment loss, or responsibility given, suffered or undertaken by the other." Most cases can be analysed in terms of a detriment suffered by the promisee and a corresponding benefit flowing to the promisor in exchange for her promise.

2. The bargain theory

In more recent cases the dominant view has focused on the idea of bargain and the ele-

---

❶　deed. A written document that must make it clear on its face that it is intended to be a deed and validly executed as a deed. see Oxford Dictionary of Law, P177, Oxford University Press.

❷　*Currie v Misa* (1875) LR 10 Ex 153 at 162.

ment of exchange and define consideration as the price paid for a promise. "An act or forbearance of one party, or the promise thereof, is the price for which the promise of the other is bought, and the promise thus given for value is enforceable. "❶

5.5.3   Consideration conditions

1. Consideration must move from the promisee to promisor, not to third party

As a general rule, a person can enforce a promise made to her only if she herself provided the consideration for that promise-traditionally expressed by the statement that consideration must move from the promisee. This rule is closely related to the common law doctrine of privity of contract which provides that only a person who is a party to the contract can sue on the contract or be bound by it.

2. Consideration must be sufficient

Consideration must be sufficient-ie. if the promisee provides something of 'value' that is sufficient. Generally the courts will not enquire into whether adequate value has been given for the promisor's promise, a contract may be held valid when the exchange involved in it is very unequal. The courts will not enquire into whether the parties have made a fair bargain or exchange.

3. Consideration must not be past

The necessary price can be paid, either by a promise to do something or by actually doing it. Hence consideration may be provided either by a promise or by an act. A promise confers a benefit in law and an act provides a benefit in fact or a practical benefit, as it is sometimes called. An exchange of promises may provide consideration and so may the exchange of an act for a promise. In the latter case the act must be referable to or respond to the promise, otherwise it will not constitute consideration in law. An act already done without reference to a promise does not satisfy the concept of an exchange which underpins the law of consideration. That is why past consideration, ie the conferring of a benefit in the past, is no consideration in law.

5.6   Steps to sign a successful construction contract

To sign a successful construction contract, you are suggested to follow next nine steps:

5.6.1   Review your bid

When you get called that you are the successful bidder, don't get excited and put the cart before the horse. Before gearing up to sign a contract or start work, review your bid carefully. Have your bookkeeper check the math. Have your field superintendent and foreman check the labor and equipment figures. Call your major suppliers and subcontractors to confirm their bids. Remember, only you decide if you will sign the contract and a-

---

❶ *Dunlop Pneumatic Tyre Co Ltd v Selfridge & Co Ltd* [1915] AC 847 at 855 per Lord Dunedin.

gree to all the terms. If all looks good, go on to the next step.

5. 6. 2 Review complete plans

General contractors and subcontractors don't always get to see the complete set of plans, specifications, addendas, general conditions, proposed contract format and complete contract documents when asked to submit their bids. Before signing a contract, review all plans and project documents including: architectural, structural, civil, plumbing, mechanical and electrical plans; soils reports; addendum; finish schedules and the City conditions of approval.

5. 6. 3 Review all specifications

Because specification books are often three inches thick, many contractors only read the section that affects their trade. It is imperative, however, to review all specification sections before you sign a contract. You are contractually liable for all requirements included in the complete document. The general conditions section, for example, contains contractual requirements for job site safety, submittals, cleanup, change orders and how to get paid. Never - Never - Never sign a contract without reviewing the complete specifications.

5. 6. 4 Visit the job site

Always send your field superintendent to the jobsite to look for any unforeseen conditions, conflicts with the project plans and logistic concerns that can cause you grief later. Every job looks different in person than they do on paper. Things to consider include: ① Access; ②Parking; ③Mobilization; ④Staging area; ⑤Power availability; ⑥Phone availability; ⑦Water availability; ⑧Project office location; ⑨Storage yard access; ⑩Soil conditions; ⑪Demolition required; ⑫Clearing required; ⑬Neighboring property; ⑭Protection Required; ⑮Hazards; ⑯Street improvements; ⑰Location of underground.

5. 6. 5 Review the job schedule

Before committing to any project, make sure you completely understand and agree with the project schedule. Lost job profits generally can be attributed to improper scheduling of crews, poor supervision and lack of field coordination. Be careful to verify your major subcontractor and suppliers can make the project to meet the schedule. Look for delay and damage clauses contained within the contract. Also, look at how delay charges will be transferred through to subcontractors if they don't perform. Consider issues like weather delays, strikes, material shortages, etc. when reviewing every contract. Verify how you can remedy situations where you are being delayed by the project owner or a subcontractor not performing as well.

5. 6. 6 Complete a project checklist

When reviewing construction contracts, please use this simple project checklist so you and your project team will not overlook important items. On the list be sure to include: ①Scope of work; ②Inclusions & exclusions; ③Plans & specifications; ④Project schedule & manpower; ⑤Insurance requirements; ⑥Bonding requirements; ⑦Payment procedures；⑧Cash flow requirements；⑨Person（s）authorized to sign；⑩Change order procedures；⑪Dispute resolution methods；⑫Notice required on issues；⑬Delay，claims & protests；⑭Request for information；⑮Shop drawings & submittals；⑯Meetings required to attend；⑰Safety requirements；⑱Permit requirements；⑲Site access，logistics & parking；⑳Special tools & equipment required；㉑Contract close-out procedures；㉒Final payment procedures.

5.6.7   Verify project funding

Every general contractor and subcontractor has the right to know that projects have adequate funds to complete them plus a reasonable reserve for unforeseen changes and contingencies. So，always ask for proof of funding.

5.6.8   Read complete contract

Signing a contract prepared by someone else can be scary. The days of a handshake contract are long gone. Today，contractingis about contracts! If you don't understand what you are signing，you won't stay in business very long. Many contacts contain clauses that are one-sided and unfair. Carefully look over contract clauses dealing with such issues as：①Payment，retention & pay when paid；②Indemnification；③Authorizations，notices，approvals & administration；④Conflict resolution and disputes；⑤Arbitration vs. court；⑥Schedule issues、Failure to perform、Delays and weather、Acceleration & termination、Liquidated damages；⑦Change orders & back-charges；⑧Cleanup & supervision.

5.6.9   Execute contract

The construction business is risky enough without unfair contracts. So，before you execute any contract，follow these nine steps and start out every project on a fair and level playing field.

☞ 疑难词句 ☜

1. A pragmatic approach 务实的态度

2. Default rules 是指可以被合同、信托、遗嘱或其他具有法律效力的协议所取代的（判例法规则）

3. Doctrine of privity of contract 合同相对性原则

4. Errs in 犯错误

5. The supervening 随后发生

6. With reasonable promptness 合理的时间内

7. In transit 在运输中

8. Outlay 之处，花费

9. Stretching beyond 伸展，超出.

10. Signing a contract prepared by someone else can be scary. The days of a handshake contract are long gone 签订别人准备的合同可能是件可怕的事情，握手合同的时代一去不复返了。

11. "Red-flag" clauses 危险条款

12. Cross out the inappropriate clauses 删去不合适的条款

13. Be awkward to 难以，不适合于

14. Dryly-worded document 枯燥无味的文件

15. Costs plus a markup 成本加利润

16. Put the cart before the horse 前后颠倒，本末倒置

17. Before gearing up to sign a contract or start work 在签订合同或开工之前

18. Field superintendent and foreman 现场负责人和工头

☞ 中文综述 ☜

5.1 合同订立概述

大多数人认为签订合同仅仅是一个形式问题。其实，是否恰当地签署了合同，决定了合同各方能否顺利地进行交易或者卷入一场混乱的法庭诉讼。一般而言，签订合同要注意以下几点：

1. 确定将要签署的合同是你同意签署的合同

如果合同经历了数轮谈判或修正，合同内容发生了很大的变化，因此，不要侥幸放在你面前的合同还是你熟悉和认知的。在签署之前，一定要重新审视，完全了解和理解合同的主要条款。根据美国密歇根州的法律，即使你不知道合同的内容，你也必须对签署的合同承担责任。除非你能证明合同对方存在欺诈或其他不法行为，否则你将被要求遵守合同。

2. 合同日期

合同上的日期是一个重要的法律问题。例如，承包商可以声称，为期一或两年的售后服务协议是 10 年前签署的，现在已经过期很久了。没有合同上所列的日期，你无法证明不是这样的。

3. 确保双方签署合同

没有更好的方法通过展示签署的合同文件来证明合同一方希望受到合同条款约束的意图。如果合同双方不能同时签署合同，可以考虑在合同中加入一个条款：除非合同双方签字，否则合同将不具有法律约束力。如果双方确实签署了合同的不同副本，他们必须同意，他们的每一个签字页构成合同的有效组成部分，是可执行的协议。这就是为什么合同中经常有这样的条款："本合同一式两份，甲乙双方各执一份，每一份都被视为原件，所有文本构成一份合同。"

4. 确保对最后修改合同条款的可知性

这将有助于确保各方在拟签署的协议上不存在误解。但是，如果不能在合同签署前对合同进行修改和重印，则应确保对合同所作的任何修改都是由合同各方同意的。

5. 双方签署合同应在其权利范围内进行

如果合同一方是一个实体，该实体应保证合同内容是在该实体授权范围内的，例如不同建筑工程要求不同级别的技术资质，在签订合同前，承包商应确认其资质符合项目要求。

5.2　邀约承诺模式与实践中的合同

我国《合同法》第二条中规定:"合同是平等主体的自然人、法人、其他组织之间设立、变更、终止民事权利义务关系的协议。"既然合同为一种协议,就须由当事人各方的意思表示的一致即合意才能成立。当事人为达成协议,相互为意思表示进行协商到达成合意的过程也就是合同的订立过程。根据我国《合同法》第十三条规定,以及大陆法系国家的法律实践,合同订立一般经过要约与承诺两个阶段。要约是指一方当事人以缔结合同为目的,向对方当事人提出合同条件,希望对方当事人接受的意思表示。发出要约的一方称要约人,接受要约的一方称受要约人。承诺是指受要约人同意接受要约的全部条件而缔结合同的意思表示。

我国属社会主义法律体系,与大陆法系相似。在判断合同效力与可执行问题上,邀约与承诺是合同的构成要件,只要满足邀约与承诺,合同成立,也就可以执行。然而,英美法系国家,在判断合同效力和是否可执行方面,更注重合同对价(Consideration)是否已经成立,没有对价的合同是无效的,不可以执行的。

5.3　要　　约

5.3.1　要约的含义

要约是一方当事人向另一方当事人提出订立合同的条件,并希望对方能完全接受此条件的意思表示。发出要约的一方称为要约人,受领要约的一方称为受要约人(承诺人)。要约一般由下列几个因素构成:

(1)要约须具有订立合同的意图。所谓订立合同的意图,是指要约人通过文字表述使受要约人感受要约人希望与之订立合同的愿望和条件。

(2)要约须是要约人向与之缔结合同的受要约人发出。一般认为,要约应当向特定人发出,这个特定人就是要约人希望和他订立合同的人。而特定不限于一个,也可以是几个,但必须都是确定的。

(3)要约的内容必须具体确定。所谓具体确定,是指要约中应包含有合同的主要条款,让受要约人看了以后可以决定是否同意订约并作出承诺。

(4)要约必须送达受要约人。要约只有到达受要约人,受要约人才有可能了解要约的内容,并决定是否承诺。

与要约相近的概念有要约邀请。《合同法》第十五条规定,要约邀请是希望他人向自己发出要约的意思表示。寄送的价目表、拍卖公告、招标公告、招股说明书、商业广告等为要约邀请。

要约与要约邀请最根本的区别就在于要约有成立合同的具体确定的内容,而要约邀请则不必也不应具备满足合同成立的内容,否则其就成为要约而不是要约邀请。要约一经相对方承诺,合同即告成立,如未按规定履行,则要承担违约的后果。要约与要约邀请有以下三个不同点:第一,要约邀请是一方邀请对方向自己发出要约,而要约是由一方发出订立合同的意思表示。第二,要约是当事人旨在订立合同的意思表示,含有要约人愿意接受要约拘束的意旨,而要约邀请不含有当事人愿意承受拘束的意旨,不具有法律上的约束力。第三,要约在内容上应具备愿与他人订立合同的必要条款,要约邀请则一般不必具备足以使合同成立的必要条款。

5.3.2 商业广告的要约属性判断

商业广告,一般属于要约邀请,但内容符合要约规定的,可以视为要约。所谓符合要约规定,即商业广告表达了希望和收到广告者订立合同的愿望,并且其内容具体确定,表明一经相对人承诺,广告发出者即受该意思表示的约束。但要约邀请是否构成要约,最终判断和决定权在法官。

《合同法》第十五条第二款规定:"商业广告的内容符合要约规定的,视为要约。"《最高人民法院关于审理商品房买卖合同纠纷案件适用法律若干问题的解释》(法释〔2003〕7号,以下简称"司法解释")第三条规定:"商品房的销售广告和宣传资料为要约邀请,但是出卖人就商品房开发规划范围内的房屋及相关设施所作的说明和允诺具体确定,并对商品房买卖合同的订立以及房屋价格的确定有重大影响的,应当视为要约。该说明和允诺即使未载入商品房买卖合同,亦应当视为合同内容,当事人违反的,应当承担违约责任。"

5.4 承 诺

5.4.1 承诺的含义

承诺是指受要约人同意接受要约的条件以缔结合同的意思表示。承诺的法律效力在于一经承诺并送达于要约人,合同便告成立。在法律上,承诺必须具备以下条件,才能产生法律效力:

(1)承诺必须由受要约人向要约人作出。由于要约原则上是向特定人发出的,因此只有接受要约的特定人即受要约人才有权作出承诺,受要约人以外的第三人无资格向要约人作出承诺。同时,承诺必须向要约人作出,如果向要约人以外的其他人作出承诺,则只能视为对他人发出要约,不能产生承诺效力。

(2)承诺必须在规定的期限内到达要约人。《合同法》第二十三条规定:"承诺应当在要约确定的期限内到达要约人"。承诺的期限通常都是在要约人发出的要约中规定的,如果要约规定了承诺期限,则应当在规定的承诺期限内到达;在没有规定期限时,如果要约是以对话方式作出的,承诺人应当及时作出承诺,如果要约是以非对话方式作出的,承诺应当在合理的期限内作出并到达要约人。

(3)承诺的内容必须与要约的内容一致。受要约人必须表明其愿意按照要约的全部内容与要约人订立合同。也就是说,承诺是对要约的同意,其同意内容须与要约的内容一致,才构成意思表示的一致即合意,从而使合同成立。承诺的内容与要约的内容一致,意味着承诺不得限制、扩张或者变更要约的内容,换言之,承诺不得对要约的内容作出实质性的修改。

根据我国《合同法》第三十一条,"承诺对要约的内容作出非实质性更改的,除要约人及时表示反对或者要约表明承诺不得对要约的内容作出任何变更的以外,该承诺有效,合同的内容以承诺的内容为准"。这就是说,即使是非实质性内容的变更在以下两种情况下承诺也不能生效。第一,要约人及时表示反对,即要约人在收到承诺通知后,立即表示不同意受要约人对非实质性内容所作的变更,如果经过一段时间后仍不表示反对,则承诺已生效。第二,要约人在要约中明确表示,承诺不得对要约的内容作出任何变更,否则无效,则受要约人作出非实质性变更也不能使承诺生效。

（4）承诺的方式必须符合要约的要求。《合同法》第二十二条规定，"承诺应当以通知的方式作出。"这就是说，受要约人必须将承诺的内容通知要约人，但受要约人应采取何种通知方式，应根据要约的要求确定。如果要约规定承诺必须以一定的方式作出，否则承诺无效，那么承诺人作出承诺时，必须符合要约人规定的承诺方式，在此情况下，承诺的方式成为承诺生效的特殊要件。例如要约要求承诺应以发电报的方式作出，则不应采取邮寄的方式。如果要约没有特别规定承诺的方式，则不能将承诺的方式作为有效承诺的特殊要件。

5.4.2　在建设工程招投标过程中的要约与承诺

在招标投标过程中，从《合同法》意义上讲，招标是指招标人采取招标公告或者招标邀请书的形式，向法人或其他组织发出要约邀请以吸引其投标的意思表示。因此，招标属于要约邀请的性质，而投标是一种法律上的要约行为，是指投标人按照招标人提出的要求和条件，在规定的期限内向投标人发出的包括合同主要条款的意思表示。

我国《招标投标法》第四十五条规定，"中标人确定后，招标人应当向中标人发出中标通知书，并同时将中标结果通知所有未中标的投标人。中标通知书对招标人和中标人具有法律效力，中标通知书发出后，招标人改变中标结果的，或者中标人放弃中标项目的，应当承担法律责任。"中标通知书就是招标人对其选中的投标人的承诺，是招标人同意某投标人要约的意思表示。

5.4.3　投标是否创造了一个有约束力的合同？

投标是承包商向业主发出的愿意按照招标文件所示条件承建工程项目的邀约。根据我国的法律实践，如果业主没有接纳某个承包商的投标，业主与该承包商之间并没有产生合同法律关系。但是，在英美法系国家，投标被视为投标过程合同（Process Contract），如果业主违背了招标文件中的某些许诺，就某一承包商投标行为而言，业主可能会被法官判定违反了投标过程合同（Process Contract）。

5.5　对　　价

5.5.1　对价的含义

对价是英美合同法上的效力原则的概念，其本意是"为换取另一个人做某事的允诺，某人付出的不一定是金钱的代价"，也许是"购买某种允诺的代价"。对价原则的功能在于区别可执行和不可执行的许诺，一般来说，英美法院不会执行一个没有对价的许诺。在英美法系国家，对价服务于以下两大功能：一是证据功能。对价的存在对合同各方签订有约束力的合同提供了客观的证据。二是警告功能。合同各方清楚地意识到，一方给出对价将使另一方的承诺得到强制执行。因此，各方在签订合同，给出对价之前要格外小心。

5.5.2　对价的条件

（1）对价必须从被邀约人向邀约人进行，而不是向第三方进行。作为一般规则，一个人可以向另一人要求执行承诺，其前提是另一个人对该承诺提供了对价。传统意义上的表述为，对价必须从受邀约人向邀约人进行。

（2）对价必须是充分的有价值的

对价必须是充分的——也就是说，承诺人提供的"价值"是充分的。对价应该是有价值的。爱情和喜爱并不具有现金价值，因此爱情和喜爱的承诺不构成对价。对价必须是价值可以客观确定的。

（3）过去的对价不是对价

必要的对价是可以通过承诺做某事或实际做某事来完成。因此，对价可以通过承诺或行为来实现。承诺赋予法律上的利益，行为产生事实上的利益。交换承诺可以提供对价，履约也是对价的表现形式。但是履约行为必须针对许诺，否则不构成法律上的对价。没有按照许诺实施的行为不符合对价的交换原则，因此不构成对价，这就是为什么过去的对价，即过去给予的利益承诺，在法律上不构成对价。例如，父亲去世后，将住房留给妻子，并遗嘱说当他的妻子也去世后，由 2 个孩子继承这个房产。这位妻子在丈夫去世后与其中的一个孩子居住在这件房子里，为了改善房屋的居住环境，与母亲一起居住在房子里的孩子拿出 500 元对房子进行修缮，另外一个孩子知道此事并承诺，在母亲去世，处理此房产时，将 500 元房子修缮费计算其中，其承担 250 元。但是在母亲去世后，处理该处房产时，承诺负担 250 元修缮费的孩子违背了他的承诺，理由是过去的对价不是对价。他的理由也得到了法官的支持。

5.6　签订建筑工程合同应注意的几个问题

5.6.1　仔细阅读标书、准备完整的施工计划

当获得中标通知书时，回顾和检查投标文件是非常重要的。作为承包商，在与雇主签订合同前，根据标书的条件，检查合同条款的规定是否与投标文件一致，这里包括阅读和理解合同文本的通用条件和附录。是否存在需要进一步与雇主协商的问题；检查是否对现场管理团队进行了有效的组织和安排，是否有充分的人力资源；现场设备的租赁与购置；与供应商和分包商是否就采购和分包工程达成一致。同时，开工需要相应的水、电、气等基础条件，也需要各种政府出具的允许开工的项目文件，这些都是完整施工计划的有效部分。

5.6.2　检查所有规格和技术参数

对于一个大型工程，技术规格与参数有几本书厚。有些承包商只阅读和其有直接关系的部分，而忽视了其他部分。作为承包商，不仅应当阅读和掌握与自己有关的部分，也要阅读与分包商或者其他工程项目参与者的部分，只有全面掌握了项目所有规格和技术参数，才可签订合同，才能更好地履行合同。

5.6.3　考查施工现场和检查工作进度计划

合同签订前，甚至投标前，对项目现场实地考察十分重要。根据 FIDIC 等国际工程施工标准合同文本，承包商在签订合同进入现场施工后，如果现场地表以下及水文条件产生预想不到的问题，承包商可能对因此增加的施工成本承担责任。对项目现场考查包括但不限于：现场进入；停车；道路改善；建设区段划分区域；电力供应；通信；水供应；现场项目办公地点；货场通道；土壤条件；需要拆除的设施；清洁；项目邻产；保安；危险；道路改善等。

在检查工作进度计划时，确保主要分包商和供应商按照项目计划完成工作。关注合同中延迟与损坏条款。同时也要关注气候原因引起的延迟条款，罢工条款和材料短缺条款等。

5.6.4　完善项目清单

当审查工程合同时，几个重要项目是不容忽视的，主要是：工程项目范围；包含和排除；计划与技术参数；工程计划表与人力资源；保险；担保要求；支付程序；现金流要求；签字授权人；工程变更通知程序；纠纷解决方法；纠纷通知要求；延期、索赔和抗议；信息要求；施工图和审核记录；要求参加的会议；安全要求；许可；现场进入，物流和停车；专用工具与设备要求；合同终止程序；尾款支付程序。

5.6.5　核实项目资金来源

资金的合理安排是项目顺利进行的关键。因此，主承包商与分包商有权利知道项目资金的安排情况，资金的来源。以确保主承包商与分包商及时得到支付。

5.6.6　理解和掌握合同完整内容

建筑工程合同往往不是单一合同文本，而是以雇主与主承包商之间签订的主合同为核心的合同体系。因此，合同各方首先应当清楚合同体系的构成，各合同主体之间的关系与地位。其次，要了解合同约定的内容。作为分包商，不仅要理解和熟悉其与主承包商签订的分包合同的内容，更应了解和熟悉雇主与主承包商之间签订的合同的内容。

Questions

1. How to properly sign a contract so it will be enforceable?

2. How do you understand offer and acceptance?

3. Discuss how to sign a successful construction contract?

4. How do you understand the consideration? Does civil law countries recognize the doctrine of consideration? Why?

Chapter 6　Standard Form Construction Contract

6. 1　What is standard form of construction contract

One of the distinctive features of the construction industry is the widespread use of standard conditions of engagement in respect of :

(1) contracts for professional services;

(2) construction contracts;

(3) construction subcontracts.

Many of these are national in origin and intended for use in the national sphere, although some of them may be suitable for use outside the jurisdiction in which they were developed. FIDIC, NEC, AIA and many others provide a series of popular form of construction. Large corporations have their own forms of contract and their own peculiar boilerplate.

Standard form contracts help give private construction transactions predictability and efficiency and have provided the framework for the development of construction. Because most industry drafted documents are developed through a process in which other industry groups and organizations participate or give feedback on proposed terms and conditions, these documents represent prevailing customs and practices and are good sources of industry best practices. Therefore, even if the parties choose to draft their own contract forms, industry standard forms serve as invaluable references for the parties' forms drafting and negotiations.

Industry standard forms are popular because they are familiar to industry players. This familiarity with standard terms and conditions reduces drafting and review time. Familiarity with standard terms and conditions provides contractors and subcontractors with the necessary comfort to offer lower bids or negotiated prices. Another reason to support the use of industry standard forms is that drafting a multi-part construction contract from scratch in a short time is an ambitious task for the inexperienced. Despite their usefulness, construction industry standard form contracts should not be used without noting certain cautions:

(1) Standard forms should not be used without modifications. Because they are drafted for broad use, standard form contracts cannot account for all specific transactional and jurisdictional terms that the parties need to insert in their agreements.

(2) When modifying a standard form, be wary of the "ripple effect." Because standard form construction contracts are complex documents that often reference other parts of the contract, changes made in one may have effects in another. Pay particular attention

when changing the definition of a word or term.

(3) Do not become "contract complacent. " Read the contract, even if it is a standard form. New projects and circumstances may necessitate a "fresh look" at specific boiler plate language.

(4) Custom-drafted and industry-drafted forms do not mix. Industry-drafted forms usually are coordinated only with other industry-drafted forms from the same organization (for example, AGC forms with other AGC forms). It is difficult to make custom forms compatible with industry-drafted forms. In addition, industry-drafted forms from different organizations usually are not compatible.

(5) Every contract form, including those drafted by industry organizations, contains the bias of the drafter. Any contract contains a bias, whether drafted by an industry organization or by counsel for one of the contracting parties. Therefore, you should know both the terms and conditions of and when to use the various standard forms published by different industry organizations.

6. 2　FIDIC

6. 2. 1　Introduction

FIDIC is a French language acronym for Fédération Internationale Des Ingénieurs-Conseils, which means the international federation of consulting engineers. It was started in 1913 by the trio of France, Belgium and Switzerland. The United Kingdom joined the Federation in 1949. FIDIC is headquartered in Switzerland and now boasts of membership all over the world. Over the years, FIDIC has become famous for its secondary activity of producing standard form contracts for the construction and engineering industry.

FIDIC published its first contract, titled "The Form of contract for works of Civil Engineering construction," in 1957. As the title indicated, this first contract was aimed at the Civil Engineering sector and it soon became known for the colour of its cover. It has become the tradition that FIDIC contracts are known in popular parlance by the colour of their cover.

6. 2. 2　FIDIC available documents

In 1999, FIDIC published a completely new suite of contracts, the 'Rainbow Suite', including:

(1) Red Book: Conditions of Contract for Construction (for Building and Engineering Works designed by the Employer) (1st Edition 1999).

(2) Yellow Book: Conditions of Contract for Plant and Design-Build (for electrical and mechanical plant, and for building works, designed by the Contractor) (1st Edition 1999).

(3) Silver Book: Conditions of Contract for EPC / Turnkey Projects (1st Edition 1999)

(4) Green Book: Short form of Contract (1st Edition 1999)

Other FIDIC contracts published before or after that date include:

(1) Pink Book: A version of the Red Book approved for use by the Multilateral Development Banks. The Islamic Development Bank and the World Bank worked with FIDIC in developing this contract form.

(2) Orange Book: Conditions of Contract for Design & Build and Turnkey (1st Edition 1995).

(3) Gold Book: DBO Contract - Conditions of Contract for Design, Build and Operate Projects (1st Edition 2008)

(4) Sub-consultancy Agreement (1st Edition 1992)

(5) White Book: Client/Consultant Model Services Agreement (4th Edition 2006)

(6) Form of Contract for Dredging and Reclamation Works (Dredgers Contract; First Edition, 2006).

(7) Conditions of Subcontract for Construction: for use with the Red Book and the Pink Book (Test Book was published in 2009, 1st edition 2011).

6. 2. 3 Introduction of FIDIC 2017

On 5 and 6 December 2017 in London the International Federation of Consulting Engineers (commonly known as FIDIC) launched its long-awaited FIDIC Suite 2017.

At first glance FIDIC Suite 2017 appears to be more prescriptive but at the same time more proactive than its predecessor FIDIC 1999. The primary aim of the newly launched FIDIC Suite 2017 is to introduce increased clarity and certainty for the purposes of reducing the risks of disagreements between the parties on the one hand and to further increase the probability of a successful project on the other. Broadly speaking the new 2017 FIDIC Suite is also intended to: (i) encourage more active contract management, (ii) reflect international best practice, (iii) remodel and emphasize dispute avoidance.

The structure of FIDIC Suite 2017 remains largely the same as the earlier 1999 edition. The contract consists of an Optional Contract Agreement, General Conditions and Particular Conditions. The Particular Conditions have been split into Contract Data (formerly called the "Appendix to Tender"), the project specific information which is to be completed by the parties and Special Provisions which are specific contractual provisions agreed between the parties.

In terms of structural amendments, there are now 21 clauses (as opposed to the 20 clauses in the 1999 edition) and this is due to the split of former clause 20 to separate 'day-to-day' parties' claims (Employer's and Contractor's Claims) from parties' disputes (Disputes and Arbitration). New definitions, now in alphabetical order, have been added, i. e. among others "Claim", "Delay Damages", "Extension of Time", whilst some have been renamed, i. e. "Force Majeure" to "Exceptional Events". More detailed contract management obligations have been imposed on both parties through: (i) introduction of the so- called concept of "Advance Warning" of any future events which may have an adverse effect on performance of the Works, increase of the Contract Price or delay in execution of the Works (Sub-Clause 8. 4), (ii) significant extension of details concerning the Contractor's programme, e. g. start and end dates for each activity, the float and critical path (Sub- Clause 8. 3), (iii) new management meetings (Sub-Clause 3. 8) and an updated quality management system (Sub-Clause 4. 9).

Undoubtedly, the significant increase of the rights and obligations of the parties which are based on the principle of reciprocity can be found throughout the text of the new 2017 edition, e. g. obligation to assist the Employer in obtaining its permits (Sub-Clause 1. 13 (c)), obligations not to poach staff (Sub-Clause 6. 3), advance warning obligations (Sub-Clause 8. 4). This further provides a fair and balanced approach to risk allocation.

An enhanced, strengthened and clarified role of the Engineer has been marked in the 2017 edition (Sub-Clause 3. 7), pursuant to which the obligation of the Engineer's neutrality has been confirmed and details of the Engineer's role in dealing with parties' claims through a step-by-step procedure has been re-introduced.

Considerable modifications have been incorporated to the design provisionsin relation to the so-called Fitness for Purpose (FFP) requirements (Sub-Clause 4. 1), under the new version of which *"if no purpose is stated in the Employer's Requirements, then the Works must be fit for their ordinary purpose"*. The foregoing modification is further backed up by: (i) the indemnity clause, according to which the Contractor is required to indemnify the Employer for failures of the Works or any Section or any major item of Plant not being FFP (Sub-Clause 17. 4), and (ii) the Contractor's obligation to hold professional indemnity insurance against its liabilities for failure to achieve FFP requirements (Sub-Clause 19. 2. 3).

Best practice provisions have also been incorporated in the new 2017 FIDIC Suite, e. g. Sub-Clauses 2. 3 and 6. 9, pursuant to which individuals engaged in fraud, corruption and similar practices can be removed at the request of one of the parties. Similarly, safety provisions (Sub-Clause 4. 8) and quality assurance provisions (Sub-Clause 4. 9) have been expanded and updated.

There are new Procedural Regulations for DAB Dispute Avoidance/Adjudication proceedings (now called DAAB proceedings), and templates of other contract documents such as the Letters of Tender, Performance Security documentation (such as Parent Company Guarantee and Performance Bonds) and an advisory note to users about Building Information Modelling. A new dispute avoidance role has been assigned to DAAB (Dispute Avoidance and Adjudication Board), whereby it can also provide 'informal assistance' to the parties. DAAB is thus now intended to have a more prominent role to attempt to resolve any disputes between the parties.

6. 3　Institution of Civil Engineers (ICE)

The Institution of Civil Engineers (ICE) is an independent professional association for civil engineers and a charitable body which exists to deliver benefits to the public. Based in London, ICE has nearly 89, 000 members, of whom three quarters are located in the United Kingdom, while the rest are located in more than 150 countries around the world. ICE supports the civil engineering profession by offering professional qualification, promoting education, maintaining professional ethics, and liaising with industry, academia and government. Under its commercial arm, it delivers training, recruitment, publishing and contract services. As a professional body, ICE is committed to support and promote professional learning (both to students and existing practitioners), managing professional ethics and safeguarding the status of engineers, and representing the interests of the profession in dealings with government, etc. It sets standards for membership of the body; works with industry and academia to progress engineering standards and advises on education and training curricula.

6.3.1   Available Documents

(1) ICE Conditions of Contract Measurement Version 7th Edition: July 2004

(2) ICE Conditions of Contract Design and Construct 2nd Edition: July 2004

(3) ICE Conditions of Contract Minor Works 3rd Edition: July 2004

(4) ICE Conditions of Contract Term Version: July 2004

(5) ICE Conditions of Contract Ground Investigation 2nd Edition: July 2004

(6) Agreement for Consultancy Work in respect of Domestic or Small Works: amendments Dec 1999

6.3.2   Brief Summary

(1) ICE Conditions of Contract, 7th Edition: July 2004

This Contract is based on the traditional pattern of engineer designed contractor built works with valuation by admeasurement. The traditional role of the engineer in advising the client, designing the works, supervising construction, certifying payment and adjudicating in cases of dispute is fully maintained.

(2) ICE Conditions of Contract Design and Construct 2nd Edition: July 2004

This contract radically departs from the normal ICE Conditions of Contract concept with the contractor responsible for all aspects of design and construction, including any design originally provided by or on behalf of the employer. The Form of Tender provides for payment on a lump sum basis but other forms of payment may be used.

(3) ICE Conditions of Contract Minor Works 3rd Edition: July 2004

Intended for use in contracts where:

1) the potential risks involved for both the employer and the contractor are adjudged to be small;

2) the works are of a simple and straightforward nature;

3) the design of the works, save for any design work for which the contractor is made responsible is complete in all essentials before tenders are invited;

4) the contractor has no responsibility for the design of the permanent works other

than possibly design of a specialist nature;

5) nominated sub-contractors are not employed; and

6) the contract value does not exceed £500, 000 and the period for completion of the contract does not exceed 6 months except where the method of payment is on either aday-work or a cost plus fee basis.

(4) ICE Conditions of Contract Term Version: July 2004

The concept of a term contract is to carry out routine maintenance and remedial work within a set geographical area. A contractor is appointed to carry out such work for an a-greed period of time (the term) carrying out such packages of work as may be required by the employer under conditions set out in the Term Version. The contract should be suit-able for planned and reactive maintenance or refurbishment work as well as for new work and emergency works where a contractor may be on call. Each package of work to be car-ried out is identified in a works order which defines the works required and their location, sets any programming needs and also states any special requirements or payment terms. Payments will normally be valued by measurement using rates set down in the term con-tract but specially agreed prices or a cost plus arrangement may also be used.

(5) ICE Conditions of Contract Ground Investigation, 2nd Edition: July 2004

The conditions are very closely based on the ICE General Conditions of Contract 5th Edition. The contract conditions specify that the work will be under the full direction and control of the engineer, and on site, under the supervision of the engineer's representative or other person appointed by the engineer. The company or firm undertaking the physical work is referred to as the contractor. With limited exceptions, the role of the contractor is to perform the physical works and testing included within the contract documents, the control, direction and interpretation of such work generally being in the hands of the engi-neer or his representatives. In following the ICE General Conditions of Contract 5th Edi-tion, the contract price is determinated at tender stage and is only finally derived on final measurement of the work undertaken.

(6) Agreement for Consultancy Work in respect of Domestic or Small Works: amend-ments Dec 1999

ICE has produced this contract for domestic or small works in the form of a checklist for discussion with the client. It is divided into five sections, four of which reflect the type of services most often provided and the fifth deals with payment.

6.4   The New Engineering Contract (the NEC)

6.4.1   Introduction

The NEC was developed by ICE in the early 1990s with the aim of introducing a new form of non-adversarial form of contract strategy which would contribute towards the more effective and smoother management of projects. NEC is now in its Third Edition-NEC3 and has projected as the preferred form of contract for works relating to the 2012 Olympics in London. It is radically different from other English style forms of Building and Civil Engineering Contracts, in that it has a core contract form, written in simple terms. The choice of options will have to be a subject for advice in each case.

The first NEC contract-then known as the "New Engineering Contract" -was published in 1993. It was a radical departure from existing building and engineering contracts, being written in plain language and designed to stimulate rather than frustrate good management. The second edition, called the NEC Engineering and Construction Contract, appeared two years later together with a new Professional Services Contract, Adjudicator's Contract and a back-to-back set of short forms and sub-contracts. A decade of extensive international use followed, culminating in the development and launch of the NEC3 contract suite in 2005. This included a new Term Service Contract and Framework Contract, joined in 2010 by a Supply Contract. The suite was updated and enlarged to 39 documents in April 2013, including a Professional Services Short Contract-which has been selected by the Association for Project Management as its standard form for appointing project managers-and an enhanced set of guidance documents. The NEC3 suite is now endorsed by governments and industry worldwide and has an unrivalled track record for delivering projects on time and on budget- including the London 2012 Olympic and Paralympic Games venues.

The NEC is a legal framework of project management procedures designed to handle all aspects of the management of engineering and construction projects. It is in use across the spectrum of engineering and construction activities by a wide range of clients, consultants and contractors. Its use encompasses projects both large and small, civil engineering and building, national and international. It comprises a suite of contract documents and range of support services consisting of training, consultancy, software and a users group. Since the original launch of the main engineering and construction contract and subcontract, the NEC has been extended to include a professional services contract, an adjudicator's contract and a short contract. Further extensions of, for example, a term services contract, are under development.

6. 4. 2   NEC Characteristics

The NEC is a family of standard contracts, each of which has these characteristics:

(1) Its use stimulates good management of the relationship between the two parties to the contract and, hence, of the work included in the contract.

(2) It can be used in a wide variety of commercial situations, for a wide variety of types of work and in any location.

(3) It is a clear and simple document - using language and a structure which are straightforward and easily understood.

The NEC3 complies fully with the Achieving Excellence in Construction (AEC) principles. The Efficiency & Reform Group of The UK Cabinet Office recommends the use of NEC3 by public sector construction procurers on their construction projects.

6. 4. 3   A suite of contracts of NEC

The NEC contracts now available within the suite are:

(1) Engineering and Construction Contract (ECC)

Suitable for any construction based contract between an Employer and a Contractor. It is intended to be suitable for any sector of the industry, including civil, building, nuclear, oil & gas, etc. Within the ECC contract there are six family level options of which the Employer will choose what he deems to be the most suitable and give him the best option/ value for money on that project:

Option A: Priced contract with activity schedule

Option B: Priced contract with bill of quantities

Option C: Target contract with activity schedule

Option D: Target contract with bill of quantities

Option E: Cost-reimbursable contract

Option F: Management contract

(2) The Engineering and Construction Subcontract Contract (ECS)

Very similar in detail and complexity of contractual requirements to the ECC contract above, but allows the contractor to sub-let the project to a subcontractor imposing most of the clauses that he has within his headline contract. There is very little difference between the ECC and the ECS, other than the names of the parties are changed (contractor and subcontractor) and some of the timescales for contractual responses are altered to take into account the timescales required in the ECC contract.

(3) The Engineering and Construction Short Contract (ECSC)

This is an abbreviated version of the ECC contract and most suitable when the contract is considered " low risk" (not necessarily low value) on a project with little change expected. This contract is still between the employer and contractor but does not use all of the processes of the ECC making it simpler and easier to manage and administer.

(4) The Engineering and Construction Short Subcontract (ECSS)

Allows the contractor to sub-let a simpler lower risk contract down the line to a subcontractor. It is back-to-back with the ECSC but is frequently used as subcontract when the main contract is under the ECS.

(5) The Professional Services Contract (PSC)

This contract is for anyone providing a service, rather than doing any physical construction works. Designers are the most obvious party that fit into this category. Whilst they are producing a design for an employer or contractor, they would sign up and follow the clauses within the PSC. Most of the clauses within this contract are the same or similar to those in the main ECC contract, so that all contractors, designers and subcontractors have pretty much the same obligations and processes to follow as each other.

(6) The Professional Services Short Contract (PSSC)

This was added to the family in April 2013 and was co-developed with the Association for Project Management. It is for simpler less complex assignments than the PSC, such as the appointment of small team for managing an ECC contract on the Employer's behalf. E. g. the Project Manager and Supervisor. It is frequently used as a subcontract to the PSC for design work.

(7) Framework Contract (FC)

Parties enter into a "framework" of which work packages will then be let during the life of that framework. Any individual projects will then be awarded using one of the other contracts within the suite, meaning that the parties follow the headline clauses within the framework contract (which is a fairly slim contract) and then the individual clauses within the chosen contract for that package. Different work packages can be let using different contracts during the life of the framework.

(8) Term Service Contract (TSC)

For parties on a project that is operational or maintenance based, e. g. maintaining highway signage, where the contract is to ensure that a certain standard is maintained. This contract is not generally used for constructing new works, but can include some amount of betterment. There is also a "Term Service Short Contract" where the project is a relatively low risk project and/or the work is primarily re-active. It is an abbreviated version of the main TSC.

(9) Adjudicator's Contract (AC)

If there is a dispute between the parties on a project then the Adjudicator will follow the clauses within this contract in order to come to a decision.

(10) Guidance Notes and Flowcharts

For each of the different contracts listed above each comes with its own set of guidance notes and flowcharts which should aid understanding of the intent of the drafted clauses. The guidance notes expand on each clause to give extra substance and intent of the original drafters as to how a clause should be understood and interpreted. The flowcharts then map out each of the main processes within each contract and demonstrate how it should operate and what to do next if a party has or has not carried out the next contractual action.

6.5　The Joint Contracts Tribunal (JCT)

6.5.1　Introduction

The Joint Contracts Tribunal was established in the 1930s by the Royal Institute of British Architects (RIBA) and the National Federation of Building Trades Employers (NFBTE), to consider future proposals for amending the Form of Contract which had been published in 1931. Important new editions of the form were published in 1939, 1963 and 1980, and after the JCT had become a limited company further revised editions were published in 1998, 2005 and 2011. JCT Contracts are currently published by Sweet and

Maxwell Thomson Reuters.

In 2012 the publication was announced of JCT Contracts discovery: the education and learning module from the Joint Contracts Tribunal. This was described as an education and learning module for education and training providers, in-house training teams and independent tutors, providing materials for a comprehensive understanding of JCT contracts and JCT contractual procedures and looking at the roles of contractors, employers, subcontractors and contract administrators and how JCT provisions deal with matters such as payment, control of the works and control of time.

6.5.2   Available Documents of JCT

(1) Major Project Form

(2) PCC 2005 Standard Form of Prime Cost Contract

(3) WCD 2005 Standard Form of Building Contract With Contractor's Design

(4) 2005 Standard Form of Building Contract

(5) MC 2005 Standard Form of Management Contract

(6) IC 2005 Intermediate Form of Building Contract

(7) MW 2005 Agreement for Minor Building Works

(8) MTC 2005 Standard Form of Measured Term Contract

In addition JCT publish subcontracts, trade contracts and forms of warranty to be used with the particular contract in question. In addition forms of framework agreement and facilities management agreements are available.

6.6   The American Institute of Architects (AIA)

6.6.1   Introduction

The American Institute of Architects (AIA) published its first form contract in 1888. The document, referred to as the "Uniform Contract", was an agreement between an owner and a contractor and consisted of a mere three pages. As the industry evolved, however, so did the AIA's Contract Documents. Since the AIA first published the Uniform Contract, the AIA's Contract Documents have expanded in scope, length, and complexity to respond to industry needs. The AIA now publishes over 100 Contract Documents, which are the most widely used standard form agreements in the design and construction industry.

In order to keep the documents current and fair in terms of the modern construction industry, the AIA periodically revises the Contract Documents, generally on a 10-year cycle. In doing so, the AIA solicits and receives input from numerous organizations within the design and construction industry. The AIA thoroughly addresses the comments it receives, and periodically meets in person with industry representatives to clarify their positions. Through this inclusive process, the AIA endeavors to achieve a fair balance among the various interests affected. In recent years, the AIA Documents Committee has undertaken the substantial effort of reviewing and revising the Conventional (A201) Family (hereinafter "A201 Family") of documents. As a result, the AIA is set to roll out its latest edition of the A201 Family in late 2007. As was the case with the 1997 edition, the AIA designed the latest iteration of the A201 Family to define and control the responsibilities of the various parties involved in a typical design-bid-build construction project. The A201 Family consists of a standard general conditions document, as well as standard form agreements between the owner/contractor, owner/architect, contractor/ subcontractors and architect/consultants. Within the A201 Family, however, it is the general conditions document and the owner/architect agreements that largely define the role of the architect on a design-bid build construction project.

The 2007 documents represent the culmination of a four-year long drafting process in which the AIA Documents Committee solicited, received, considered, and addressed comments from dozens of organizations in the construction industry, including owner, contractor, subcontractor, legal and design organizations. Based on these comments, as well as internally identified issues, the AIA Documents Committee edited and revised the A201 Family with the goal of creating a set of documents that reflects current industry practices and is fair to owners, contractors, subcontractors, architects, and consultants. As a result, the 2007 documents have undergone a number of changes.

6.6.2 Organization

More than 88,000 licensed architects and associated professionals are members. AIA members adhere to a code of ethics and professional conduct intended to assure clients, the public, and colleagues of an architect's dedication to the highest standards in professional practice.

There are five levels of membership in the AIA:

Architect members are licensed to practice architecture in the United States.

Associate members are not licensed to practice architecture but they are working under the supervision of an architect in a professional or technical capacity, have earned professional degrees in architecture, are faculty members in a university program in architecture, or are interns earning credit toward licensure.

International associate members hold an architecture license or the equivalent from a licensing authority outside the United States.

Emeritus members have been AIA members for 15 successive years and are at least 65 years of age or are incapacitated and unable to work in the architecture profession.

Allied members are individuals whose professions are related to the building and design community, such as engineers, landscape architects, or planners; or senior executive staff from building and design-related companies, including publishers, product manufacturers, and research firms. Allied membership is a partnership with the AIA and the American Architectural Foundation.

☞ **疑难语句** ☜

1. From scratch 白手起家，从头做起

2. Ripple effect 连锁反应

3. Compatible with 与……匹配

4. Trio 三个一组

5. Liaise with 保持联系，熟悉

6. Training curricula 培训课程

7. Admeasurement 分配，计量

8. Remedial work 补救工作，修补工作

9. The contract price is determinated at tender stage and is only finally derived on final measurement of the work undertaken. 合同价格在投标阶段确定，但最终结算价格以实际承担的工作量为准。

10. Unrivalled track record 无与伦比的业绩记录

11. London 2012 Olympic and Paralympic Games venues 轮动奥林匹克奥运会和残奥会运动场馆

12. Betterment 改善，改进

13. Flowcharts 流程图

14. Caters to 迎合

15. Make resort to 求助于

☞ **中文综述** ☜

6.1　建筑工程标准化合同文本概述

自 19 世纪以来，标准格式合同一直是建筑行业商业实践的重要组成部分。这些标准格式合同由建筑师（美国建筑师协会，AIA）、工程师（国际咨询工程师联合会，FIDIC）和承包商（美国联合总承包商，AGC）等专业机构和行业协会起草并推广使用。

标准格式合同有助于提高建筑活动的可预测性和效率，并为工程项目建设的发展提供了支撑。由于大多数起草的合同文本都是在行业团体参与或反馈建议的过程中不断发展和成熟起来的，因此，这些合同文件代表了行业共识的惯例和实践，是行业实践的最佳总结。因此，即使有些项目中，合同各方起草自己的标准合同，行业标准形式也可以作为各方起草和谈判的宝贵参考。

行业标准格式合同之所以流行，是因为它对业内人士来说是熟悉的。熟悉标准条款和条件会减少起草和审查消耗的时间，熟悉标准条款和条件也为承包商就合同条款的最终达成提供心理安慰。支持使用行业标准合同形式的另一个原因是，在短时间内从头开始起草一份多主体参加的工程合同对于缺乏经验的人来说是一项很难完美完成的任务。尽管如此，行业标准合同虽然有用，但不应在没有专业咨询的情况下使用。

（1）标准合同不应未经修改而使用。因为标准化合同是工程行业组织为广泛使用于工程领域而起草的共性多，个性不足的合同文本，不能完全代表所有合同各方自身特有的特殊利益诉求。

（2）修改标准合同时，要注意"连锁反应"。因为标准格式施工合同是复杂而逻辑性很强的文件，合同中的很多条款是相互引用的，所以对一个合同条款的修改可能会对另一个条款的应用产生影响。在改变一个词或词的定义时要特别注意。

（3）不要过于自信自己对某个版本标准合同的了解和掌握。在使用标准合同文本之前，应认真阅读合同，因为新的项目和环境可能需要对特定合同条款进行重新审视。

（4）注意区分定制起草和行业起草标准合同文本的区别。行业起草的标准合同文本通常只与来自同一组织制定的其他合同文本合同条款匹配、协调（例如，AGC 标准合同与其他 AGC 标准合同；FIDIC 合同文本相互之间）。而定制的标准合同文本与行业起草的标准合同文本很难兼容。此外，不同组织，例如 FIDIC，AIA 等行业起草的标准合同文本通常是不兼容的。

（5）每一份合同表格，包括由行业组织起草的合同，都含有合同起草者的观点。无论是由一个行业组织起草的，还是由一个缔约方的律师起草的任何合同也都包含起草者的观点。因此，了解和掌握不同行业组织发布的各种标准合同文本的条款和条件是非常重要的。

6.2　FIDIC

6.2.1　FIDIC 简介

FIDIC 是以法语为官方语言的三个欧洲国家比利时，法国和瑞士于 1913 年在比利时根特发起设立的，它的全称是国际咨询工程师联合会（Fédération Internationale Des Ingénieurs Conseils），FIDIC 是法文第一个字母的缩写合拼。目前有近百个成员国加入 FIDIC，分属于四个地区性组织，即亚洲及太平洋地区会员协会（ASPAC）、欧洲共同体会员协会（CEDIC）、非洲会员协会组织（CAMA）、北欧会员协会组织（RINORD）。FIDIC 是最具有权威性的咨询工程师组织，它建立以来，有效地推动了全球范围内高质量的工程咨询服务业的发展。目前，FIDIC 总部设在瑞士洛桑，主要职能机构有：执行委员会、土木工程合同委员会、雇主与咨询工程师关系委员会、职业责任委员会以及秘书处。1996 年，中国工程咨询协会代表我国加入了 FIDIC，成为其正式成员。

6.2.2　FIDIC 主要合同范本

1994 年，FIDIC 成立特别工作小组，根据国际建筑工业发展现状，FIDIC 决定升级红皮书和黄皮书，同时进一步发展橘皮书。这个小组的努力工作使其在 1999 年发布了 4 个新的合同文本。

（1）《建筑工程合同条款（Conditions of Contract for Construction）》（新红皮书）。

在 1999 以前，FIDIC 组织分别在 1957 年，1963 年，1977 年和 1987 年出版了 FIDIC 红皮书第 1 版，第 2 版，第 3 版和第 4 版。从第 3 版起，FIDIC 红皮书就得到了欧洲建筑业国际联合会、亚洲及西太平洋承包商协会国际联合会、美洲国家建筑业联合会、美国普通承包商联合会等协会的共同认可。经世界银行推荐，FIDIC 的红皮书第 3 版也纳入了世界银行与美洲开发银行共同编制的《工程采购招标文件样本》。正因有前面四个版本的红皮书，所以 1999 年修订出版的红皮书被称为"新红皮书"。新红皮书是 FIDIC 组织推荐的适用于由雇主负责设计的建筑施工工程，其最大特点有以下两个方面，其一是雇主支付承包商的依据是工程量清单；其二，工程师的纠纷解决职能被 DAB 机构所取代。

（2）《生产设备与设计－建造合同条款》（Conditions of Contract for Plant and Design－Build for Electrical and Mechanical Plant，and for Building and Engineering Works，Designed by the Contractor）（新黄皮书）。

新黄皮书适用于大型工程的设备提供和施工安装，承包工作范围包括设备的制造、运送、安装和保修几个阶段。这个合同是在建筑工程合同条款（新红皮书）基础上编制的，针对相同情况制定的条款完全照抄建筑工程合同条款的规定。与"新红皮书"的区别主要表现为：一是该合同涉及的不确定风险的因素较少，但实施阶段管理程序较为复杂；二是工程设计任务由承包商承担。这个合同一般适用于大型项目中的部分工程。黄皮书于1963 年出第 1 版，并在 1980 年和 1987 年出版第 2 版和第 3 版。因此，1999 年出版的黄皮书被称为"新黄皮书"。

（3）《设计采购施工（EPC）/交钥匙项目合同条款》（银皮书）（Conditions of Contract for EPC Turnkey Projects（First Edition，1999））（the " Silver Book"）。该合同文本是在 1995 年 FIDIC《设计－建造与交钥匙工程合同条款（橘皮书）》基础上重新编写的。"银皮书"适用于以交钥匙方式为雇主承建工厂、电力、石油开发以及基础设施的"设计－采购－施工"的总承包项目。该合同范本适用于建设项目规模大、复杂程度高、承包商提供设计、承包商承担绝大部分风险的情况。根据银皮书（EPC）的条款，承包商将负责工程"设计－采购－施工"的全部工作，（在工程完工后）向雇主提交拿钥匙即可进驻的工程产品。在银皮书条件下，承包商承负的时间和费用风险要比黄皮书条件下大得多。

（4）《简明格式合同（Short Form of Contract）》（绿皮书）。绿皮书的宗旨在于使该合同范本适用于投资规模相对较小的民用土木工程，如：（1）造价在 50 万美元以下以及工期在 6 个月以下；（2）工程相对简单，不需专业分包合同；（3）重复性工作；（4）施工周期短。

同时，FIDIC 也意识到，为了适应不断变化的工程条件，发布新的合同文本已经成为一种客观要求。除了上述四个合同文本，FIDIC 在 1999 年前后又分别发布了其他一些合同文本。

（1）MDB（multilateral development banks ）（粉皮书）是红皮书的协调版（harmonised edition），初版 2005 年 5 月制定，修订于 2006 年 3 月和 2010 年 6 月。粉皮书（Pink book）是 FIDIC 与世界银行等国际金融组织合作专门编制的用于国际多边金融组织出资的建设项目，其条款并不是很适合其他资金来源的项目，比如，MDB 版本对采购地就有明确而严格的限制。

（2）《设计、建造和项目运营合同条款》（Conditions of Contract for Design，Build and Operate Projects）（金皮书）。金皮书将设计、建设、运营和维护于一体，项目的运行试验要经受 20 年运营与维护的考验，在此期间，承包商要实现运作目标，并根据合同条件，将项目的运营权转给雇主。FIDIC 声明金皮书的起草的目的在于减少项目移交后由于项目设计、工艺和材料质量问题引起的风险。因此，金皮书适用于需要长时间使用的，并需要长期维护的基础设施项目，例如 PPP 和 BOT 建设项目。

（3）《设计建造与交钥匙工程合同条款（橘皮书）》Conditions of Contract for Design－Build and Turnkey（1st Edition 1995）.

橘皮书发布于 1995 年，为 FIDIC 合同的工作小组起草合同提供样本。在 1999 年

FIDIC 发布了新红皮书和新黄皮书后，就很少使用橘皮书了。

（4）《招标程序（Tendering Procedure）》（蓝皮书）。国际咨询工程师联合会在 1982 年出版了《招标程序》，反映了国际上建设行业当今招投标的通行做法，它提供了一个完整、系统的国际建设项目招标程序，具有实用性、灵活性。

（5）《雇主与咨询工程师标准服务协议书（Conditions of the Client/Consultant Model Services Agreement）》（白皮书）。白皮书是雇主为了工程项目的顺利进行与咨询机构签订的关于工程咨询服务的合同。

（6）《土木工程施工分包合同》。FIDIC 编制的《土木工程施工分包合同》是与 FIDIC 施工合同条款配套使用的分包合同范本。FIDIC 分包合同制定与 1994 年，2011 年进行了修订。

6.2.3 2017 版 FIDIC 介绍

2017 年 12 月 5 日和 6 日，国际咨询工程师联合会 FIDIC 在伦敦推出了期待已久的 FIDIC2017 合同范本，包括红皮书，黄皮书和银皮书。2017 年的 FIDIC 合同范本比其前身 FIDIC 1999 更具规范性，也更具前瞻性。其主要目标是增加透明度和确定性，一方面减少各方之间出现分歧的风险，另一方面进一步增加项目成功的可能性。总的来说，新的 2017 版 FIDIC 合同范本较为突出地表现在：①鼓励更积极的合同管理，②反映国际最佳的工程实践，③重塑并强调避免争议的重要性。2017 版合同范本结构与 1999 版基本相同。合同由可选择合同协议、一般条款和特殊条款组成。具体条款分为合同资料（前者称"投标附件"）、双方拟完成的项目具体资料和双方约定的具体合同条款。

在结构方面，2017 版有 21 条，1999 版为 20 条，即 2017 版对 1999 版第 20 条进行了分割，将索赔与纠纷解决分开，独立为 20 条和 21 条。同时，按英文字母顺序增加了新的定义，包括"索赔"、"延误损害赔偿"、"延长时间"等，并将一些定义重新命名，即"不可抗力"改为"例外事件"等。

同时，2017 版通过以下方式，使双方承担了更详细的合同管理义务：①引入所谓"预警"概念，对合同履行可能会产生相反的效果，增加合同价格或履行中的延迟（第 8.4 款）；②承包商工作细节的扩展，例如，每个活动开始和结束日期，实施的关键路径（子条款 8.3）；③新的管理会议（第 3.8 款）和更新的质量管理体系（第 4.9 款）等。

在 2017 版 FIDIC 中，以互惠原则为基础的当事人的权利和义务的增加贯穿整个文本，例如义务协助雇主获得许可（副条款 1.13（c）），义务不挖角（第 6.3 款），预警义务（副条款 8.4）。这进一步提供了一种公平和平衡的风险分配方法。

值得注意的是，在 2017 年的 FIDIC 版本（第 3.7 款）中，工程师的角色得到了增强、加强和明确。工程师的中立义务得到了确认，并重新引入了工程师通过适当程序处理各方索赔的角色细节。

在 2017 新版本中，在所谓"符合目的"（FFP）规定（第 4.1 款）的条件下，对设计条款进行了重大修改，如果雇主的要求没有在合同中具体列明，则工程必须符合一般目的。上述修改进一步支持：①赔偿条款，据此承包商被要求对失败的工作或任何部分或任何重大项目不"符合目的"FFP（第 17.4 款）进行赔偿；②承包商应购买职业赔偿保险，以承担没有完成"符合目的"（FFP）的责任（副条款 19.2.3）。

最佳实践条款也被纳入新的 2017 版中，例如根据第 2.3 和 6.9 款规定，从事欺诈、腐败和类似行为的个人可以在一方的要求下被删除。同样，安全条款（第4.8款）和质量保证条款（第4.9款）也得到了扩充和更新。

在纠纷解决程序上，2017版FIDIC更新了1999版的DAB机制，推出了争议回避/裁决程序（现称"DAAB程序"），以及其他合同文件范本，例如投标书、履约保证文件（如母公司保证书及履约保证），以及用BIM向用户提供的咨询文件。争端避免和裁决委员会（争端避免和裁决委员会）被赋予了一个新的回避争端的角色，在这个角色上，它还可以向当事各方提供"非正式援助"。因此，新版FIDIC希望DAAB发挥更加突出的作用，以解决合同双方之间的任何争端。

6.3　英国行业机构编制的主要合同范本

6.3.1　英国土木工程师学会合同范本（ICE）

1. ICE简介

ICE是英国土木工程师学会（The Institution of Civil Engineer）的简称，该学会创建于1818年，在英国是代表土木工程师的专业机构及资质评定机构。该学会拥有8万多名会员，其中1/5会员是在英国以外的150多个国家和地区。该学会已有200年的历史（截至2018年），已成为世界公认的学术中心、资质评定组织及专业代表机构。ICE在土木工程建设合同方面具有高度的权威性，它编制的土木工程合同条款在土木工程中具有广泛的应用。

2. ICE主要合同文本

（1）ICE合同条款（2004年7月第七版）

这个合同文本是基于传统的工程师设计承包商建造的，通过测量进行估值的建筑工程。工程师的工作主要侧重咨询、设计、监理、认证支付和调解雇主与承包商之间纠纷。

（2）ICE设计建造合同条款（2004年7月第二版）

这个合同文本在本质上已不同于传统的ICE合同条款的概念，承包商对所有的设计和建造负责，包括最初由雇主设计的或代理雇主设计的部分。支付采用总价合同形式，与FIDIC银皮书（EPC）总包付款合同相似。

（3）ICE小型工程合同条款（2004年7月第三版）

小型工程合同条款类似于FIDIC《简明格式合同（Short Form of Contract）》（绿皮书），主要适用于：

1）雇主和承包商可能遇到的潜在风险较小；

2）工程简单而直接；

3）设计工作，除了由承包商负责设计的工作，在招标之前已经全部完成。

4）承包商只设计专业性强的工程，对于永久性工程不负责设计；

5）指定分包商不予接受；

6）合同价值不超过50万英镑，合同期限不超过6个月，支付方式采用日工或成本加费用的方式进行。

（4）ICE合同条款固定版本（2004年7月）

定期合同是为了在一定地理区域内执行日常维护和修补工作。承包商被指定在一定期限内，根据与雇主的约定承担这些工作。合同适合有计划的适应性维护或翻新工作，或者一些新的或紧急的工作。每项将进行的工作通过施工通知加以认证，包括约定的工作要求、工作地点、工作程序要求或者支付条件等。

（5）ICE 土地勘察合同条款（2004 年 7 月第二版）

ICE 土地勘察合同条款是基于 ICE 通用合同条款第五版制定的。该合同条款强调了工程师的作用。除了个别情况，承包商的任务是根据合同条款完成工程的具体工作和工程试验，但是对工程的指导，控制和解释的权利掌握在工程师或工程师代表手里。

（6）国内或小工程咨询合同（1999 年 12 月修订）

国内或小工程咨询合同是 ICE 为英国国内或小工程咨询制定的，包括 5 个部分，四个部分是服务的内容，第五个部分是支付条款。

6.3.2 新工程合同（NEC）

1. NEC 简介

NEC 是 ICE 在 20 世纪 90 年代初建立和发展起来的，其目的在于介绍一种新型的非对抗性的合同策略，适用于更加有效和方便的项目管理。目前，NEC 合同系列已经颁发了第三个版本 NEC3，NEC3 不同于英国其他的建筑与土木工程合同，合同制定过程中更多地考虑了合同的通识性，做到简单易懂，得到了英国政府商务部（Office of Government Commerce）的支持和推荐，被推荐为伦敦奥林匹克运动会场馆建设首选合同文本。

NEC 合同第一个版本颁发于 1993 年，第二个版本于 1995 年出版，称作 NEC 工程施工合同。NEC 合同文本经过 20 多年在国际工程中的反复使用，使 NEC 得到良好的发展。在 2005 年 7 月，NEC 颁发了新的合同系列，并得到不断的升级，到 2013 年 4 月，合同文件已经上升到 39 个。其中雇主服务简易合同已被（英国）项目管理协会选为制定项目管理的标准格式合同。NEC3 系列合同为全世界很多政府和企业选用，并保持无与伦比的业绩记录，包括 2012 伦敦奥运会和残奥会场馆项目也使用了这一合同文本。

NEC 合同文本是项目管理程序的重要法律文件，设计的目的在于满足工程和建筑项目管理的需要，其应用的项目有大有小，有国内的，也有国际的。目前，NEC 被用于包含任何或全部传统科目的土木工程、电气工程、机械工程和建筑工程。根据不同合同版本的应用，承包商可以负担全部设计责任，也可以负担部分设计责任或者不承担设计责任。

2. NEC 特点

与 ICE 相比，NEC 代表了英国建筑工程合同体系发展的最新成果，在合同理念和设计思想上都有很多独到之处。NEC 合同有如下一些特点：

（1）NEC 的使用促进了合同主体间的良好合作，体现了"伙伴关系"（Partnering）理念的项目管理方法，提高了工程的管理质量。

（2）NEC 使用范围广泛，适用于各种商业环境，各种工程和不同的地点。NEC 不是针对任何特定的法律体系而编写的，其使用也并不仅限于英国。

（3）NEC 是简单明了的合同文件，它的语言和文字表达直接，容易理解。NEC 在编写过程中避免使用复杂的长句子，尽量避免了只有专家才能理解的法律术语和措辞。

NEC3 认真全面遵守了实现卓越建筑的原则，英国内阁效率与改革领导小组推荐公共部门的建设项目使用 NEC3 系列合同文本。

3. NEC 合同系列

目前，NEC 已成为一套完整的合同体系，并被冠以"伞"型合同。在 1993 年，第一版 NEC 合同还是简单的"新工程合同"，后来 NEC 发展为工程建筑的领域的主导合同"工程施工合同"。现在，NEC 的系列合同已经发展为能够适用于各种工程项目和各方当事人的合同系列。这些合同主要包括：

（1）工程施工合同（ECC）

适用于任何承包商与雇主之间签订的建筑合同，它适用于所有领域的工业建筑，包括土木工程，建筑工程，核工业，石油和燃气等。在工程与建筑合同系列中，有 6 个系列可供雇主选择。

选择 A：价格合同附带日程安排

选择 B：价格合同附带工程量清单

选择 C：目标合同附带日程安排

选择 D：目标合同附带工程量清单

选择 E：成本补偿合同

选择 F：管理合同

（2）工程施工分包合同（ECS）

工程施工分包合同（ECS）与工程施工合同（ECC）合同构架类似，允许承包商将工程分包给分包商去做。工程分保的比例可以从 0~100%。

（3）工程设计与施工简易合同（ECSC）

适用于结构简单，风险较低，对项目管理要求相对简单的工程项目。

（4）工程设计与施工简易分包合同（ECSS）

适用于结构简单，风险较低，对项目管理要求相对简单的分包工程项目，它与工程设计与施工简易合同（ECSC）是配套使用的，但是也经常与 ECS 配套使用，当 ECS 为主合同时。

（5）专业服务合同（PSC）

适用于聘任专业咨询人员，项目经理，设计师，工程师等专业技术人员或机构。合同的主要条款与 ECC 合同条款类似或相同，所以、所有的承包商，设计师和分包商与 ECC 合同具有几乎对应的责任与工作程序。

（6）专业服务简易合同（PSSC）

专业服务简易合同（PSSC）颁发于 2013 年四月，比专业服务合同（PSC）更加简便易行。

（7）框架合同（FC）

这是 NEC3 新增加的合同范本，用于在雇主与承包商之间在确定项目内容之前建立的一种工作关系。

（8）定期服务合同（TSC）

该合同文本主要用于长期运营和维护的合同主体之间，而不适用于新开工的工作。

（9）评审员合同（AC）

如果合同各方之间产生了纠纷或争执，那么调解人将根据合同约定条款进行和解和评判。

6.3.3 合同审定联合会合同范本 (JCT)

JCT 合同审定联合会创建于 1931 年。创始机构有英国皇家建筑师学会和全国建筑职业联合会 (National Federation Of Building Trades Employers，NFBTE)。建立这个机构的主要目的是制定并修订标准化的建筑施工合同。在 2005 年合同族中，每一合同类型均包括主合同和分包合同标准文本，以及其他能够跨越不同合同版本的标准文件。2005 年版合同族主要合同文件类型及其主合同文件如下：

(1) 小型工程建筑合同 (Minor Works Building Contract)

(2) 中型工程建筑合同 (Intermediate Building Contract)

(3) 标准建筑合同 (Standard Building Contract，分为有工程量清单、有估计工程量、无工程量清单三种)。

(4) 设计建造合同 (Design and Build Contract)。

(5) 大型工程施工合同 (Major Project Construction Contract)。

(6) JCT 高绩效伙伴合同 (JCT－ Constructing Excellence Contract)。

(7) 施工管理专业合同 (Construction Management Trade Contract)。

(8) 管理建筑合同 (Management Building Contract)。

(9) 住宅许可工程建筑合同 (Housing Grant Works Building Contract)。

(10) 测量条件合同 (Measured Term Contract)。

(11) 成本加酬金建筑合同 (Prime Cost Building Contract)。

(12) 修复和维护合同 (Repair and Maintenance Contract)。

(13) 框架协议 (Framework Agreement)。

(14) 合同争议评判员协议书 (Adjudication Agreement)。

JCT 和上文 ICE 合同是英国建筑业使用最为广泛的合同，但 JCT 合同更常用于房屋建筑项目中。

6.4 美国行业机构编制的主要合同范本

美国合同范本的历史起源于美国建筑师学会 (AIA) 于 1888 年制定的早期合同范本。当时发布的仅仅是一份雇主和承包商之间的协议书，称为"规范性合同" (Uniform Contract)。1911 年 AIA 首次出版了"建筑施工通用条款" (General Conditions for Construction)。经过多年的发展 AIA 形成了一个包括 90 多个独立文件在内的复杂体系。和英国合同范本相比，AIA 合同范本的主要特点是为各种工程管理模式制定不同的协议书，而同时把通用条款作为单独文件出版。

6.4.1 美国建筑师协会合同范本 (AIA)

始创于 1857 年的美国建筑师学会 (AIA) 是美国主要的建筑师专业社团。该机构致力于提高建筑师的专业水平，促进其事业的成功并通过改善居住环境提高大众的生活标准。该机构通过组织与参与教育、立法、职业教育、科研等活动来服务于其成员以及全社会。AIA 的成员主要是来自美国及全世界的注册建筑师，目前总数已超过 83000 名。

AIA 的一个重要成就是制定并发布了一系列的标准合同范本，在美国建筑业界及国际工程承包界特别在美洲地区具有较高的权威性。AIA 随时关注建筑业界的最新趋势，每年都对部分文件进行修订或者重新编写：例如，2004 年共更新了 12 份文件，2005 年共更新了 6 份文件。而每隔 10 年左右会对文件体系及内容进行较大的调整。在 2007 年 AIA 对整个文件的编号系统以及内容都做了较大规模的调整。2007 年修改后的 AIA 系列合同范本更根据文件性质的不同大致分为了 A、B、C、D、E、G 六个系列。

A 系列：雇主与总承包商、CM 经理、供应商之间，总承包商与分包商之间的合同文件、施工合同通用条件以及与招投标有关的文件等。

B 系列：雇主与建筑师之间的合同文件；

C 系列：建筑师与专业咨询机构之间的合同文件；

D 系列：建筑师行业有关文件；

E 系列：电子文件协议附件；

G 系列：合同和办公管理中使用的文件。

AIA 合同范本的核心文件是施工合同通用条件，有包括 A201-2007 在内的多个不同版本。

6.4.2　美国总承包商协会合同范本（AGC）

美国总承包商协会（AGC）是美国最大的、历史最为悠久的建筑业行会组织。AGC 通过向其成员提供一系列的服务来提高建筑工程质量，保护公众的权益。AGC 是 1918 年应当时的美国总统威尔逊的要求创立的。创立的初衷是建立一个代表整个建筑行业的组织与政府商讨有关建筑行业的事宜。AGC 目前代表美国全国 32000 多个建筑企业，分属于美国各地的分会组织。这些成员包括总承包商，专业承包商，各种分包商和供应商等。AGC 成员在美国经济发展过程中起着重要的作用，代表来自建筑行业的声音。AGC 作为承包商的行业组织独立制定一套与 AIA 文件功能用途相近的标准合同文件范本。和 AIA 文件相比，此套文件更加照顾承包商的利益。

除了独立编制自己的 AGC 合同范本外，AGC 还积极参与 AIA 等其他组织主持编制的合同范本。随着美国建筑业的发展，2008 年年初，AGC 联合代表雇主的行业组织等，对 AGC 现有的合同进行全面的修订，并将修订后的版本称为"合议文件"（Consensus DOCS），并得到了 28 个与工程建设业相关的主要协会的认可。

合议文件系列包括 90 多个合同范本文件，覆盖了所有工程建设模式下的合同文件需求，包括六大系列：

200 系列：用于传统模式；

300 系列：用于项目多方合作；

400 系列：用于设计－建造模式；

500 系列：用于风险型 CM 模式；

700 系列：用于分包合同；

800 系列：用于雇主的项目管理以及代理性 CM 管理。

6.4.3　工程师联席合同文件委员会合同范本（EJCDC）

工程师联席合同文件委员会（EJCDC）是几个在美国建筑业有广泛影响的专业组织为了制定标准文件范本而成立的专门机构，至今已有 30 余年的历史。EJCDC 的成员组织包括美国工程公司委员会（American Council of Engineering Companies，ACEC），美国土木工程师学会（American Society of Civil Engineers），美国总承包商协会（AGC），以及美国全国职业工程师学会（National Society of Professional Engineer，NSPE）等。该机构的成员组织主要来自于工程设计方面，因此制订的合同范本主要用于土木工程类项目。合同范本的修订与审阅工作主要通过专家委员会来进行。

EJCDC 在 2016 年发布了备受期待的 2016 版 EJCDC 设计建筑合同系列。2016 年版代表了对设计建筑合同系列的重大修订。2016 年版的 EJCDC 设计构建系列包含了 16 个文件，包括 10 个完整的全新文件，以及 7 个现存的进行了不同程度修改的文件。

EJCDC 合同文件由经验丰富的工程设计和施工专业人员、业主、承包商、职业责任和风险管理专家组成的委员会对每一份 EJCDC 合同文件进行系统的准备、审查和分析，并提供法律顾问的参与和建议。40 多年来，EJCDC 一直在发展和支持质量合同文件，鼓励他们通过教育和推广加以使用。

自 2009 年以来，EJCDC 更新的文件包括：

（1）D-500，业主与业主顾问之间的协议；

（2）D-505，设计建设者与工程师之间的协议；

（3）D-520，业主与设计建设者之间的协议（规定价格）；

（4）D-525，业主与设计建设者之间的协议（成本加成）；

（5）D-610，设计建设履约保证文件；

（6）D-615，设计建设付款保证文件；

（7）D-700，业主与设计建设者之间的一般合同条款。

EJCDC 合同文件有如下特点：

（1）EJCDC 合同文件是由经验丰富的行业专家制定，并经同行评审；

（2）减少了冲突和诉讼机率

（3）包含平衡和公正的条款。

（4）以用户友好的 MS WORD 格式发布并易于定制；

（5）是最全面、组织最好的标准合同文档。

Questions

1. Please introduce the Rainbow Suite of FIDIC contracts?

2. What are main feather of NEC? Describe development of NEC?

3. Please introduceAIA A201-2007?

Chapter 7   Important Contract Clauses

This chapter addresses the main clauses in a typical construction contract. We believe that focusing on these clauses prior to commencing a construction project will reduce the likelihood of disputes during and after the work. For each clause, we spell out the issue and its importance to the project, then set out the most common approaches used by owners, contactors, and designers. In the chapter we will make reference to the clauses of AIA A101 and A201, as well as clauses of FIDIC New Red Book since those are comprehensive and widely-used standard in the building industry.

7. 1   Payment

One of the most sensitive areas for all parties involved in a construction project is the payment process. While all parties bear a significant risk in this area, it is important to understand each parties' unique concerns. Owners, as well as their lenders, are concerned about overpaying the general contractor before the work is completed and failing to hold back adequate retainage as security. On the other hand, general contractors and subcontractors are concerned about prompt payment. Any delay in the cash flow can essentially force the general contractors or subcontractors to finance the project, which may ultimately result in the contractors' insolvency. Neither the owners, nor the contractors, of course, desire this result. Accordingly, the terms of payment clauses should be designed to balance the parties' concerns.

7. 1. 1   What documents must be submitted for payment?

The AIA form contracts require progress payments for projects of any considerable size. The contractor initiates the process by submitting an "Application for Payment" to the architect on a monthly basis. Meanwhile, owners will require supporting back-up documents such as lien waivers, certified payrolls (for public sector work), schedule updates, and test results on work performed to date. Lien waivers are of particular importance as they protect the owner and lender, if applicable.

7. 1. 2   How quickly will the contractor get paid?

According to S9. 4. 1 of AIA201, the Architect will, within seven days after receipt of Contractor's application for payment, either issue to the Owner a certificate for payment, with a copy to the Contractor, for such amount a s the Architect determines is properly due, or notify the Contractor and Owner in writing of the Architect's reasons for withholding certificate in whole or in part as provided in Section 9. 5. 1. Therefore, the Architect in AIA 201 has three options: (1) to certify the payment amount due applied for and forward it to the Owner or Employer; (2) to certify a lesser amount and forward the certificate to the owner, or (3) to reject the contractor's application.

7.1.3   Pay-When-Paid Clauses

Most of the clauses discussed so far involve the relationship between the owner and general contractor. Equally as important is the relationship between the general contractors and subcontractors. An often-litigated issue concerning whether the general contractor's obligation to pay the sub-contractor is conditioned on payment from the owner.

The dispute arises in circumstances under which nonpayment by the owner is unexcused or another subcontractor has breached. General contractors believe that they should not have to pay until they are paid and that any loss should be shared equally. Subcontractors, in response, note that the general contractors are in the best position to evaluate the owner's financial position. Accordingly, subcontractors believe that they are not on equal footing with the general contactors.

Payment clauses that seek to allocate these risks technically fall into either one of the following categories: ① pay-when-paid or ② paid-if-paid. Pay-when-paid clauses allow reasonable delay before the general contractor must pay the subcontractor. On the other hand, under pay-if-paid clauses, the general contractor's obligation does not arise until the owner has paid the general contractor. That is, payment from the owner is a condition precedent.

The Contractor shall promptly pay each Subcontractor, upon receipt of payment from the Owner, out of the amount paid to the Contractor on account of such Subcontractor's portion of the Work, the amount to which said Subcontractor is entitled, reflecting percentages actually retained from payments to the Contractor on account of such Subcontractor's portion of the Work. The Contractor shall, by appropriate agreement with each Subcontractor, require each Subcontractor to make payments to Sub-subcontractors in a similar manner.

7.2   Differing site conditions

Contractors are forced to make assumptions about the difficulty of the project when they price the work. One of the hardest areas of costs to estimate in advance is that which is not visible. It is not uncommon for a contractor to encounter a physical condition, usually subsurface, that was not anticipated by the parties at the time of contracting. Underground rock, water, or objects, such as unused tanks or buried structures, add to the cost of completing the construction project. These cost increases are often significant, and as a result, unanticipated physical site conditions, or "differing site conditions," provide the grounds for many construction claims. Depending on the contract and the facts, the results can go both ways. In some cases, the owner is ordered to pay the contractor for any cost increases caused by the differing site condition. In other cases, the contractor is forced to bear the increased costs on its own. It is imperative, therefore, for both owners and contractors to undertake certain precautions and employ certain strategies to minimize the risk that a differing site condition will be encountered during the course of a project.

7.3   Dispute clauses

Procedures to resolve claims and disputes are necessary components to all construction contracts. Diverse parties, shifting relationships, and high levels of risk inevitably result in disputes. Many form contracts, such as those available from AIA and FIDIC, use a three-tiered approach to dispute resolution. First, the parties attempt to resolve the dispute themselves in good faith. Failing that, the parties then turn to an interest-based process such as mediation. If mediation does not resolve the dispute, the parties then turn to either the courts or to some variation of arbitration. Thus, it is imperative to create an appropriate roadmap by which the parties can resolve their differences. This process must be able to work both during construction and after substantial completion.

7.3.1   What type of dispute procedure is best for the project?

Most form construction contracts employ a process by which claims and disputes are first heard and decided by the design professional. If necessary, they proceed next to mediation and conclude in arbitration. In most cases, this three-tiered approach is the best process, but that is not always so. Thus, the most fundamental question is what type of dispute resolution process is best for the project.

To answer this question, one should consider a number of factors: project size, project complexity, number of parties to the project, complexity of contractual relationships, risk distribution, owner status, and length of construction. After weighing all factors, the three-tiered provision may prove to be inefficient and overly-burdensome for a small-scale project; or it may prove too simplistic to address the technicalities of a large commercial construction job.

Arbitration may be the best method to resolve technical disputes or issues of law, as arbitrated issues are typically decided by attorneys with knowledge of these technicalities and legal issues. But arbitration may not be the best choice if a quick resolution to the dispute is required. While still usually faster than the courts, Arbitration is no longer the simplified, shorter, and cheaper option of years past.

In the end, the dispute resolution process must be able to work both during the construction and after substantial completion. What works best for one project may not for another. Therefore, it is in a contractor's best interest to give thoughtful consideration to dispute resolution provisions in form contracts, even if doing so requires taking a nap break.

7.3.2 Standard Clauses

Most form contracts use the standard three-tiered dispute resolution process, as embodied in the 1997 edition of most AIA documents. This elemental structure has proven effective over decades, and it is wise to use when drafting a non-form contract and prudent to maintain when using a form contract.

The effectiveness of this three-tiered system, or any process, depends upon the provisions supporting it. Necessary provisions include the following six elements:

(1) Parties must put all claims in writing, and claims should be addressed to a previously designated individual. Written claims create a record. They also add gravitas to the situation, requiring parties to focus immediate attention on the problem. They force the claimant to perform some cursory due diligence prior to making a claim, and they are an effective way to communicate issues.

(2) Parties must make claims within a finite time from discovery. The industry standard requires that claims are made within twenty-one days. A finite time period has many benefits including that it brings to light claims or potential claims so they may be addressed before further consequential harm is realized. It also forces parties who wish to mitigate damages to begin sooner rather than later.

(3) Parties must continue performing other obligations, notwithstanding claims. Design professionals must continue to administer the contract; contractors must continue to prosecute the work; and owners must continue to pay undisputed amounts.

(4) Parties must commence mediation within a finite period of time from when the claim is submitted to the design professional or when the design professional renders a decision.

(5) Parties must file arbitration demands within a finite period of time from the same benchmark.

(6) Parties must designate an applicable set of rules (or jurisdiction) as well as the location for both mediation and arbitration.

7.4 Liquidated damages

Liquidated damages are specified daily charges deducted from moneys otherwise payable to the contractor for each day the contractor fails to meet a milestone and/or contract completion date. Another way of looking at liquidated damages, is that it is the price the contractor must pay per day for working beyond the required completion dates. Liquidated damages are a contract based remedy for late completion of the contract. It must be agreed to by the parties in the construction contract and normally takes the following or similar form:

"If the contractor fails to complete the work within the contract time or fails to achieve any of the contract milestones, the contractor agrees to pay the owner $ X per day as liquidated damages to cover losses, expenses and damages of the owner for each and every day which the contractor fails to achieve completion of the milestone work or the entire project. "

7.4.1   Enforceability of liquidated damages

To be enforceable, a liquidated damages provision must be a reasonable estimate of the damages an owner would incur if the contractor fails to complete the project by the required completion date. If the liquidated damages amount is unreasonable and considered an attempt to coerce or penalize the contractor, the clause will be deemed an unenforceable "penalty. "

U. S. courts take two approaches when determining the enforceability of a liquidated damages clause. A majority of courts use a "prospective" approach that looks at the reasonableness of the liquidated damages amount as of the time the parties entered into the contract. If the amount was a reasonable estimate at the time of contract formation, it will be enforced, regardless of the actual damages.

A minority of U. S. courts use a "retrospective" approach, which determines the reasonableness of the liquidated damages provision based on the facts at project completion. In this case, a liquidated damages amount that was reasonable when the parties entered into the contract may be held to be an unenforceable penalty if the amount is way off kilter at the time of the delay in completion compared to the actual damages being incurred by the owner.

In one recent case, the owner of a power plant collected more than $20 million in liquidated damages from its EPC contractor. An arbitration panel dismissed the EPC contractor's assertion that the recovery of the stipulated liquidated damages amount would result in a windfall for the owner because of a change in power market economics.

7.4.2   Elements of liquidated damages

In the for-profit sector it is not difficult to decide on liquidated damages figures. The sum should be a combination of the lost profits from late completion and administrative expenses from continued oversight of the project, coupled with the cost of disruption to move-in plans.

In the public and non-profit sector, the equation is not so simple. One approach is to take the daily interest cost of the capital cost of the project as of the completion. Another approach would include evaluating the cost based upon the value that the project is intended to ultimately provide its users.

In most cases, enforceable liquidated damages must have 5 principal elements (this varies from state to state and country to country, so you and your lawyer must check applicable law very closely):

(1) Actual damages must be difficult to quantify;

(2) The amount must be liquidated (i. e. , agreed on and set in advance);

(3) The amount must be reasonable;

(4) They must be compensation, not a penalty;

(5) They must be exclusive (i. e. , the only remedy available).

7.5 Delay and extensions of time

Every construction project has a schedule that determines, in advance, the sequence of work. For the owner, a schedule provides the answer to the owner's number one concern: "When will it be finished?" For the general contractor or construction manager, a schedule is a crucial tool in managing a particular project.

Unfortunately, it is a rare occurrence for a construction project to progress to completion without some disruption to the original schedule. In most cases, these disruptions cause delays, which in turn cost the owner or contractor, or both, time and money. The contract documents dictate which party is responsible for the delay and whether the contractor is entitled to an extension of time or for reimbursement of costs incurred as a result of the delay. If the delay is caused by the owner, the contractor will often be entitled to recover the costs incurred as a result of the delay. Some contracts, however, contain exculpatory clauses that restrict a contractor's right to recover compensatory damages.

For those involved in the construction business, various types of delays often pervade progress; however, there are ways to contract around these delays by including various remedies under standard contract documents for each type of delay.

7.5.1 Inexcusable delays

Generally, inexcusable delays are those delays caused by, or within the control of, the contractor or its subcontractors. Examples of inexcusable delays include equipment problems, slow work, poor management, or poor coordination. In such cases, the contractor bears all of the responsibility and will not be entitled to any additional time or money.

7.5.2 Excusable Delays

Excusable delays, on the other hand, are typically those delays that are outside the control of either party. Causes of excusable delays include unusually severe weather, labor disputes (such as union strikes), or national shortage of materials. In situations involving excusable delays, the owner is required to give the contractor additional time to finish the project. The contractor is not, however, entitled to compensation from the owner for costs incurred as a result of the delay.

In some cases, the owner may nevertheless require the contractor to finish by the originally-scheduled completion date. When this happens, the owner has "accelerated" the work and must pay the contractor for costs incurred as a result of such acceleration. Often, these costs are substantial because acceleration requires over-time and double shifts. An owner should evaluate the situation carefully and should never accelerate for the purpose of mitigating delay damages. It is almost always cheaper to pay delay damages than to pay for the costs of acceleration.

7.5.3 Compensable delays

Compensable delays are those delays for which the owner bears responsibility and must give the contractor additional time and compensation. Examples of Compensable delays include design changes or errors that slow down the progress of the work, interference with site access not anticipated by the contractor, failure by the owner to secure necessary permits, or decision making by the owner that results in work delays.

7.5.4 Concurrent Delays

Occasionally, two different types of delays will overlap on a particular project. Such occurrences are commonly referred to as " concurrent delays. " In order to determine whether two delays are concurrent, the parties must independently identify and evaluate each delay. If each delay would cause the project to be delayed for a similar period of time, the delays are considered concurrent.

7.5.5 Delays cause by Force Majeure

Force majeure is defined generally as any event or condition, not existing as of the date of signature of the contract, not reasonably foreseeable as of such date and not reasonably within the control of either party, which prevents, in whole or in significant part, the performance by one of the parties of its contractual obligations, or which renders the performance of such obligations so difficult or costly as to make such performance commercially unreasonable.

Under most national laws, force majeure events must meet four criteria:

(1) Beyond a Party's control;

(2) The Party could have not reasonably anticipated;

(3) The Party could not have reasonably avoided;

(4) Which is not substantially attributable to the other Party.

In AIA, standard form agreements allow Contractors to claim time extensions and/or damages when so-called "force majeure" delays occur, if the Contractor bears no responsibility for the delays. Force majeure delays, in addition to "acts of God," may include labor disputes, material shortages, government agency actions and delays caused by the Owner or Architect. Contractor delay damages, in addition to basic costs, may include price escalations, acceleration costs and extended home office/field office overhead and costs.

Of course, if the Contractor bears responsibility for project delays, the Owner will not approve additional time or money. Most agreements provide in such cases for Contractor acceleration of the work, at no cost to the Owner, to overcome Contractor-caused delays. Owners also often include "liquidated damage" provisions that provide for payment of a fixed daily sum to the Owner if the Contractor fails to timely achieve the contractual Substantial Completion date.

7. 6　Indemnification and insurance

An important function of the contract drafting process is identifying risks and negotiating their allocation among the parties. The party most apt to handle the risk should assume it, provided that the party is adequately compensated; however, the party with the greatest bargaining power will often insist on shifting risk to the other party to a contract. These risks are especially great in construction where smooth progress can so easily be disrupted at great expense to the parties, and where the consequences of lapses in safety can be so great.

At the first level is allocating the risk for project completion, which may be accomplished through various provisions, usually placing the contractor at risk to complete the job. The owner, however, bears the risk of contractor insolvency. The owner may require bonding the project, but because it is the owner's risk, the cost of bonding can be passed back to the owner. Similarly, the contractor must consider risks implicated by owner insolvency. The AIA A201 addresses such risks, though not in their entirety, by allowing the contractor to request in writing evidence of financial arrangements made to fulfill the owner's obligations to the contractor as a precondition to commencement or continuation of the work.

At the next level are the risks inherent with construction activities, owning property, or providing a professional service. Where these risks should lie are self evident. Though standard contract provisions place most building risks on the contractor, they do not completely protect the owner or design professional against third-party injury claims. Because safety is best controlled by the contractor, other contractual tools, such as indemnification and insurance, are necessary.

There are two types of indemnification clauses. The first provides indemnity for all work-related incidents regardless of guilt. The second provides indemnity for work-related incidents arising from an indemnitor's wrongful conduct. It is important to note with respect to the former indemnity clause that many courts and state statutes prevent indemnification of a person whose own negligent acts caused the injury.

Insurance fills gaps left by indemnity. Moreover, it provides incentive to the indemnitor to assume indemnity obligations since it can insure them and pass the cost back to the indemnitee, usually the owner.

When drafting contract provisions that require a party to obtain insurance, it is important to ① require inclusion in that policy as an additional insured; ② require that the policy continues without interruption until completion; and ③ require notice of cancellation of any policies. The policies typical to a construction project are commercial general liability, project management liability, property, loss of use, off-site storage, boiler and machinery, and professional liability.

7.7 Notice-of-claim requirements

Most construction contracts require parties who are asserting a claim to provide prompt notice to the other party. Such notices most commonly apply when a contractor encounters a field condition that will delay the work or cause cost overruns. The typical clause requires notice of a claim within a certain number of days of the time the claimant learns of the facts leading to the claim and in any event prior to the date on which the claimant begins to expend extra funds for which it will seek compensation. While the specific timing and method of notice vary, there are several consistent principles underlying notice requirements.

First, notice of a claim gives the recipient an opportunity to gather information relating to the claim before it is lost. For example, upon receiving notice of a claim for additional costs due to subsurface conditions, the owner will want to measure, photograph, or sample the buried structure or rock that the contractor claims will lead to additional costs.

Second, notice may enable the parties to reach agreement regarding the amount of loss. When both parties investigate a claim simultaneously, they share the benefits and burdens of finding a solution which tends to minimize the chances of any future dispute regarding proper remediation methods.

Third, notice requirements may help assess whether a claim is genuine. In some situations, owners believe that once a contractor completes a project and discovers that the project lost money, the contractor will begin asserting claims in an attempt to recoup the loss. Requiring prompt notice at the time of the event in question helps avoid after-thoughts.

Fourth, owners have to manage the budget of a construction project and make decisions based on information regarding the prospective costs of the job. If the owner does not learn until late in the job that there will be cost overruns, the owner has less ability to arrange additional financing or change parts of the project so as to save the money needed to cover the claim.

There are, however, limitations on the enforceability of clauses requiring notice of claims. The best advice for all parties is to strictly follow the contractual notice requirements, even if notice of a claim is also provided in another manner (often less formal). Doing so is likely to eliminate the need to litigate any notice issues. However, failure to comply strictly with contractual notice requirements may not be fatal to a claim. In some instances, a court or arbitrator will not enforce technical requirements of a notice clause where the purpose of the clause has been met, such as where minutes of job meetings confirm actual discussion and consideration of a potential claim.

7. 8   Termination clauses

Perhaps the worst thing that can happen on a construction project is contract termination. Everyone loses money in that situation, and some parties will lose a significant amount of money. Litigation very frequently follows terminations. Terminations arise in three situations: terminations for convenience by the owner; terminations for cause by the owner; and terminations for cause by the contractor.

When a relationship with a contractor or construction manager has turned sour, a construction project owner has two termination options: ①For cause, which is based on a contract breach or default, and often leads to litigation or arbitration; ②Without cause—"termination for convenience" — where there is no such claim of breach/default.

7. 8. 1   Termination for convenience

Termination for convenience clauses are standard in public and private construction projects, permitting a party to terminate a contract without actually breaching the contract itself. The provision will require that the non-terminating party be properly compensated for the work performed and materials furnished to date, but excluding compensation for profits and overhead for work not yet performed and materials not yet furnished. Typically, a termination for convenience clause contains a notice provision, outlines what the non-terminating party must do upon receipt of notice, and the further actions the non-terminating party must take to receive compensation as a result of the terminating party's decision to terminate.

Similar to a prenuptial agreement, "termination for convenience" is when no court action (or arbitration) takes place—the parties simply agree to dissolve their relationship based on previously agreed-upon financial terms and then part ways. Owners typically go this route when the project has become unworkable, i. e. , project abandonment, which can occur for a number of reasons, such as a loss of financing or failure to obtain necessary public authority approvals.

7. 8. 2   Owner's termination for cause

The worst case scenario for an owner is a contractor that has stopped performing. When all else fails, the owner's remedy is termination of the contract. Form A201 contains the basic clause concerning owner termination. It provides that the owner may terminate the contract if the contractor: 1) persistently fails or refuses to supply enough properly-skilled workers and/or materials; 2) fails to pay subcontractors; 3) persistently disregards applicable laws, ordinances or rules; or 4) is otherwise guilty of a substantial breach of the contract (the "catch-all"). Once the architect certifies any of the above causes, the owner may, without prejudice to other rights and remedies, terminate the contractor after providing seven days' written notice to the contractor and its surety, if applicable. If the cost to complete the work exceeds the unpaid balance of the contract sum, which is almost always the case，the contractor is responsible for the amounts over and above the contract sum.

7.8.3　Termination For Cause by Contractor

Contractors seldom wish to terminate contracts. However，in some instances，job conditions may become so unbearable that a contractor decides to take such drastic action. Some contracts contain a clause which provides that a contractor may terminate if the owner fails to make payment for thirty days or the architect fails to recommend payment for thirty days，through no fault of the contractor. The contractor is required to provide seven days' written notice to the owner and architect. Thereafter，the contractor is entitled to be paid for all work performed together with proven loss with respect to materials and equipment and even reasonable overhead and profit.

Because termination is a drastic remedy，contractors should carefully consider whether termination will serve to limit their liability as opposed to increasing it. Contractors should also be mindful of any obligations that they might owe the surety as a result of cancellation，as sureties' rights to indemnification in these situations are generally quite broad.

☞ **疑难语句** ☜

1. Retainage 保留款，尾款

2. Lien waivers 留置权放弃

3. Payrolls 工资单

4. Inequities 不公平待遇

5. Usury laws 高利贷法

6. Truth-in-lending 真实贷款，诚实贷款

7. On equal footing 平等地位

8. Sprinkler systems and stairwells 自动喷水灭火系统和楼梯井

9. Turn-around times 周转时间

10. Incumbent 有义务的，义不容辞的

11. Exculpatory 申明无罪的，辩解的

12. In the interest of brevity 为了简短起见，为了方便起见

13. Touch on 提及，谈及

14. Imperative 不可避免的

15. Roadmap 路径，路线图

16. Consolidated litigation 合并诉讼

17. Joinder 联合诉讼，共同诉讼

18. Liquidated damages（合同中确定的）违约赔偿金

19. In the tens of thousands of dollars 几万美元

20. Grossly disproportionate 很不成比例的

21. Immense disruption 巨大的破坏，毁坏

22. Coupled with 加上，外加

23. Inexcusable delays 不可原谅的延迟
24. Compensable Delays 可补偿的延误
25. Concurrent Delays 共同延误
26. Field condition 现场条件，野外条件

☞ **中文综述** ⌘

这个章节介绍国际工程合同的主要条款，以美国 AIA A201 和 FIDIC 新红皮书为例，对相关国际工程合同条款进行解读和讨论。在签订国际工程合同前，关注这些条款，了解这些条款的含义和应用，将有助于减少施工阶段或工期结束后的纠纷。

7.1 支 付 条 款

支付条款一直是工程合同最为重要的条款之一，也是承包商和雇主最为关心和敏感的条款。雇主应拥有充足的资金，并按合同约定进行支付，这是雇主的基本义务。任何延迟付款都可能增加承包商的融资成本或造成承包商不能按时完成工作。同时雇主也应注意，在承包商完工前，其是否充分持有承包商的保留金，以对抗承包商的违约或修补工作。因此，各方当事人在支付问题上要认真对待，避免产生纠纷。

7.1.1　承包商付款请求需提交相应的文件

根据美国 AIA 合同条款，雇主应对承包商承建的项目进行分期付款，而付款程序的开始是承包商按照合同约定，在规定的时间内，向工程师提出付款申请，付款申请书需附上证明承包商付款权的相关证据。雇主在审核付款申请时，可能会要求承包商提供相关付款支撑性文件，例如放弃建筑物留置权的法律文件，经认证的工单，工程计划的更新，已完工作的检测结果等等。放弃对建筑物的留置权是雇主或项目贷款人非常关心的。在现实中，贷款人在决定贷款前，会要求承包商或分包商放弃对建筑物的留置权。

7.1.2　承包商如何尽快得到付款

在建筑工程合同中，雇主和承包商约定付款支付程序，通过签订合同，确定支付条件和最后支付日期。支付的最后日期是实用而有效的条款，承包商必须加以注意。同时，承包商也应清醒地认识到，雇主融资渠道的不同，会对约定付款最后日期有一定的影响。

根据大多数建筑工程合同，雇主从进度付款中保留规定比例的保留金，并一直到合同终止为止，这对于雇主对抗承包商违约或者分包商行使留置权有一定的积极作用。同时，雇主持有一定比例的保留金对于激励承包商完成项目工作十分重要。一般来说，保留金的数额是工程款项的百分之五到百分之十。由于直到工程结束，验收合格，承包商和分包商一般得不到这笔款项，因此，现实中就要求承包商或分包商有一定的融资能力。目前，在美国的一些州，已经颁布相关法律来限制雇主持有保留金的比例，以便减少承包商的融资压力，以最终平衡雇主与承包商之间的关系。

7.1.3　延迟支付的罚息

为了避免延迟付款，合同各方可以协商决定延期付款部分的罚息利率，一般认为，该罚息利率最好与雇主贷款利率相同，这样安排的结果，使雇主意识到利用承包商的垫资没有任何便宜可占。

7.1.4　Pay-When-Paid 条款

Pay-When-Paid 是承包商与分包商之间适用的支付条款。承包商承担工程项目工作的款项是由雇主支付的，雇主支付了承包商工程款，承包商才有了可供支付分包商的资金来源。所以 Pay-When-Paid 就是说，承包商获得雇主支付后，才可能支付分包商。但是，在现实中，承包商与分包商之间的支付仍暴露诸多法律问题，其中承包商对分包商的支付是不是有条件的成为问题的焦点。

在讨论 Pay-When-Paid 条款之前，考虑合同各方的观点是非常重要的。如果不支付是由于承包商原因引起的，承包商不能以雇主不支付为借口拒绝支付分包商；如果雇主不支付是由于分包商不能有效地完成工作或者提交付款申请文件等原因引起的，承包商拒绝向分包商付款的问题似乎很好解决；但是，尽管如此，分包商认为，分包商不与雇主直接接触，沟通存在障碍，出现了问题，应归因于承包商管理缺欠，承包商应承担责任。

在总包商与分包商之间的付款条件上，有两个版本：一是 pay-when-paid 总包商得到付款后，向分包商付款。这个条款是说在承包商得到雇主付款后，不必马上向分包商付款，允许适当的宽限期，雇主已经向总承包商付款是总承包商向分包商付款的先决条件；二是 paid-if-paid 条款，即如果承包商得到了付款，分包商也得到了付款。这就要求承包商一旦得到雇主付款，应马上或立刻支付对分包商的应付款项，而得到付款的分包商同样要向其下属的分包商第一时间支付应付款项。

7.2　不可预测的现场条件

投标期间，承包商在确定投标价格时，应当对项目的难度和潜在风险有所考虑。而对潜在风险预估是通过肉眼看不到的，例如地下物理条件，也就是说对于地下物理条件，在投标和合同签订时是很难在投标文件中列明或者在合同中准确约定。因此，没有预料到的地下物理条件，或不同的场地条件，为工程索赔创造了条件。根据合同和事实情况，不同的场地条件，在 FIDIC 条款中，其结果可能是双向的，在某些情况下，雇主被要求向承包商支付因场地条件不同而造成的费用增加；在其他情况下，承包商被迫自行承担增加的费用。因此，雇主和承包商都必须采取某些预防措施和策略，尽量减少在项目建设过程中遇到的不同现场条件的风险。

根据 1999 年版 FIDIC 新红皮书第 1.1.6.8 项的规定，"不可预见"是指一个有经验的承包商在提交投标书日期前不能合理预见。第 4.12 款的规定，"物质条件"是指承包商在现场施工时遇到的自然物质条件、人为的及其他物质障碍和污染物，包括地下和水文条件，但不包括气候条件。第 4.10 款也规定，承包商应被认为在提交投标书前，已视察和检查了现场、周围环境、上述数据和其他得到的资料，并对所有有关事项已感到满足要求。

在发生不可预见的物质条件时，将第 1.1.6.8 项和第 4.10 款的内容联系起来，从雇主的观点出发，很难判断和说清楚一个有经验的承包商不能预见的物质条件的范围和程度。但从举证的角度而言，当承包商遇到不可预见的物质条件时，承包商将承担举证责任，他不仅需要证明导致延误的物质条件是一个有经验的承包商无法预见的，而且还需要证明他在投标和准备进度计划时无法预见会遇到此类物质条件的风险。

FIDIC 定义的物质条件中"不包括气候条件"的含义是热带风暴和飓风等属于季节性

的气候现象，是可以预见的。但根据 1999 年版新红皮书第 8.4 款，承包商可因极端恶劣的气候条件要求延长工期。在发生了不可预见的物质条件时，根据 1987 年版 FIDIC 红皮书第 12.2 款、1999 年版新红皮书、新黄皮书第 4.12 款的规定，承包商可以要求延长工期和补偿费用。

7.3 纠纷解决条款

解决索赔和纠纷的条款是所有施工合同的必要组成部分。不同的合作主体，不断变化的法律关系，以及各种风险的干扰必然导致争端。很多国际工程合同范本，例如 AIA 和 FIDIC 提供的合同范本，都采用了三层结构方法来解决争议。首先，争议各方以最大诚信通过协商解决争端。如果协商没有结果，双方就会转向第三方介入的纠纷解决程序，比如调解。如果调解没有成功，双方就会诉诸法律或通过仲裁渠道解决问题。因此，制定一个争议解决的路线图，使各方能够在争议出现后得以迅速解决。同时，这个争议解决路线图不仅针对施工期间出现的争议，同时也要应对完工后可能出现的问题。

7.3.1 什么类型的争议程序对项目最好？

大多数的工程合同范本都采用了争议事件第一时间由现场工程师或设计师指导并予以调节处理的方法。必要时，可以请第三方对争议进行调解，调解不成，争议方可申请仲裁。在大多数情况下，这种三个层次的纠纷解决方法是最好的、最合理的。但这个方法并不适用所有类型纠纷。在国际工程实践中，对纠纷的解决应侧重考虑这样几个因素：即项目规模、项目复杂性、项目参与方数量、合同关系的复杂性、风险分配、所有者状态和工期长度。在权衡了所有因素后，三层次纠纷解决规则对于一个小规模项目来说是低效和过度繁琐的；但是，对于解决大型商业建筑项目的技术性争议问题，工程师或设计师的指导与调节可能是过于简单化了。仲裁是解决技术纠纷或法律纠纷的最佳方法，因为仲裁裁决通常是由掌握技术的专家仲裁员和法律专家仲裁员做出的。但如果需要迅速解决争端，仲裁可能不是最好的选择。尽管仲裁通常比法院更快捷，但与其他争议解决方式比较，仲裁不再是程序简化，时间短和更经济的最佳选择。一个好的方法一定满足施工期间和完工后的因工程施工产生的争议解决的需要，一种方法对一个项目可能是最有效的，但不一定适用另一个项目。因此，在合同条款中恰当的落笔争议条款对承包商利益保护至关重要。

7.3.2 标准条款

大多数范本合同使用标准的三层结构方法解决合同期间的争议问题，这在 FIDIC，AIA 等合同条款中都有所体现。这种争议解决方法在过去几十年里，在国际工程实践中得到了积极的证明。因此，在起草一份非格式合同时，在合同中规定这个纠纷解决方法是明智的，并且在使用合同范本时也要认真维护该方法的使用。

（1）合同各方须将所有索赔以书面形式提交，并按照程序向合同指定的负责受理索赔事务之人提出索赔。书面申请应附上相关索赔证据，让被索赔方意识到索赔的严肃性，并立即将注意力集中在问题解决上。书面索赔要求可以迫使索赔人在提出索赔之前进行一些必要的尽职调查，确认索赔的充分性，这是解决争议的有效沟通方式。

（2）当事人须在有限的规定时间内提出索赔。FIDIC 要求承包商在发现索赔事实 21 天内提出索赔。提出索赔时间的限制可以避免索赔事件的继续发生或者避免造成事件继续恶化，也迫使索赔尽早开始并减轻损害的后果。

（3）尽管索赔已经进入程序，但各方须按照合同约定继续履行义务。

（4）当事人必须在提交索赔后的合理时间内进入调解状态，调解人也应在规定的时间内做出调解。

（5）当事人应在调解失败后规定的时间内提出仲裁。

（6）各方必须共同选择或指定一套适用的调解和仲裁规则（或管辖）。

7.4　违约赔偿金

违约赔偿金是指承包商违反合同约定或者未能完成合同任务，从支付给承包商的款项中扣除的费用。另一种情况是，在超过规定的完工日完工情况下，承包商对工程延误承担的罚金。

7.4.1　违约赔偿金的执行

如果承包商未能按规定的完工日期完成项目工作，违约金的数额应该能够合理地反映出对雇主造成的损害。如果违约金数额超出合理限度，并被认为是企图胁迫或处罚承包商，该条款将被视为不可执行的"处罚"。在确定违约金条款的可执行性时，美国法院采取两种方法。大多数法院采用一种"前瞻性"的方法，即在当事人订立合同时，考虑到违约金的合理性。如果金额是合同成立时的合理估算，无论实际损失如何，都将执行。少数美国法院采用"溯及既往"的方法，根据项目实际完成情况确定违约金条款的合理性。在这种情况下，当合同双方签订合同时，如果违约赔偿金额与雇主实际发生的损害相比不是匹配的，违约赔偿金可能会被认为是不可执行的。

7.4.2　违约赔偿金的要素

违约赔偿金款项应该是由延迟完工造成的损失和对项目持续监督产生的管理费用的结合体。在大多数情况下，可强制执行的违约金应参考以下 5 个因素，但是这 5 个因素因国家和地区不同而有所不同：①实际损害赔偿难以量化；②数额必须经过测算；③金额必须合理；④是补偿，而不是惩罚；⑤是唯一的补救办法。

7.5　工期与工期延误

7.5.1　工期

工期指单位工程或建设项目从开工到竣工交付使用所需要的时间，即建筑物在施工过程中所耗用的全部时间，以天数表示。施工工期决定着建设工程能否尽快交付投入使用、发挥投资效益。施工工期的长短，反映了建设的速度和建筑企业经营管理水平，是考核建筑企业经济效益的重要指标。根据 FIDIC 标准合同有关工期要求的规定，在建筑和土木工程施工合同中，与工期相关的主要问题涉及了开工、进度计划、进度控制、暂停施工、试验、竣工、工期延长以及缺陷通知期限等。在 1999 年 FIDIC 红皮书中，以第 8 条为工期的核心条款。

在英国法中，由于履约时间不是合同成立的一个要件，因此，如果合同当事人希望在某个特定日期完成履约行为，则合同当事人通常应在合同中明示规定履约时间。如果合同明示规定了履约时间或工期，则合同当事人应在合同明示规定的时间内完成履约。如果合同没有明示规定履约时间，则应默示合同当事人应在合理的时间内（within the reasonable time）完成履约。

在所有的施工合同，例如 FIDIC、ICE、JCT、NEC、AIA 等标准合同格式中，合同均规定了承包商完成工程项目的具体时间要求，这些标准合同格式的明示规定，表明时间，或称工期构成了施工合同的要件。按照合同明示规定的工期要求，承包商有义务在规定的工期内实施、完成工作任务和修复工程中的缺陷。在工程施工过程中，如果承包商遇到了可原谅的延误事件，承包商有权提出工期延长索赔，并应在工程师或建筑师批复的工期延长的期限内竣工。

在施工合同没有明示规定工期时，承包商应在合理的时间内完成工程项目。但如何界定合理时间却是一个令人头痛的问题。根据英美有关判例，在施工合同中，确定合理时间的长短取决于：第一、承包商是否在施工作业中使用了充分的或者合理的人力、设备或材料等资源；第二、承包商是否以应有的勤奋和努力，以应有的速度和毫不耽搁地施工工程项目。关于承包商实施工程所需的资源，承包商应当提供充分的资源，或退一步讲，应提供合理的资源，而'充分的'和'合理的'用语并没有什么明显的界限，需根据具体项目的情况作出判断。

7.5.2 延期与工期延长的一般规定

每个建设项目都有一个时间表，决定着工作的先后顺序。时间表是雇主最为关注的，对于总承包商或施工经理来说，时间表是管理项目的重要依据。在大多数情况下，工程施工过程中经常会有突发事件导致工程延迟，从而引起雇主和承包商对合同时间和金额认识发生改变。通常情况下，合同文件规定了延迟责任的归属，以及承包商是否有权延长时间或有义务偿付因延迟而产生的费用。

1. 不可原谅的延迟

一般来说，不可原谅的延误是由承包商或其分包商原因造成的。不可原谅的延误的例子包括设备问题、工作缓慢、管理不善或协调不力。在这种情况下，承包商承担所有的责任，将无权获得任何额外的时间或金钱补偿。

2. 可原谅的延迟

可原谅的延迟一般是指任何一方无法控制的延迟。造成可原谅延误的原因包括异常恶劣的天气、劳资纠纷（如工会罢工），或国家物资短缺，以及国家政策变化等。在涉及可原谅延迟的情况下，雇主需要给承包商额外的时间来完成项目。在通常情况下，雇主会要求承包商提前完工。当这种情况发生时，雇主已经要求承包商"加速"了工作，因此，雇主必须向承包商支付由于这种加速而产生的费用。通常，提前完工的成本是巨大的，因为加速需要超时工作。

3. 可补偿的延误

可补偿的延误是雇主原因引起的延误，必须给予承包商额外的时间和补偿。可补偿延误的例子包括：设计变更或错误使工作进度慢下来，雇主因现场访问带来的干扰，或雇主的决策导致工作延迟。

4. 并发延误

在某些情况下，两种不同类型的延误会在某个特定的项目上重叠。这种情况通常被称为"并发延误"。为了确定是否并发了两个原因引起的延误，各方必须独立地识别和评估每起延误。如果每起延迟都会导致项目延误到类似的时间，那么延迟被认为是并发的。

7.5.3　不可抗力引起的延期

"不可抗力"（Force Majeure）就是违约免责的一种情况。不可抗力（Force Majeure）是指非由当事人的主观意志决定，也非当事人能力能抗拒的客观情况。不可抗力事故包括自然原因引起的，如地震、海啸、水灾、风灾、旱灾、大雪等，也包括社会原因引起的，如战争、罢工、政府封锁、禁运。不可抗力事故发生后的法律后果，一般均可以使当事人有解除合同或要求延迟履行合同的权利。具体须视不可抗力的大小和持续时间决定。如不可抗力使合同的履行成为不可能，则可解除合同。如只是暂时阻碍了合同的履行，则只能延迟履行合同。

FIDIC 新红皮书明确指出，一个事件或情况只有在同时满足 19.1 款中的 4 个条件时，才能称为不可抗力。在 FIDIC 合同中也列举了一些事件或情况，但不局限于此。只要合同双方当事人同意，可以把其他可能发生的情况列入不可抗力的范围之内。

AIA 标准范本合同允许承包商在所谓的"不可抗力"发生的情况下，在非承包商责任的前提下，申请延长时间和/或提出损害赔偿。除了自然原因引起的不可抗力外，引起不可抗力的原因可能包括劳资纠纷、物资短缺、政府机构的行动和由雇主或建筑师造成的延误。除了基本成本外，承包商延迟损害赔偿还包括价格上升、成本增加和其他费用。当然，如果承包商对项目延误负有责任，雇主不会批准额外的时间或金钱。承包商自己承担费用，加速工作，以补偿承包商原因给雇主造成的损失。

7.6　保　障　与　保　险

合同起草过程的一个重要功能是识别风险，并将风险在合同各方之间进行有效的分配。然而，合同协商过程中，占优势的一方往往会坚持将风险转嫁给另一方。而这些风险在建设过程中会阻碍工程的顺利进行，也会给工程安全带来问题。

首先，项目的风险分担是通过合同条款的约定来实现的，例如，如果工期时间约定过短，对承包商不利，使承包商按工期完工风险增大；对于雇主和承包商的任何一方都面临对方在施工期间破产的风险：雇主承担着承包人施工期间破产的风险，承包商也会考虑雇主破产可能给承包商带来的风险。AIA a201 对这类风险有所考虑，允许承包商提出书面请求，要求雇主提供充分的财务证据，作为承包商开始或继续工作的先决条件。

其次，建筑活动的风险存在对于雇主和承包商是不言而喻的。绝大多数标准合同文本将大部分建筑风险分配给了承包商，承包商也通过商业保险购买的方式分散了这些风险的承担。但是，由于承包商最易控制现场建筑活动引起的风险，而雇主或设计专业人员缺乏直接管控风险的机会，因此考虑雇主或设计专业人员不受第三方的伤害索赔相关保险安排是非常必要的。

损害赔偿是工程施工过程中不可避免的，而保险为损害赔偿的落实提供了保障。此外，保险法鼓励商事行为人为商业交易行为购买保险，保险人承担赔偿义务，被保险人得到应有的保险保障。

7.7　索　赔　通　知　条　款

大多数的工程施工合同都要求有索赔人及时通知被索赔人，特别是当承包商遇到与合同约定差异较大的现场条件，并且该现场条件可能拖延工期或导致成本超支时。典型索赔通知条款要求索赔人在了解可能导致索赔的事件后一定时间内进行。虽然具体的通知时限和方法各不相同，但有几个一致的原则是索赔者应当遵守的：

首先，索赔通知给被索赔方收集和准备与索赔有关的信息或证据的机会。例如，在收到由于地质物理条件造成额外费用的索赔通知后，雇主将要求测量、检测或取样承包商声称将导致额外费用的地下结构或岩石样本证据。

第二，索赔通知可以使双方就损失金额达成协议。当双方同时探究索赔解决方案时，他们会分享解决方案的好处和负担，减少因此项索赔可能带来的其他争议的可能性。

第三，索赔通知要求可能有助于评估索赔是否成立。在某些情况下，雇主认为一旦承包商完成了一个项目并发现项目因雇主或非承包商原因损失了资金，承包商应立即开始主张索赔以弥补损失。雇主会在合理时间内接受索赔申请，避免事后再生事端。

第四，雇主必须管理建设项目的预算，并根据有关工作的费用信息作出决定。如果直到项目后期才知道预算存在问题，费用超支，雇主可能没有能力再行资金安排。

就国际工程项目索赔而言，各方应严格遵循合同约定的索赔通知要求，遵守索赔通知的格式要求和实践要求，这样做可能有效的消除仲裁或诉讼的可能性。

7.8　合　同　终　止　条　款

在建设项目中最糟糕的事情就是合同终止。在这种情况下，合同各方都会招受损失，其中一方可能会损失巨大，同时，诉讼也经常伴随合同终止而发生。国际工程合同终止一般有三种情况：雇主为方便而终止；因雇主原因而终止；因承包商原因而终止。

当雇主与承包商或项目经理的关系恶化时，雇主有两个终止选项：其一是因承包商违约而提出终止，这往往导致诉讼或仲裁的发生；或没有理由，即"为了方便而终止"，没有所谓的违约作为前提。

7.8.1　为了方便终止

为了方便而终止是公共和私人建设项目工程合同的标准条款，即允许一方在对方不违反合同的情况下终止合同。该规定要求提出终止一方应适当地补偿被终止一方所完成的工作和提供的材料，但不包括对尚未履行的工作和尚未提供材料的利润和费用的补偿。一般情况下，为了方便而终止包含了通知条款，规定了被终止方在收到通知后必须做的事情，以及被终止方必须采取的进一步行动，因为终止方决定终止时，必须对被终止方提供补偿。FIDIC 合同条款对此做了相应规定❶。

7.8.2　雇主终止合同

对于雇主来说，最糟糕的情况是承包商已经停止了合同履行。当所有其他方法都失败时，雇主的补救办法就是终止合同。美国 AIA a201 包含了关于雇主终止的基本条款。它规定，(1) 如果承包商坚持不履行或拒绝提供足够的技术工人和/或材料，雇主可以终止合同；(2) 承包商未支付分包商款项的；(3) 对适用的法律、条例或规则不遵守的；(4) 严重违反合同规定。一旦建筑师证明上述任何原因，雇主可以在不损害其他权利和补救的情况下，在向承包商和其担保人提出书面通知 7 天后终止合同。FIDIC 新红皮书 15.2 条也规定了雇主有权终止合同的情况。

---

❶　见 FIDIC 新红皮书 16 条。

7.8.3　承包商终止合同

承包商很少希望终止合同。然而，在某些情况下，特别是工作条件变得难以忍受，以至于承包商决定采用终止合同的方法来缓解自己的压力。FIDIC 新红皮书 16.2 条规定承包商应有权终止合同的几种情况❶。由于合同终止是一项重大事件，承包商应仔细考虑终止是否会增加责任，以及承包商也应注意因终止合同而发生的与担保人之间的责任或义务。

Questions

1. Why do many owners require retainage on contracts even though the contractor has provided the owner with a performance bond?

2. Give a good example scenario of consequential damages associated with owner-caused delay.

3. Please discuss the owner's payment responsibilities?

4. What is the contract time? And to which situation the contract time can be extended?

---

❶　见 FIDIC 新红皮书 16.2 条。

Chapter 8　Subcontracts

8.1　Introduction

8.1.1　Definition

A subcontractor is a person who is hired by a general contractor (or prime contractor) to perform a specific task as part of the overall project and is normally paid for services provided to the project by the originating general contractor. While the most common concept of a subcontractor is in building works and civil engineering, the range of opportunities for subcontractor is much wider. The incentive to hire subcontractors is either to reduce costs or to mitigate project risks. In this way, the general contractor receives the same or better service than the general contractor could have provided by itself, at lower overall risk. Many subcontractors do work for the same companies rather than different ones. This allows subcontractors to further specialize their skills.

Building construction is a common example of how the contractor-subcontractor relationship works. The general contractor takes prime responsibility for seeing that the building is constructed and signs the contract to do so. The cost of the contract usually a fixed sum and may have been derived from a bid submitted by the contractor. Before offering the bid or before contract negotiations begin, the general contractor normally asks the subcontractors to estimate the price they will charge to do their part of the work. Thus, the general contractor will collect information from electricians, plumbers, dry wall installers, and a host of other subcontractors.

Once construction begins, the general contractor coordinates the construction schedule making sure the subcontractors are at the building site when needed so that the project remains on schedule. The sequencing of construction and the supervision of the work that the subcontractors perform are key roles for the general contractor.

Subcontractors sign contracts with the general contractor that typically incorporate the agreement between the general contractor and the owner. A subcontractor who fails to complete the work on time or whose work is not acceptable under the general contract may be required to pay damages if the project is delayed because of these problems.

The subcontractor's biggest concern is getting paid promptly for the work and materials provided to the project. The general contractor is under an obligation to pay the subcontractors any sums due them unless the contract states otherwise. Some contracts state that the subcontractors will not be paid until the general contractor is paid by the owner.

If the owner refuses to pay the general contractor for work a subcontractor has performed, the subcontractor has the right to file a mechanic's lien against the property for the cost of the unpaid work.

8. 1. 2　Major pitfalls as a subcontractor

Working as a subcontractor oftentimes put sit in a challenging position where lacking the power to enforce its rights and may find it difficult to fulfill its responsibilities due to factors beyond its control. The fact is, a lot can go wrong when working as a subcontractor, and it is essential for subcontractor to learn how to protect themself from many potential risks.

1. Liability rolls downhill

A subcontractor is essentially the bottom rung of the ladder that comprises a contracted job. If something goes wrong with the job, the employer is going to put a lot of heat on the general contractor, who will in turn try to deflect as much liability for the issue onto the subcontractors as he or she possibly can. Even if the subcontractors were not directly responsible for the issues.

2. Lack of communication with employer

Oftentimes as a subcontractor, it will not have a direct line of communication with the actual Employer. The subcontractor may find itself with only the instructions of the general contractor to work off and it is very easy for things to get lost in translation. This lack of communication with the employer will prevent the subcontractor from setting up proper expectations for the work it will conduct, and creates barriers towards its understanding of exactly what the employer is looking for.

3. Payment issues

As a subcontractor, it will be at the mercy of a general contractor for invoicing and collecting payment for its work. If the employer is dissatisfied with any aspect of the work, even if it is not subcontractor's work, they may withhold payment to the general contractor, who may in turn neglect to pay in a timely manner.

4. Lack of control over safety

Subcontractors must usually go to someone else's worksite to conduct their work, which means they will likely have little control over the quality of safety measures at the worksite. The idea of a safe work environment may be very different from that of the general contractor, but you will be expected to complete your work either way, which puts subcontractor at risk of injury or being sued for refusing to work in such an environment.

8. 2　Types of Subcontractors

8. 2. 1　Domestic subcontractor

Adomestic sub-contractor is one selected and employed by the general contractor, for whom the general contractor is solely and entirely responsible. A subcontractor who contracts with the general contractor to supply or fix any materials or goods or execute work forming part of the main contract. Essentially this contractor is employed by the general contractor.

8. 2. 2   Nominated subcontractor

A nominated sub-contractor is one selected by the employer but employed by the main contractor. If a sub-contractor is nominated then the employer usually retains some liability. Employers sometimes wish to exert influence over the subcontractors employed on their project. Most standard forms of building contract enable the Employer to select a subcontractor, who is subsequently employed by the Contractor, via a " nomination" procedure. Employers may want this for a number of reasons, not least the peace of mind of working with a subcontractor with whom the Employer is familiar, and knowing that subcontractor is experienced, dependable, and, most importantly, solvent.

8. 2. 3   Named subcontractors

Naming sub-contractors allows the employer to influence the general contractor's selection of sub-contractors, whilst leaving responsibility for their performance with the general contractor. To name sub-contractors for a particular package, the employer first identifies a list of potential sub-contractors. They may invite these potential sub-contractors to submit bids for the package. The employer then names a short-list of acceptable sub-contractors in the tender documents for the main construction contract. When tendering for the main contract, the general contractor makes allowances for mark up, attendance and programme in relation to the sub-contract package. Once appointed, the successful contractor seeks tenders for the package from the named sub-contractors (although they may reasonably object to any of the named sub-contractors). Under this arrangement the general contractors assumes responsibility for the sub-contractor's performance. In effect the named sub-contractor becomes a domestic sub-contractor, they are paid by the general contractor and the general contractor is responsible for their works.

The JCT Intermediate Building Contract 2011 is one of the few contracts that expressly provides for named sub-contractors, albeit it still leaves a few questions unanswered.

8. 3   Subcontractors in FIDIC

8. 3. 1   Clause 4. 4 Subcontractor (Red Book 1999)

The Contractor shall not subcontract the whole of the Works. The Contractor shall be responsible for the acts or defaults of any Subcontractor, his agents or employees, as if they were the acts or defaults of the Contractor. Unless otherwise stated in the Particular Conditions:

(1) the Contractor shall not be required to obtain consent to suppliers of Materials, or to a subcontract for which the Subcontractor is named in the Contract;

(2) the prior consent of the Engineer shall be obtained to other proposed Subcontractors;

(3) the Contractor shall give the Engineer not less than 28 days' notice of the intended date of the commencement of each Subcontractor's work, and of the commencement of such work on the Site; and

(4) each subcontract shall include provisions which would entitle the Employer to require the subcontract to be assigned to the Employer under Sub-Clouse 4. 5 [Assignment of Benefit of Subcontract] (if or when applicable) or in the event of termination under Sub-Clause 15. 2 [Termination by Employer].

8.3.2　FIDIC Subcontract 2011

In 2011 FIDIC has published the FIDIC Subcontract for Works which goes back-to-back with the FIDIC Red Book (for Construction). This new format shall help Contractors being involved in the construction of a project under the FIDIC Red Book, 1999 Edition to subcontract parts of the Works to a subcontractor in a way which avoids unnecessary gaps in the chain of liabilities. The Subcontractor accepts to execute the Subcontract Works as if the Main Contractor would carry out the Works. If he fails to provide his services properly and this results in liability of the Main Contractor the Subcontractor shall hold harmless the Contractor from such liability. Additionally the Subcontractor shall enable the Main Contractor to proceed properly under the Main Contract. Sub-Clause 20. 1 of the Conditions of Subcontract requires the Subcontractor to give all notices and to keep all records which are necessary in order to allow the Main Contractor to comply with the claims clauses under the Main Contract.

The Subcontract is not easy to read. Users should start to study the Subcontract together with the Main Contract. A typical feature of the Subcontract is that it merely refers to a clause under the Main Contract rather than to provide the reader with a full set of information. The parties to the Subcontract shall then read the Main Contract as if it had been changed for the purposes of the Subcontract, for example whenever the Main Contract uses the term "Contractor" then for the purposes of the Subcontract the "Subcontractor" is meant. Words under the Subcontract are used as defined in the Main Contract. However, there is never a rule without exception. Thus, users should be very careful in reading the Subcontract.

Once the parties to the Subcontract have acquainted themselves with the concepts and the wording they will understand that the General Conditions of Subcontract reflect the Main Contract (Red Book) in terms of the number of Clauses and the numbering of clauses. Thus, the Subcontract incorporates 20 Clauses. The clause headings are similar or the same than under the Main Contract.

The FIDIC Subcontract 2011 is intended for use with the FIDIC " Red Book" 1999 edition. The Subcontract is intended to be used when the Red Book is the main contract on a project. The Subcontract is drafted in a way which assumes that all the obligations of the Contractor under the Main Contract are passed down to the Subcontractor via the Subcontract and that the numbering of both the Main Contract and Subcontract are unchanged.

8. 4   Nominated Subcontractors

8.4.1   Definition of nominated Subcontractor

FIDIC provides:

In the Contract, nominated Subcontractor means a Subcontractor:

(1) who is stated in the Contract as being a nominated Subcontractor; or

(2) whom the Engineer, under Clause 13 [Variations and Adjustments], instructs the Contractor to employ as o Subcontractor.

Previous FIDIC Contracts had a definition of nominated Subcontractors which included anyone who supplied Goods for which a Provisional Sum had been included in the Contract, as well as those who executed work. Sub-clause 5. 1 now refers only to Subcontractors who are either named in the Contract or are the subject of a Variation under Clause 13. Subcontractors are defined at Sub-clause 1. 1. 2. 8 to include a person who is appointed as a Subcontractor for a part of the Works and Materials are defined at Sub-clause 1. 1. 5. 3 as forming part of the Permanent Works. Hence, under FIDIC, a material supplier who is nominated would appear to be a nominated Subcontractor and be covered by the provisions of Clause 5.

8.4.2   Why Nominate?

Nomination is used because there are benefits for the Employer in using the system. The key benefit for the Employer is control over the choice of, and performance required from, Nominated Subcontractor. Above all, the Employer reserves to itself the choice of subcontractor.

Nominated subcontractors may offer the lowest bid or highest quality design input or some combination of price and quality benefits. Nominated subcontractors may have a proven track record for good work. The Employer may have developed a long-term business relationship with Nominated subcontractors. The Employer may wish to use a proprietary system offered by Nominated Subcontractor. Further, the Employer can, if he wishes, control the terms of the subcontract, including the price and scope of Nominated subcontractor's work.

Another benefit is the potential for reduced procurement times. Some specialist subcontract work requires a longer lead time than the construction programme would allow – such work must be started before general contractor has been chosen. Nomination allows for continuity when a specialist subcontractor has been selected before the general contractor is in place.

8.4.3   Objection to Nomination

Under FIDIC (1999), the Contractor shall not be under any obligation to employ a nominated Subcontractor, the Contractor may raise reasonable objection by notice to the Engineer as soon as practicable, with supporting particulars. An objection shall be deemed reasonable if it arises from (among other things) any of the following matters, unless the Employer agrees to indemnify the Contractor against and from the consequences of the matter:

(1) there are reasons to believe that the Subcontractor does not have sufficient competence, resources or financial strength;

(2) the subcontract does not specify that the nominated Subcontractor shall indemnify the Contractor against and from any negligence or misuse of Goods by the nominated Subcontractor, his agents and employees; or

(3) the subcontract does not specify that, for the subcontracted work (including design, if any), the nominated Subcontractor shall:

1) undertake to the Contractor such obligations and liabilities as will enable the Contractor to discharge his obligations and liabilities under the Contract, and

2) indemnify the Contractor against and from all obligations and liabilities arising under or in connection with the Contract and from the consequences of any failure by the Subcontractor to perform these obligations or to fulfill these liabilities.

8.5　Dispute resolution of Subcontractor

Clause 20 of the 2011 Subcontract provides a dispute resolution procedure whereby disputes arising under the Subcontract are first referred to the Subcontract DAB (Dispute Adjudication Board) and thereafter to arbitration for final determination. The Guidance for the Preparation of the Particular Conditions of Subcontract (the " Guidance") gives two optional alternative dispute resolution provisions - the first being a simple dispute resolution procedure involving only arbitration; the second setting out a complex mechanism that is intended to make the Subcontractor bound by Main Contract DAB decisions and arbitration awards on disputes related to those under the Main Contract.

The clause is separated into sub-clauses dealing with the Subcontractor's claims for extensions of time and/or additional payment under the Subcontract (sub-clauses 20.1 to 20.5) and disputes (sub-clauses 20.6 to 20.8).

For claims for extensions of time and/or additional payment, the Subcontractor is required to give notice within 21 days of when it becomes (or should have become) aware of the event or circumstance giving rise to the claim (sub-clause 20.1).

Such claims are then separated into "Related Claims" (claims that arise from circumstances which may also give rise to a claim under the Main Contract or otherwise concern existing claims or disputes under the Main Contract) and "Unrelated Claims". Any disagreement between the parties on whether a claim is "Related" or "Unrelated" will ultimately be referred to the ICC (the International Chamber of Commerce) ❶pre-arbitral referee procedure (sub-clause 20.2).

---

❶ During the course of many contracts, especially those made for long-term transactions, problems can arise which require an urgent response. It is frequently not possible to obtain in the time required a final decision from an arbitral tribunal or from a court.

Accordingly, the International Chamber of Commerce (ICC) has set out the following Rules for a Pre-Arbitral Referee Procedure in order to enable parties that have so agreed to have rapid recourse to a person (called a "Referee") empowered to make an order designed to meet the urgent problem in issue, including the power to order the preservation or recording of evidence. The order should therefore provide a temporary resolution of the dispute and may lay the foundations for its final settlement either by agreement or otherwise. Use of the Pre-Arbitral Referee Procedure does not usurp the jurisdiction of any entity (whether arbitral tribunal or national court) that is ultimately responsible for deciding the merits of any underlying dispute.

For Unrelated Claims, the Subcontractor puts forward its detailed claim to the Contractor. If agreement cannot be reached in respect of the claim, the Contractor is required to make a "fair determination" (sub-clause 20. 3).

Under sub-clause 20. 4, the Contractor is obliged to submit Related Claims to the Engineer under the Main Contract and must use "all reasonable endeavours" to secure the claim from the Employer. The Subcontractor is entitled to be involved in any meetings with the Engineer which concerns the Related Claim, although there is nothing in the Red Book that obliges the Engineer to allow the Subcontractor to be present. Unless the Subcontractor is present in those meetings, or refuses to attend where permitted to do so, the Contractor is not allowed to reach agreement with the Engineer on the Related Claim without "prior consultation" with the Subcontractor.

Sub-clause 20. 4 goes on to state that, where the Engineer and Contractor reach agreement on the Related Claim, or the Engineer issues a determination, such that the Contractor is entitled to an extension of time and/or additional cost under the Main Contract, the Contractor is required to pass the share of the benefit applicable to the Related Claim to the Subcontractor. However, the Contractor is only liable to pass on monetary benefits if it first receives payment from the Employer, which is likely to be controversial. If the Contractor and Subcontractor disagree what the Subcontractor's share of the benefit will be, the Contractor will make a "fair determination", which the Subcontractor will be bound by if it does not issue a notice of dissatisfaction on time. If however the Engineer and Contractor agree, or the Engineer determines, that no additional payment and/or extension of time is due to the Contractor under the Main Contract, then the Subcontractor will be bound by this unless it serves a notice of dissatisfaction within the prescribed period.

Similar to Claims, Subcontract Disputes are categorised into "Unrelated Disputes" and "Related Disputes". Disputes arising from "Unrelated Claims" and "Related Claims" automatically constitute "Unrelated Disputes" and "Related Disputes" respectively (sub-clause 20. 6). A procedure is followed to determine the nature of disputes which do not arise out of either an Unrelated Claim or Related Claim, and any disagreement between the parties on this issue will again ultimately be resolved by the ICC pre-arbitral referee procedure.

Under sub-clause 20. 7, Unrelated Disputes can be referred by either the Contractor or Subcontractor for adjudication by the Subcontract DAB. If either party issues a notice of dissatisfaction in relation to the Subcontract DAB's decision the parties shall attempt to amicably settle the dispute or proceed directly to ICC arbitration.

☞ 疑难词汇 ☜

1. Repetitiveness 重复
2. Payroll 工资名单

3. Profitability 盈利能力

4. Goes without saying 不言而喻

5. Be squeezed by their main contractors 勉强得到承包商的认可

6. Project solutions or project processes 项目解决方案和项目过程

7. Traced back to 追溯到

8. Preferred supplier 首选供应商

9. Liaison 联络

10. Expediting 催货，催交

11. Quantity surveying 工料测量，数量估计

12. Follow up on 追踪，跟踪

13. Batch 一批，批次

14. Fleshed out 充实，具体化

15. At the mercy of 受……支配

☞ **中文综述** ☜

8.1　概　　述

8.1.1　分包的含义

分包商是指由承包商雇用的，完成整个工程项目一部分工作，对承包商负责，并由承包商支付价款的独立承包商。虽然分包商的概念最常用于建筑工程领域，但分包商的机会范围不限于此。而承包商雇佣分包商的动机除了降低成本或减轻项目风险外，某些专有技术和工程建造资质也是考虑因素之一。通过分包方式，承包人得到比其自身承担该工作相同或更好的服务，从而降低总体项目风险。许多分包商长期从事某一领域的专门工作，这使得分包商的专业化技能进一步加强。

转包可能是个冒险的行为，也就是说，如果没有适当的法律保护，转包是有风险的。在我国，转包是非法的，转包合同可能会被认定为无效合同。在当今充满活力和不断增长的建筑业中，与分包商合作共同完成和交付一个项目是一种常见的做法，因此，分包合同的重点是承包商与分包商之间关系，其关系的内容视具体项目的规模而定。在大型商业建设项目中，由于存在大量的错综复杂的合同安排，对这些合同关系进行有效的管理是十分重要的。如果承包商缺乏有效管理其与分包商之间关系的能力，发生纠纷的可能性就会大大增加。在大型商业项目建设过程中，发生纠纷是不可避免的，这是由于承包商与分包商之间的相互关系决定的，主要是表现为：①分包协议和合同条款；②暴露于高水平的财务风险（从双方的角度来看）；③保护当事人自身的利益或者动机；④基于时间、金钱和资源的约束。

8.1.2　分包的种类

1. 自雇分包商

自雇分包商是由承包人承包建设工程后，由承包人选择并雇用的，将其承包的某一部分工程或某几部分工程，再发包给其他承包人，与其签订承包合同项下的分包合同。分包商与承包商签订合同，为承包商供应材料或分包某一部分工程，执行主合同的某一部分。

承包人分包建设工程的，应当符合以下条件：①承包人只能将部分工程分包给具有相应资质条件的分包人；②为防止承包人擅自将应当由自己完成的工程分包出去或者将工程分包给雇主所不信任的分包人，分包工程应通知雇主或经过雇主的同意。

2. 指定分包商

指定分包商是由雇主指定、选定，完成某项特定工作内容并与承包商签订分包合同的特殊分包商。合同条款规定，雇主有权将部分工程项目的施工任务或涉及提供材料、设备、服务等工作内容指定分包商实施。大多数标准合同文本允许雇主选择几个分包商，然后由承包人通过"提名"程序雇佣他们。雇主这样做有很多原因，包括但不限于雇主与熟悉的分包商合作的心态，分包商是有经验的、可靠的、有偿付能力的等。

3. 提名分包商

提名分包商允许雇主影响承包商对分包商的选择，同时将责任留给承包商。为了达到指定分包商的目的，雇主首先确定一个潜在的，可接受的分包商的短名单，并邀请这些潜在的分包商来投标。提名分包商的存在缓和了雇主与承包商在指定分包商方面存在的矛盾。也映衬了 FIDIC 合同条款关于承包商有拒绝指定分包商权利的规定。2011 年的 JCT 中级建筑合同是为数不多的明确提出提名分包商的标准范本合同，尽管仍有一些问题未得到解答。

8.2　FIDIC 关于分包合同的规定

1. 新红皮书 4.4 条规定

承包商不得将整个工程分包出去。承包商应将分包商、分包商的代理人或雇员的行为或违约视为承包商自己的行为或违约，并为之负全部责任。除非专用条件中另有说明，否则：

（1）承包商在选择材料供应商或向合同中已注明的分包商进行分包时，无需征得同意；

（2）其他拟雇用的分包商须得到工程师的事先同意；

（3）承包商应至少提前 28 天将每位分包商的工程预期开工日期以及现场开工日期通知工程师；以及

（4）每份分包合同应包含一条规定，即雇主有权按照第 4.5 款【分包合同利益的转让】（如果可行）或出现第 15.2 款【雇主提出终止】中规定的终止合同的情况时要求将此分包合同转让给雇主。

同时，新红皮书对分包合同利益转让做出了规定：如果分包商的义务超过了缺陷通知期的期满之日，且工程师在此期满日前已指示承包商将此分包合同的利益转让给雇主，则承包商应按指示行事。除非另有说明，否则承包商在转让生效以后对分包商实施的工程对雇主不负责任。

2. FIDIC 分包合同 2011

FIDIC 在 2011 年出版了 FIDIC 的分包合同，该分包合同范本与 FIDIC 新红皮书是配套使用的，是有连续性的。这种新的合同格式将帮助承包商参与到项目中，将工程分包给分包商，以避免在责任链中不必要的空白。分包商同意执行分包工程，就像承包商履行主合同项下工程义务一样。如果分包商不能正确地提供服务，导致承包商的责任，分包商有义务使承包商免于承担这种责任。此外，分包商应使承包商在主合同下正常进行工作。分包条款 2011 第 20.1 条要求分包商提供所有通知，并保留所有必要的记录，以便承包商遵守主合同下的索赔条款。

没有对承包合同的阅读为基础，分包合同并不容易读懂，因此，要理解分包合同，得首先研究主合同，并且将两个合同一起研究。分包合同的一个典型特征是，它仅仅是指主合同项下的一个条款，而并不提供完整的信息。例如，当主合同使用"承包商"一词时，则"分包商"指的是为分包合同的目的而设。分包合同中使用的文字应在主合同中有所定义。因此，用户在阅读分包合同时应该非常小心。

一旦分包商了解了合同条款的含义和措辞，他们就会明白分包合同的一般条款对应了主合同（红皮书）的条款和条款的编号。因此，分包合同包含了 20 个条款，条款的标题与主合同的标题相似或相同。

8.3　指　定　分　包　商

8.3.1　概述

根据行业定义，指定分包商是由雇主选择的承包商，他们随后直接与承包商签订合同，以执行特定的工程范围。指定分包商通常是专业的承包商，提供设计和施工服务。对雇主而言，发现和邀请潜在的指定分包商参与某种形式的采购或投标活动是很常见的做法。雇主将与成功的分包商商议商业和法律条款，然后由承包商根据预先商定的条款与指定承包商签订分包合同。

为了满足雇主对指定分包商在采购等方面的需要，承包合同通常会允许雇主直接选择和任命分包商。一个重要的例证就是 1987 年 FIDIC 红皮书第 59 条的规定。作为回报，承包商通常会以利润和工时形式从雇主获得更多的资金，作为其可能失去利润的一种补偿，而这种失去利润可能是因为承包商放弃自雇分包商而引起的。

除金钱补偿外，在指定分包商签订的合同条款中，指定分包商对主承包商的赔偿也是常见的做法。赔偿的目的是保护承包商在履行其在分包合同下的义务时，因分包商违约或过失行为引起的损害。此外，为了保护承包商的利益，合同条款还规定分包商应确保承包商在主合同项下不因指定分包商的行为而违约。许多标准合同也规定了如果指定分包商完工延期，承包商有权要求雇主延长整体项目时间。例如 JCT 标准建筑合同文本。

8.3.2　指定分包商的含义

FIDIC 合同条款 5.1 条规定指定分包商是指一个分包商，并且合同中指明作为指定分包商的，或者工程师依据 FIDIC 第 13 款【变更和调整】规定指示承包商将其作为一名分包商雇用的人员。因此，指定分包商是指由雇主（或工程师）指定、选定，完成某项特定工作内容并与承包商签订分包合同的特殊分包商。FIDIC 合同条款规定，雇主有权将部分工程项目的施工任务或涉及提供材料、设备、服务等工作内容发包给指定分包商实施。

提名分包商之所以被定义或使用，是因为雇主会从中获得好处。雇主的主要利益来自于对标准适用要求的选择和执行的控制，有些利益也来自于雇主维系关系的需要。同时提名分包商在先，指定分包商在后，可以避免雇主与承包商之间的矛盾。被指定的分包商有良好的工作经验，并且雇主可能与指定的分包商已经建立了长期的业务关系，指定分包商的另一个好处是可以减少采购时间。一些专业分包工作可能需要比主体建设项目更长的时间，这样的工作必须在承包商被选定之前开始。当一个专业分包商在承包人就位之前被选中时，提名允许继续。

8.3.3 对指定分包商的反对

承包商有反对指定分包商的权利，承包商反对指定分包商可以向工程师提出（FIDIC条件下），并附上相关的证据资料。如果因为（但不限于）下述任何事宜而反对，则该反对应被认为是合理的，除非雇主同意保障承包商免于承担下述事宜的后果：①有理由相信分包商没有足够的能力、资源或资金实力；②分包合同未规定指定分包商应保障承包商免于承担由分包商、其代理人、雇员的任何疏忽或对货物的错误操作的责任；③分包合同未规定指定分包商对所分包工程（包括设计，如有时），应该：①向承包商承担该项义务和责任以使承包商可以依照合同免除他的义务和责任，以及②保障承包商免于按照合同或与合同有关的以及由于分包商未能履行这些义务或完成这些责任而导致的后果所具有的所有义务和责任。

如果承包人不希望雇佣指定的分包商，他必须尽快提出异议。如果指定的分包商在投标文件中被指定，承包商在签订合同之前就有机会提出异议。反对理由不限于FIDIC新红皮书5.2条（a）至（c）段所述的事项，但必须是合理的。任何关于反对理由是否合理的争论都可能导致相当大的问题和工期延误。如果承包人不希望雇用某一分包商，而雇主坚持使用，就会出现问题。

8.4 分包关系中应注意的主要问题

作为一个分包商，其与承包商的法律关系往往使其处于一个具有挑战性的境地，即分包商受制于承包商，其行使权利的欲望可能受制于合同条款的约束，同时，相对于雇主而言，分包商与承包商负有连带责任。因此，分包商学习如何保护自身利益，免受潜在风险的侵害是很重要的。

8.4.1 责任下移

在建筑工程合同链条中，分包商处于合同链条底部，如果工程出了问题，雇主就会给承包人带来很大的压力，而承包人反过来也会把这个责任转嫁给分包商来承担，分包商与承包商对雇主承担连带责任。分包商的风险部分来自于承包商，承包合同中约定的承包商对雇主的风险被转交给分包商，分包商被认为是"完全了解主合同的相关条款"。因此，分包合同是根据主合同的"背靠背"原则起草的，分包商必须履行"主合同项下承包商的与分包工程有关的义务和责任"。例如，在FIDIC分包合同2011版文本中，第20.1条（FIDIC Subcontract 2011）中给出了通知的时间限制，分包商的时间限制比主合同中相应的时间限制要短。

8.4.2 缺乏与雇主直接沟通的渠道

根据合同关系，分包商不会与雇主有直接的沟通。分包商一切活动的指令来自于分包合同，同时这个分包合同内容要体现承包合同条款的主要精神，但是，在传递这种主要精神的过程中，丢失和误传也是常有的事。这种与雇主沟通的缺失会阻碍分包商对其所从事的工作建立适当的期望，并为其确切的理解雇主的意图造成障碍。

8.4.3 付款纠纷

作为一个分包商，它的工作成果由承包商检验，为其工作支付报酬。如果雇主对承包商工作的任何方面不满意，即使不是分包商所为，分包商也可能受到牵连，例如，雇主可能对有缺欠的工作延时付款，而承包人可能会借故停止支付分包商，尽管不是由于该分包商的过错引起的。在 FIDIC 分包合同 2011 年版本中，分包商必须在分包商缺陷通知期结束后 28 天提交他的最终声明（与主合同项下的缺陷通知期相关）。如果承包商无法核实最终声明的相关部分，则可能需要分包商提供额外的信息。承包商必须在分包商的缺陷通知期结束后 56 天内支付分包商价款余额。承包商如果未得到工程师的认可或已通过工程师认可但没有得到雇主支付的金额，对分包商的支付问题将给承包商和分包商之间的关系带来麻烦。

8.4.4　缺乏对安全的控制

分包商通常必须与其他分包商交叉工作，或者去承包商的工地进行工作，这意味着他们很可能无法控制工地上的安全措施的质量。而分包商对现场安全的理解和要求可能与承包商非常不同，这就可能使分包商受到风险威胁，或者因为拒绝在这样的环境中工作而被索赔。

8.4.5　与其他分包商的合作

承包商负责工程的整体协调和项目管理，以及分包工程与主导工程和任何其他分包工程的协调。在这个过程中，承包商占优势的管理地位，而各分包商则是被动的服从承包商的安排，或者通过承包商与雇主或其他分包商联系。FIDIC 分包合同 2011 第 6.1 条规定，如果分包商被另一分包商延迟或妨碍，他必须向承包商发出通知，通过承包商的协调，分包商可享有延长时间和获得支付费用的权利。

8.4.6　履约证书

履约证书是承包商已按合同规定完成全部施工义务的证明，因此该证书颁发后工程师无权指示承包商进行任何施工工作，承包商即可办理最终结算手续。适用于分包工程的履约证书是由工程师在主合同项下签发的证书。换句话说，直到所有工程完工并在主合同项下获得认证后，分包商的工作才得到认证。

8.4.7　分包工作的损失或损害

分包商有义务对分包工程的所有损失或损害进行修复和整改。FIDIC 分包合同条款 2011 第 17 条规定了分包商对整改费用负责的情况，但也包含了分包商对于不是由于其自身原因造成的损失或损害可以收回成本的机制。

8.5　分包商纠纷的解决

FIDIC 分包合同条款 2011 第 20 条提供了一项解决争议的程序，根据该程序，在分包合同项下产生的争议首先提交到分包商 DAB（争议仲裁委员会）解决，其后可以提交仲裁最终决定。对分包合同纠纷解决的具体条件有两种可选的解决办法：一是简单的争端解决程序，只涉及仲裁；二是复杂的解决机制，旨在使分包商在与主合同相关的纠纷中，以主合同 DAB 决定为主，以仲裁裁决为附。

FIDIC 分包合同条款 2011 第 20 条被分成若干子条款，处理分包商要求延长工期和额外支付的索赔（条款 20.1 至 20.5）和争议（条款 20.6 至 20.8）。对于延长时间和/或额外支付的索赔要求，分包商应在知晓或已知晓引起索赔的事件或情况后 21 天内提出索赔。

这样的索赔被分成"相关索赔"（根据主要合同中可能引起索赔的情况而产生的索赔，

或主合同项下现有的索赔或纠纷）和"不相关的索赔"。双方对于索赔是否"相关"或"无关"的任何分歧最终将提交给国际商会仲裁委员会仲裁解决。对于不相关的索赔，分包商将其详细的索赔要求提交给承包商。如果不能就索赔要求达成协议，则承包商需要作出"公平的决定"（第20.3条）。

根据第20.4条的规定，承包商必须在主合同项下向工程师提交相关的索赔要求，并且必须使用"一切合理的努力"来保证向雇主索赔的充分性。分包商有权参与工程师组织的涉及相关索赔的任何会议。尽管在《红皮书》中，没有要求工程师允许分包商出席任何会议。除非分包商出席这些会议，或拒绝出席，否则，承包商在不与分包商进行"事先协商"前提下，不得与工程师就相关索赔达成协议。

条款20.4规定，如果工程师和承包商就相关索赔达成协议，承包商根据主合同由此获得工期延长或者额外费用，承包商应当将上述以利益分享给分包商。如果承包商不同意分包商的利益份额，承包商需作出"公正的决定"，但是如果分承包商没有及时发出不满意的通知给工程师，分包商权益将受到损害。但是，如果工程师和承包商同意，或工程师决定，没有额外的付款和/或时间的延长是由于承包商原因所致，那么分包商如果没有在规定的期限内发出不满通知，其权益将受到损害。

与索赔类似，分包合同纠纷也被归类为"不相关的纠纷"和"相关纠纷"。由"无关的索赔"和"相关索赔"引起的纠纷，自动构成"不相关争议"和"相关争议"（第20.6条）。一项程序被遵循，确定纠纷的性质所遵守的程序并不以无关的或者相关的索赔为基础，并且双方分歧上的不同观点最终将由国际商会仲裁前裁判程序解决（ICC Pre-arbitral Referee Procedure）。

Questions

1. What types the subcontractors are defined under FIDIC 2011, what are main features of those subcontractor?

2. What is nominated subcontractor?

3. We are employed as main contractor to carry out a 40 story building. The contract used by the Employer is FIDIC Conditions of Contract 1st edition 1999. The employer has now nominated the XY works and instructed us to use the same conditions of contract to administer the subcontractor. Can you please advise the legal and administration implications of using the conditions of contract to administer the subcontractor?

Chapter 9   Variations in Contracts

9. 1   Definitions of variations

Many definitions of the word "variation" exist. The International Federation of Financial Standards issued the International Accounting Standard, which is applicable to construction contracts: "A variation is an instruction of the customer for a change in the scope of work to be performed under the contract. A variation may lead to an increase or a decrease in contract revenue. Examples of variations are changes in the specification or design of the asset and changes in the duration of the contract." This definition is sufficient for accounting purposes, but not for managing projects. Many standard contracts mention more details, in order to prevent confusion.

The FIDIC red book (1999) defines a variation as: "any change to the works as per sub-clause 13. 1, i. e. any change of quantities and quantities of items, changes to levels, positions and/or dimensions of any part of the works, omission of any part of the works, any additional work, plant, or services, including any associated tests on completion, boreholes or any other testing, changes to the sequence of timing."

The FIDIC yellow book (D&B contract) defines variation in a different way, i. e. as any change to the employer's requirements or the works; it does not mention the list of variations as mentioned in the FIDIC red book. The reason is that, in the red book, the employer is responsible for the design, while in the yellow book, the contractor is responsible for the design.

A201 of AIA clause5. 1 provides that the Changes in the work may be accomplished after execution of the contract, and without invalidating the contract, by Change order, Construction Change Directive or order for a minor change in the Work, subject to the limitation stated in this article7 and elsewhere in the Contract Documents. A201 of AIA clause5. 2 further provides that a Change Order shall be based upon agreement among the Owner, Contractor and Architect; a Construction Change Directive requires agreement by the Owner and Architect, and may or may not be agreed to by the Contractor; an order for a minor change in the Work may be issued by the Architect alone.

Therefore we may say a variation (sometimes referred to as a variation instruction, variation order or change order) is an alteration to the scope of works with required procedure in a construction contract in the form of an addition, substitution or omission from the original scope of works.

9. 2 Reasons for causing a variation order

9. 2. 1 Employer Related Changes

In some cases, the Employer directly initiates Variations or the Variations are required because the Employer fails to fulfil certain requirements for carrying out the project.

(1) Change of plans or scope by Employer: Change of plan or scope of project is one of the most significant causes of Variations in construction projects and is usually the result of insufficient planning at the project planning stage, or lack of involvement of the Employer in the design phase.

(2) Change of schedule by Employer: A change of schedule or master programme during the project construction phase may result in major resource reallocation. This is because time has an equivalent money value. A change in schedule means that the Contractor will either provide additional resources, or keep some resources idle in the construction site. In both cases additional cost is incurred.

(3) Employer's financial problems: The Employer of the project may run into difficult financial situations that force him to make changes in an attempt to reduce cost of the project. Proper financial planning and review of project cash flow would be effective in avoiding this problem to from happening.

(4) Inadequate project objectives: Inadequate project objectives are one of the causes of Variations in construction projects. Due to inadequate project objectives, the designers would not be able to develop a comprehensive design which lead to many of Variations during the project construction phase.

(5) Replacement of materials or procedures: Replacement of materials or procedures may cause major Variations during the construction phase. The substitution of procedures includes Variations in application methods. Therefore, an adjustment to the original contract value is required if there is a change in procedures.

(6) Impediment in prompt decision making process: Prompt decision making is an important factor for project success. A delay in decision making may obstruct the progress of subsequent construction activities and that may eventually delay the entire project progress.

(7) Obstinate nature of Employer: A building project is the result of the combined efforts of the professionals. They have to work at the various interfaces of a project. If the Employer is obstinate, he may not accommodate other creative and beneficial ideas. Eventually, this may cause major Variations in the later stages and affect the project negatively.

(8) Change in specifications by owner: In a multi-player environment like any construction project, change in specifications by the Employer during the construction phase

may require major Variations and adjustments in project planning and procurement activities.

9.2.2　Consultant Related Variations

In some cases, the consultant directly initiates Variations or the Variations are required because the consultant fails to fulfil certain requirements for carrying out the project.

(1) Change in design by Consultants: The changes in design are frequent in projects where construction starts before the design is finalized. Design changes can affect a project adversely depending on the timing of the occurrence of the changes.

(2) Errors and omissions in design: Design errors and omissions may lead to loss of productivity and delay in project schedule. Hence, errors and omissions in design can affect a project adversely depending on the timing of the occurrence of the errors.

(3) Conflicts between contract documents: Conflict between contract documents can result in misinterpretation of the actual requirement of a project. Insufficient details in contract documents may adversely affect the project, leading to delay in project completion.

(4) Technology change: Technology change is a potential cause of Variations in a project. During the construction phase, value engineering can be a costly exercise, as Variation in any design element would initiate and lead to Variations to other relevant design components .

(5) Lack of coordination: A lack of coordination between parties may cause major variations that could eventually impact the project adversely. Unfavourable Variations, which affect the projects negatively, can usually be managed at an early stage by paying extra focus in coordination.

(6) Design complexity: Complex designs require unique skills and construction methods. Complexity affects the flow of construction activities, whereas simple and linear construction works are relatively easy to handle. Hence, complexity may cause major Variations in construction projects.

(7) Inadequate working drawing details: To convey a complete concept of the project design, the working drawings must be clear and concise. Insufficient working drawing details can result in misinterpretation of the actual requirement of a project.

(8) Inadequate shop drawing details: Shop drawings are usually developed for construction work details for site professionals. As mentioned earlier with regard to working drawing details, likewise, inadequacy of shop drawing details can be a potential cause of Variations in the construction projects.

(9) Consultant's lack of judgment and experience: Professional experience and judgment is an important factor for a successful completion of a building project. The lack of professional experience increases the risk of errors in design as well as during construction. Eventually, this may affect the project quality and delay the project completion.

(10) Design discrepancies (inadequate design): Inadequate design can be a frequent cause of Variations in construction projects. Design discrepancies affect the project functionality and quality. Eventually, this can affect a project adversely depending on the timing of the occurrence of the Variations.

(11) Noncompliance of design with government regulations: Noncompliance of design with government regulations or policies would cost the project difficult to execute. Noncompliance with government regulations may affect the project safety and progress negatively, leading to serious accidents and delays in the project completion.

(12) Noncompliance of design with owner's requirements: A noncompliance design with the owner's requirements is considered an inadequate design. Eventually, this may cause Variations for accommodating the Employer's requirements. This may affect the project adversely during the construction phase.

9. 2. 3　Contractor Related Variations

In some cases, the contractor may suggest Variations to the project, or the Variations may be required because the contractor fails to fulfil certain requirements for carrying out the project.

(1) Lack of Contractor's involvement in design: Involvement of the Contractor in the design may assist in developing better designs by accommodating his creative and practical ideas. Lack of Contractor's involvement in design may eventually cause Variations. Practical ideas which are not accommodated during the design phase will eventually affect the project negatively.

(2) Unavailability of equipment: Unavailability of equipment is a procurement problem that can affect the project completion. Occasionally, the lack of equipment may cause major design Variations or adjustments to project scheduling to accommodate the replacement.

(3) Unavailability of skills (shortage of skilled manpower): Skilled manpower is one of the major resources required for complex technological projects. Shortage of skilled manpower is more likely to occur in complex technological projects. This lack can be a cause for Variations that may delay the project's completion date.

(4) Contractor's financial difficulties: Construction is a labour intensive industry. Whether the Contractor has been paid or not, the wages of the worker must still be paid. Contractor's financial difficulties may cause major Variations during a project, affecting its quality and progress and in some cases even the safety of the site is affected if there is an argument.

(5) Differing site conditions: Differing site condition can be an important cause of delays in large building projects. The contractor may face different soil conditions than those indicated in the tender documents. Eventually this may affect his cost estimates and schedule negatively.

(6) Defective workmanship: Defective workmanship may lead to demolition and re-

work in construction projects. Defective workmanship results in low quality in construction projects. Even the Contractor bares the cost of the defective work, but this also may affect the project negatively, leading to rework and delay in the project completion.

(7) Lack of a specialized construction manager: The construction manager carries out the construction phase in an organized way to eliminate the risks of delays and other problems. Lack of a specialized construction manager may lead to defective workmanship and delay in the construction project.

(8) Lack of communication: Detrimental Variations, which affect the projects adversely, can usually be managed at an early stage with strong and incessant communication. A lack of coordination and communication between parties may cause major Variations that could eventually impact the project negatively.

(9) Complex design and technology: Complex design and technology require detailed interpretations by the designer to make it comprehensible for the Contractor (Arain, 2002). A complex design may be experienced for the first time by the Contractor. Eventually, the complexity may affect the flow of construction activities, leading to delays in the project completion.

(10) Lack of strategic planning: Proper strategic planning is an important factor for successful completion of a building project. The lack of strategic planning is a common cause of Variations in projects where construction starts before the design is finalized, for instance, in concurrent design and construction contracts.

Contractor's lack of required data: A lack of required data may affect the contractor's strategic planning for successful project completion, leading to frequent disruptions during the construction process. This is because a lack of data can result in misinterpretation of the actual requirements of a project.

9.2.4 Other Variations

(1) Change in government regulations: Local authorities may have specific codes and regulations that need to be accommodated in the design. Change in government regulations during the project construction phase may cause major Variations in design and construction. This can affect a project negatively depending on the timing of the occurrence of the changes.

(2) Change in economic conditions: Economic conditions are one of the influential factors that may affect a construction project. The economic situation of a country can affect the whole construction industry and its participants. Eventually, this may affect the project negatively, depending on the timing of the occurrence of the Variations.

(3) Socio-cultural factors: Professionals with different socio-cultural backgrounds may encounter problems due to different perceptions, and this may affect the working environment of the construction project. Lack of coordination is common between professionals with different socio-cultural backgrounds. Eventually, project delays may occur that end up with vital changes in the entire project team.

（4）Unforeseen problems: Unforeseen conditions are usually faced by professionals in the construction industry. If these conditions are not solved as soon as possible, they may cause major Variations in the construction projects. Eventually, this may affect the project negatively, leading to reworks and delays in the project completion.

9. 3   Effective Approach to control variations

9. 3. 1   Design Stage Approach to Control Variations

（1）Review of contract documents

Comprehensive and balanced Variation clauses would be helpful in improving coordination and communication quality. Conflicts between contract documents can result in misinterpretation of the actual requirement of a project.

（2）Freezing design

Variations in design can affect a project adversely depending on the timing of the occurrence of the changes. Therefore, freezing the design is a strong control method. Many owners freeze the design and close the door for variations after the completion of the drawings.

（3）Value engineering at conceptual phase

During the design phase, value engineering can be a cost saving exercise, as at this stage, Variation in any design element would not require rework or demolition at the construction site. Value engineering at the conceptual stage can assist in clarifying project objectives and reducing design discrepancies.

（4）Involvement of professionals at initial stages of project

Involvement of professionals in design may assist in developing better designs by accommodating their creative and practical ideas. This practices would assist in developing a comprehensive design with minimum discrepancies . Practical ideas that are not accommodated during the design phase may affect the project adversely. Variation during the construction phase is a costly activity as it may initiate numerous changes to construction activities.

（5）Employer's involvement at planning and design phase

Involvement of the Employer at the design phase would assist in clarifying the project objectives and identifying noncompliance with their requirements at the early stage. Hence, this may help in eliminating Variations during the construction stage where the impact of the Variations can be severe

（6）Involvement of contractor at planning and scheduling process

Involvement of the Employer at the design phase would assist in clarifying the project objectives and identifying noncompliance with their requirements at the early stage. Hence, this may help in eliminating Variations during the construction stage where the impact of the variations can be severe.

(7) Thorough detailing of design

A clearer design tends to be comprehended more readily. This would also assist in identifying the errors and omissions in design at an early stage. Eventually, thorough detailing of design can eliminate Variations arising from ambiguities and errors in design.

(8) Clear and thorough project brief

A clear and thorough project brief is an important control for Variations in construction projects as it helps in clarifying the project objectives to all the participants. Eventually, this may reduce the design errors and noncompliance with the Employer's requirements.

(9) Reducing contingency sum

The provision of a large contingency sum may affect the construction team' working approaches. This is because the designer may not develop a comprehensive design and would consequently carry out the rectifications in design as Variations during the later stages of the construction project. Therefore, reducing the contingency sum would be helpful in ensuring that the professionals carry out their jobs with diligence.

9.3.2   Construction Stage Approach to Control Variations

(1) Clarity of Variation Order procedures

Clarity of Variation Order procedures is an integral part of effective management of Variation Orders. Early in the project construction stage, the procedures should be identified and made clear to all parties. Clarity of Variation Order procedures would help in reducing the processing time and other mishandling issues.

(2) Written approvals

Any Variation in the work that involves a change in the original price must be approved in writing by the Employer before a Variation can be executed. Any party signing on behalf of the Employer must have written authorization from the Employer. It is difficult to prove the right for compensation if there is no such authorization from the Employer. In the hectic environment of construction, many verbal agreements can be forgotten, leaving the Contractor without any legal proof to get compensation for the Variations works.

(3) Variation Order scope

A well defined scope can assist the professional team in recognizing and planning appropriately to minimize the negative impact of the Variation. The original scope should be clear and well defined to distinguish between a Variation of scope and a Variation due to design development. It is common that there are disagreement between parties in a project was about defining the Variation scope. Thus, the effective definition of the scope of work helps us to identify and manage Variations.

(4) Variation logic and justification

Variation logic and justification for implementation was one of the principles of effective change management. This principle required a change to be classified as required or elective. Required changes were required to meet original objectives of the project while e-lective changes were additional features that enhanced the project. Knowing the logic and justification behind the proposed Variations assist the professionals in promoting beneficial Variations and eliminating non-beneficial Variations.

(5) Appointment of Project manager from an independent firm to manage the project

Involvement of a project manager from an independent firm would assist in eliminating Variations that arise due to the lack of coordination among professionals. This practice may assist in reducing design discrepancies through early reviews of the contract documents and drawings.

(6) Employer's involvement during construction phase

Involvement of the Employer during the construction phase would assist in identifying noncompliance with the requirements and in approving the Variations promptly. The involvement of the Employer during the construction phase allows to keep him aware of ongoing activities and assist in prompt decision making.

(7) Avoid use of open tendering

Competitive open tendering usually encourages the Contractor to price very low to win the contract, especially in bad times when they are in need of jobs. This practice would give rise to the Contractor trying to claim more to compensate for the low price award. Avoiding the use of open tender would help in eliminating the risks of unfair bids. This may also help in reduces Variations that may arise due to the contractor's bidding strategy.

(8) Use of project scheduling/management techniques

To manage a Variation means being able to anticipate its effects and to control, or at least monitor, the associated cost and time impact. Well planned and close monitoring on the schedule plan will helps to reduce the Variations effects on the project.

(9) Comprehensive documentation of variation order

Through timely notification and documentation of Variation Orders, participants will have kept their rights and thereby their option to pursue a subsequent claim or to defend against a claim. One of the most aggravating conditions is the length of time that elapses between the time when a proposed contract modification is first announced and when the matter is finally rejected or approved as a Variation Order. Documentation of Variation and claims had assisted in tracking the effects of the Variation and claim events on time and cost. A documented source of knowledge about previous Variation instructions would be helpful in making decisions concerning the appropriate handling of Variation instructions.

9. 3. 3　Design-construction interface stage approach to control variations

(1) Prompt approval procedures

One of the most aggravating conditions is the length of time that elapses between the time when a proposed contract modification is first announced and when the matter is finally rejected or approved as a Variation. However, the longer the period between recognition and implementation, the more costly the change will be.

(2) Ability to negotiate Variation

Ability to negotiate Variation is an important factor for the effective control of Variations. Effective negotiation can assist the professional team in minimizing the negative impacts of the Variation. There are certain skills required for effective negotiation of Variations, i. e. , the knowledge of contract terms, project details, technology, labour rates, equipment, methods and communication skills.

(3) Valuation of indirect effects

Consequential effects can occur later in the downstream phases of a project. Therefore, it is essential to acknowledge this possibility and establish the mechanism to evaluate its consequences.

Professionals should thus evaluate the total overall effects a change may have on the later phases of a project, in order to manage the Variations effectively.

(4) Team effort by Employer, consultant and Contractor to control Variation

Coordination is important in a multi-participant environment as in most construction projects Detrimental Variations, which affect the projects negatively, can usually be managed at an early stage with due diligence in coordination.

(5) Utilize work breakdown structure

A work breakdown structure (WBS) is a management tool for identifying and defining work. A Contractor should consider using the this as an evaluation tool, especially on large projects. If a Variation involves work not previously included in the WBS, it can be logically added to the WBS and its relationship with the other WBS element can be easily checked. Domino effects can also be traced by the use of WBS.

(6) Continuous coordination and direct communication

Coordination, and frequent communication are essential to reduce miscommunication among team members, hence reduce the chances of occurring Variations.

(7) Control the potential for Variations to arise through contractual clauses

Selection of the appropriate standard contract form with the necessary and unambiguous Variation clauses would be helpful in the management of Variations. Clear procedures presented in the contract and fair allocation of risks can help in resolving disputes through negotiation rather than litigation.

(8) Comprehensive site investigation

Comprehensive site investigations assist in proper planning for construction activities. Differing site conditions are an important cause of delays in large building projects. Therefore, a comprehensive site investigation would help in reducing potential Variations in a project.

(9) Use of collected and organized project data compiled by Employer, consultant and Contractor

The Variations works should always be documented for future references. Hence, better controls for Variations were achievable by sharing a database compiled by all the team members

（10）Knowledge-base of previous similar projects

From the outset, project strategies and philosophies should take advantage of lessons learned from past similar projects. If professionals have a knowledge-base established on past similar projects, it would assist the professional team to plan more effectively before starting a project, both during the design phase as well as during the construction phase, minimize and control Variations and their effects.

9.4 Refused variations and disagreements

The contractor is not bound to all variations. The employer has to remain within reasonable limits. Grounds for a contractor to refuse variations are:

（1）The impossibility of obtaining the necessary goods.

（2）The variation will affect the safety or suitability of the works.

（3）The variation will have an adverse impact on the achievement of the guarantees.

（4）The variation results in work that exceeds what parties could reasonably have expected when the contract was concluded.

（5）The variation has nothing to do with the work.

Other reasons for a contractor to refuse could be the impossibility of mobilizing sufficient equipment in time or to contract necessary subcontractors or service providers. Another reason for refusing a variation might be the intolerable disruption or disorder of the activities on the site or the nonavailability of the required competencies at the contractor. Anyhow, the spirit of all standard contracts is that the contractor should cooperate with the employer in the employer's interest. Even if a specific variation clause is missing in a contract, the contractor can refuse a variation if he can prove to the employer that such a variation would endanger the employer's interests.

☞ **疑难词汇** ☜

1. Prompt decision making 及时决策

2. Fast track construction 快速通道建设

3. Socio-cultural factors 社会文化因素

4. Freezing design 冻结设计

5. Value engineering 价值工程

6. Contingency sums 预算外开资、应急费用

7. In the downstream phases of a project 项目后期阶段

8. Maneuverability 可操作性

9. Standard routine 标准程序

10. Mostly the initiative is with the engineer in charge 大多数情况下，（变更的）主动权在工程师

☞ **中文综述** ☜

9.1　工程变更的含义

关于变更的含义，在现实中有不同的版本。国际金融标准联合会颁发的国际会计准则第 11 号-建筑合同定义的变更更加适合建筑工程合同："所谓变更是指客户提出的就合同规定的施工范围做出变更。它可能导致合同收入的增加或减少。例如，对建造资产的规格或设计以及工期做出变更"。这个定义是为会计目的而设计的，很多标准合同范本对变更也有定义，其目的在于防止对"变更"概念使用的混淆。

FIDIC 新红皮书 1.1.6.9 条规定"变更"指按照第 13 条【变更和调整】被指示或批准作为变更的对工程的任何变动。13.1 条规定在颁发工程接收证书前的任何时间，工程师可通过发布指示或以要求承包商递交建议书的方式，提出变更。承包商应执行每项变更并受每项变更的约束，除非承包商马上通知工程师（并附具体的证明资料）并说明承包商无法得到变更所需的货物。在接到此通知后，工程师应取消、确认或修改指示。每项变更可包括：①对合同中任何工作的工程量的改变（此类改变并不一定必然构成变更）；②任何工作质量或其他特性上的变更；③工程任何部分标高、位置和（或）尺寸上的改变；④省略任何工作，除非它已被他人完成；⑤永久工程所必需的任何附加工作、永久设备、材料或服务，包括任何联合竣工检验、钻孔和其他检验以及勘察工作；⑥工程的实施顺序或时间安排的改变。

美国 AIA-A201 5.1 条也规定，工程变更在合同签订后可以通过工程变更通知单进行，但不能使合同丧失效力。对于微小的工程变更，变更指令或变更通知应受制于本合同第 7 条或合同其他条款的规定。同时，美国 AIA-A201 5.2 条进一步规定变更通知的内容与发出程序应基于雇主、承包商和工程师之间的约定。

经过多年的实践，工程变更已经成为工程管理的必要组成部分。引起工程变更的原因多种多样，提起工程变更的雇主、承包商或工程师也基于各自不同的目的，而变更除了引起原工程施工合同约定的内容发生变化，也会引起合同金额，合同工期，费用发生变化。因此，世界各国立法机构，标准合同范本制定者也都在研究各种手段限制变更的发生频率，应对变更带来的问题。

9.2　工程变更的提出

9.2.1　发布变更指令提出的工程变更

在合同履行过程中，工程师发出变更指示包括下列三种情况：

（1）工程师认为可能要发生变更的情形。在合同履行过程中，可能发生合同约定变更情形的，工程师可向承包商发出变更意向书。变更意向书应说明变更的具体内容和雇主对变更的时间要求，并附必要的图纸和相关资料。变更意向书应要求承包商提交包括拟实施变更工作的计划、措施和竣工时间等内容的实施方案。雇主同意承包商根据变更意向书要求提交的变更实施方案的，由工程师按合同约定发出变更指示。若承包商收到工程师的变更意向书后认为难以实施此项变更，应立即通知工程师，说明原因并附详细依据。

（2）工程师认为发生了变更的情形。在合同履行过程中，发生合同约定变更情形的，工程师应按照合同约定向承包商发出变更指示。变更指示应说明变更的目的、范围、变更内容以及变更的工程量及其进度和技术要求，并附有关图纸和文件。承包商收到变更指示后，应按变更指示进行变更工作。

（3）承包商认为可能要发生变更的情形。承包商收到工程师按合同约定发出的图纸和文件，经检查认为其中存在合同约定变更情形的，可向工程师提出书面变更建议。变更建议应阐明要求变更的依据，并附必要的图纸和说明。工程师收到承包商书面建议后，应与雇主共同研究，确认存在变更的，应在收到承包商书面建议后的 14 天内作出变更指示。经研究后不同意变更的，应由工程师书面答复承包商。

无论何种情况确认的变更，变更指示只能由工程师发出。变更指示应说明变更的目的、范围、变更内容以及变更的工程量及其进度和技术要求，并附有关图纸和文件。承包商收到变更指示后，应按变更指示进行变更工作。

9.2.2 要求承包商递交建议书后再确定的变更

变更的程序如下：

（1）工程师将计划变更事项通知承包商，并要求他递交实施变更的建议书。

（2）承包商应尽快答复。一种情况可能是通知工程师由于受到某些非自身原因的限制无法执行此项变更。另一种情况是承包商依据工程师的指令递交实施此项变更的说明。

9.2.3 承包商的合理化建议

（1）在履行合同过程中，承包商对雇主提供的图纸、技术要求以及其他方面提出的合理化建议，均应以书面形式提交工程师。合理化建议书的内容应包括建议工作的详细说明、进度计划和效益以及与其他工作的协调等，并附必要的设计文件。工程师应与雇主协商是否采纳建议。建议被采纳并构成变更的，应按合同约定向承包商发出变更指示。

（2）承包商提出的合理化建议降低了合同价格、缩短了工期或者提高了工程经济效益的，雇主可按国家有关规定在专用合同中约定给予奖励。

9.3　工程变更产生的原因

9.3.1 与雇主有关的变更

在某些情况下，雇主因受外部环境变化影响或者因为不能完成合同约定的义务，或者合同签订后改变原项目设想的，而提出变更。与雇主有关的变更包括以下几种情况：

（1）改变工程计划或工程范围。这种情况的产生一般由于在规划阶段，项目论证不充分或者缺少雇主对项目论证的参与。

（2）雇主改变时间计划。在项目建设阶段，改变时间或总进度计划会产生资源重新分配。因为时间即是金钱，工程计划时间表的改变意味着承包商将要负担额外的资源，闲置现场资源，因而增加承包商的工程费用。

（3）雇主的财务问题。在项目建设过程中，如果雇主的财务出现问题，势必会影响项目建设的顺利进行，例如修改项目预算，改变工程原有计划等。

（4）建筑材料的改变。在工程进行阶段，对建筑材料的改变必然引起工程的变更。

（5）及时决策程序受阻。及时决策程序是项目成功的关键因素，如果及时决策程序遇到障碍，工程建设进度就不能保证，整个项目的进程就会违背原有的计划。

（6）固执的雇主。建筑项目是建筑工程参与者各方共同努力的结果，工作上的协商与交流是必不可少的。如果雇主在这些方面有所缺失，就很难接受项目建设过程中产生的积极的对项目有益的意见，从而可能在项目建设后期出现问题，引起变更。

（7）雇主改变项目技术指标。如果这种情况发生，必然引起项目变更。

（8）快速施工建设。当雇主拥有充足资金，希望颠覆常规建设周期，短期内完成建设工程时，或者由于施工进度提速，而各方没有就施工图纸和技术参数达成完全一致，形成统一认识而开始施工的，都会引发相应的工程停顿，工程延期。

9.3.2　与设计师有关的项目变更

在某些情况下，如果设计师不能履行工程项目建设的约定义务，必然引发工程项目的变更。

（1）设计师改变设计。工程建设开始后，设计师改变原有设计将推迟或加速工程建设时间。

（2）设计中的错误与遗漏。设计中的错误与遗漏将导致生产力的下降和工程计划的推迟，设计中的错误与遗漏对工程变更的影响决定于错误与遗漏发生的时间。

（3）合同文件之间的冲突。合同文件之间的冲突将导致承包商或分包商在施工过程中对具体项目施工方法手段或者材料的使用等产生不同的理解。合同文件之间的冲突，以及对合同文件条款解读的不充分会导致临时停工或工期延迟。

（4）技术变化。技术变化是工程变更的潜在原因。在施工阶段，任何技术调整，变化，创新，例如价值工程等都会引起工程变更。

（5）合作不够。项目合同各方合作上的不足会影响项目工程施工的顺利进行，导致工程变更。

（6）设计复杂度。复杂的设计需要高超的技能和建造方法来实现。复杂的设计影响建筑施工的速度，如果没有充分的准备或者分包商相关技术不成熟都会推迟工程的进行。

（7）施工图细节不充分或有歧义。诠释建设项目的完整的设计理念，项目施工图必须清晰而明确，不能模糊不清或有歧义。不充分的有歧义的施工图纸将导致一系列问题的发生，包括但不限于施工团队时间的浪费，引发工程变更。

（8）设计师缺乏判断能力和经验。职业的判断能力和经验是完成工程项目设计的重要因素，缺失这种判断能力和经验将增加设计中错误的风险。

（9）设计师缺乏必要的数据支撑。在设计过程中，如果设计师缺少必要的数据支撑其设计，并且没有要求雇主方面予以提供或论证，而是利用其以往的经验和认知完成设计，这种设计的结果可能背离雇主的要求，造成不必要的工程变更。

（10）设计与当地政府规章制度不一致。在施工实践中，这种不一致将导致设计方案很难实施，也可能导致项目设计的安全性出现问题，从而引发施工过程中或完工后的一系列问题，例如，如果设计不符合当地的环保要求，可能涉及项目验收问题等等。

9.3.3　与承包商有关的变更

在某些情况下，承包商根据施工的具体情况，会建议工程的变更，或者由于承包商不能按照原定施工计划或设计要求完成施工任务，而提出工程变更。

（1）承包商缺少对工程设计的参与。承包商参与工程项目的设计将有助于工程施工的顺利进行，同时也有利于将承包商的经验和技能融入施工，从而降低施工成本，提高施工效率。反之，如果缺少承包商对工程设计的融入，可能会产生设计的变更或调整。

（2）设备或熟练技能工人缺失。建筑施工设备的缺失可能与承包商在采购或设备租赁某些环节不顺畅有关，这将影响工程的进行，产生工程变更。熟练技能工人的缺失可能是承包商人力资源准备不充分造成的，也可能是熟练技能工人临时出现离岗造成的。熟练技能工人的缺失直接导致一些复杂工序不能顺利完成，推迟工程的按时完成。

（3）承包商的财务困境。工程建筑是劳动密集型行业，不论承包商资金是否充沛，承包商应当得到及时地给工人支付薪酬，向供应商支付材料或服务价款。否则，可能引起工人罢工或工程材料服务供应的不足，引起工程工期的变更。

（4）现场条件与合同约定存在差异。如果现场条件，特别是现场水文地质条件出现与投标或合同约定存在差异，可能会存在建筑成本增加的可能，也可能存在承包商技术不能处理的情况，这将导致变更的发生。

（5）工艺缺欠。工艺缺欠可能导致重复工作或者已完工作的拆除，引发工程变更。

（6）不熟悉项目所在地情况。熟悉项目所在地情况是成功完成工程建设的重要因素。如果承包商没有意思到项目所在地的一些情况，例如当地的风俗、习惯、气候、节假日等，承包商是很难完成工程计划的。

（7）缺乏专业的项目经理。项目经理是建筑项目的组织者和实施者，有经验的项目经理通晓和熟悉现场项目管理，合理使用安排各种资源，熟悉项目文件与施工图纸，具有较好地与雇主、工程师，供应商以及当地政府的沟通技能，保证项目建设按照规划顺利进行。反之，则有可能造成工程延迟和变更。

（8）承包商诚实的错误判断。承包商诚实的错误判断是造成工程项目变更的潜在原因。造成这样一种情况的原因是承包商在缺少一手资料或直接证据的情况下，凭借固执主观判断，产生错误的结论，影响工程的进度和质量。

（9）采购流程存在问题。采购出了问题对施工有诸多负面效应，会直接影响施工的进行。

（10）沟通不畅。沟通不畅是合作瑕疵的主要表现形式，这就需要雇主，承包商，工程师之间拿出更多的时间解决工程施工中出现的问题，避免造成工程的延迟与变更。

9.3.4 其他原因引起的变更

（1）项目当地政府法规的变更。建筑项目应当遵守项目所在地的各项规章制度，并密切保持对项目所在地规章制度的研究与关注。如果在施工进行中，项目所在地规章制度的变化会直接影响施工的进行，从而引起工程的变更。

（2）经济环境的改变。大的经济环境的改变会直接影响在建项目的进行。如果发生经济危机或者金融危机，雇主的融资渠道可能会受到影响，资金出现问题，项目就可能停工或延期。

（3）社会文化因素。国际工程项目的最大特点就是项目参与者来自于不同的文化背景，有不同的信仰与习惯。如果项目参与各方没有充分的准备去融合和协调，就会出现各种问题，影响项目施工的进行。

（4）无法预料的问题出现。无法预料的问题有自然原因引起的，例如地震，海啸等；也有人为原因引起的，例如罢工，战争等。当这些问题出现时，工程项目会因此停工或延迟。

9.4　控制变更的有效方法

9.4.1　设计阶段变更控制方法

1. 审查合同文件

建筑工程合同是建筑工程项目的核心合同文件，是建筑工程施工合同体系的主合同。无论雇主、承包商、分包商，还是工程师都要对合同条款内容进行阅读和理解，如发现对某一合同条款存在不同理解，要及时沟通，避免出现问题。

2. 冻结设计

冻结设计，是指建筑设计处于技术上不再进行重大修改的阶段，图纸冻结，之后就是发图给承包商，进行施工。一些雇主为了避免变更，将设计冻结。

3. 全面详细的设计

全面详细的设计要求负责设计工作的工程师或承包商严格按照雇主要求进行设计，设计过程伴随设计者与雇主、承包商等各方的及时沟通，设计目的明确，避免设计错误与遗漏。

4. 专业管理人员在项目初期阶段的介入

专业管理人员在项目初期阶段的介入可以帮助完善设计，使设计融入创新和实践经验，使设计上的认识差异减少，从而避免或减少设计变更的发生。

5. 雇主在规划设计阶段的介入

雇主在规划设计阶段的介入可以帮助理清设计理念，识别与雇主建设目的不一致的地方，从而减少施工阶段变更发生的机率。

6. 承包商在项目计划与协商阶段的介入

承包商在项目计划与协商阶段的介入可以帮助承包商尽早理解和掌握雇主建设项目的整体规划方案和设计思路，技术参数等等。施工开始后，可以尽快进入角色。同时，承包商可以根据自身的施工实践，对项目计划和设计提出自己的意见，将可能存在的规划设计，以及图纸问题进行商讨，及时加以解决。这就有效地避免或减少了变更的发生。

7. 清晰全面的项目摘要

清晰全面的项目摘要，目录与内容是解决施工出现问题的重要依据；同时一个清晰全面的项目摘要，项目目录与内容也是将设计本身应用于并指导工程施工的有效工具。

9.4.2　施工阶段控制工程变更的方法

1. 明确变更指令程序

明确变更指令程序是控制变更的有效手段。在项目合同协议阶段，变更指令程序应当明确，并为项目各方接受，这可以避免违反运作规则，减少变更的发生率。

2. 书面批准

合同变更是施工实践中经常发生的，一般小的变更，经现场代表雇主的工程师签字，即可实施。但是对于重大事项的变更，应有雇主签字方可生效。例如合同价款的变更应得到雇主的书面批准，任何代理雇主的签字应当事先得到雇主的授权。

3. 变更指令范围

议定的变更指令范围可以减少变更带来的负面影响。合同中规定的变更指令范围应该是清晰的，并将变更范围与由于设计发展引起的变更区别开来。

4. 变更逻辑与理由

变更的逻辑和执行的理由是有效变更管理的原则之一。这一原则要求将变更分为必需的或选择性的。必要的更改是为满足项目最初的目标，而选择性更改则是增强项目的附加功能。了解变更背后的逻辑和理由，有助于专业人士促进有益的变更。

5. 从独立的公司聘用项目经理管理项目

从独立的公司聘用项目经理管理项目有助于增强项目经理与各方的合作，增强项目经理对新接触的项目的审视度，减少设计误差，减少变更的发生。

6. 雇主介入施工

在工程施工阶段，雇主的介入有利于确认不符合合同规定的变更要求，并且及时批准正常的变更请求。

7. 避免公开招标

竞争性的公开招标通常使得承包商以较低的价格赢得机会，特别是当承包商急需这个工程来缓解糟糕的财务状况时，承包商可能以非常低的价格进行投标。这种情况下中标的承包商往往通过索赔的方式来补充其投标价格的利润空白。因此，变更成为承包商追求利润的主要方式。

9.5 工程变更的限制与拒绝

在承包商递交详细的支持资料后，承包商可以拒绝执行工程师的变更指示。但根据 FIDIC 合同规定，拒绝工程变更，应在递交有关无法执行的详尽资料后由工程师做出决定，即确认、修改或撤销变更。

承包商限制或拒绝变更请求的，主要包括以下几种情况：

（1）承包商难以获得变更所需的物质；

（2）变更将降低工程的安全性和适用性；

（3）将对保证清单的完成产生不利的影响。工程师接到此通知后，应取消、确认或改变原指示；

（4）当合同终止时，变更的结果超过了双方可以合理预期的工作量；

（5）变更对在建工程没有帮助。

Questions

1. How does the contractor handle variations?

2. Discuss events resulting in variations?

3. Please discuss the effective approach to control Variations?

Chapter 10   Construction Insurance

10. 1   Construction risks

10. 1. 1   Construction Risks

By nature, construction work is hazardous, and accidents are frequent and often severe. The annual toll of deaths, bodily injuries, and property damage in the construction industry is extremely high. The potential severity of accidents and the frequency with which they occur require that the contractor protect itself with a variety of complex and expensive insurance coverages. Without adequate insurance protection, the contractor would be constantly faced with the possibility of serious or even ruinous financial loss.

10. 1. 2   Risk Management in Construction Contracts

A successful construction project depends on how well project participants manage project risks. Risks are managed through sound business and construction practices and through careful preparation and review of the project contract documents. A significant component of successful risk management begins with how well the project participants allocate risks at the contract formation stage. Following are six key risk allocation and management concepts that should be considered at the project contract formation stage.

(1) Allocate risk to the party best situated to control the risk

At the outset of each project, an employer and a contractor should anticipate and evaluate potential risks to project success and, where applicable, assign responsibility for those risks to the party or parties best situated to control them. For example, a contractor should assign the employer responsibility for design errors because the employer typically holds the design services contracts and is in a better position to work with the project designer to minimize the risk of those errors.

(2) Allocate risk through indemnity provisions

Contract indemnity provisions generally require one party to pay for losses incurred by the other party as a result of claims made by third parties. A construction contract indemnity provision typically requires the contractor to indemnify the employer against claims for bodily injury or property damage arising out of the negligent performance of work by the contractor or its subcontractors. Conversely, the employer typically is called on to indemnify the contractor against claims or losses arising from the existence of hazardous substances at the project site, at least to the extent that the contractor does not have any control over those substances.

(3) Use insurance to support indemnity provisions.

Contract provisions requiring insurance coverage provide assurance that each party can satisfy its indemnity obligations. For example, employers must require their contractors to secure commercial general liability, automobile liability and worker's compensation/ employers liability coverages. Commercial general liability insurance generally covers bodily injury and property damage resulting from contractor or subcontractor negligence. However, employers and contractors should bear in mind that liability policies typically do not cover the contractor for defective work, which is instead subject to the contractor's warranty.

(4) Require additional insured status and evidence of insurance.

Employers and contractors should always require lower tier contractors or subcontractors to add the employer and contractor as additional insureds. A central reason for additional insured status is the insurer's primary duty to defend claims made against the additional insureds. Additional insured status is obtained by endorsement; thus, the applicable endorsement should be broad enough to cover ongoing and completed operations on a primary and non-contributory basis.

(5) Include waivers of subrogation.

Subrogation allows an insurer to stand in the position of its insured to recover amounts paid on behalf of the insured for damages for which another party may be liable. A waiver of subrogation precludes the insurer from seeking reimbursement for amounts paid on claims, and thus prevents an insurer from passing assigned risk back to the other project participants. In other words, a waiver of subrogation ensures that transferred project risk stays with the insurers as contemplated by the project participants.

(6) Review documents with appropriate consultants.

Construction projects typically require multiple contracts, which need to be consistent and complementary. For example, project lender and employer requirements for payment timing and conditions should flow down through all project contracts. Dispute resolution provisions should be consistent throughout the project contracts to assure that all parties to a dispute are involved in the same proceeding at the same time and are subject to the same dispute resolution rules.

10. 2　Construction insurance

10. 2. 1　Definition

Insurance is one of the tools most often used to manage risk in connection with construction projects. In determining insurance requirements for construction contracts, it is important to identify the risks associated with the project and make sure that the policy terms and limits are adequate to cover any potential losses.

Legally, the insurance is a contract by which one party (the insurer), in exchange for consideration (i. e. , money or a premium) promises to make payments upon the destruction or injury of something in which the other party (the insured) has an interest. In construction contracts, the employer, contractor and design professional each seek protection from loss or harm related to the construction project through insurance policies. Each party is responsible for providing different types of insurance that offer protection during construction and after construction is complete.

10. 2. 2   Types of Construction Insurance

Liability insurance and property insurance are the two common types of insurance coverages available and carried by most employers, contractors and design professionals. Property insurance protects the employer or user of physical property and equipment from losses due to covered perils such as fire or explosion. Liability insurance, on the other hand, protects the insured from claims arising from damage or hazards caused by the insured. It is common on most construction projects for the employer to provide property insurance while the contractor and design professional will provide liability insurance. The most common types of construction insurance applied in construction industry are as followings:

(1) Commercial General Liability Insurance

Commercial general liability insurance, or CGL insurance, is provided by the contractor and covers the costs that the contractor is legally obligated to pay for causing bodily injury or property damage arising out of "occurrences" with the contractor's operations. "Occurrence" is defined under the policy of insurance (or the insurance contract) to include "accidents". The "accident" may or may not be the result of the contractor's negligence. For example, if one of the contractor's employees drops a hammer from a scaffold and hits a car parked below causing damage to the car, the property damage to the car would be covered by the contractor's CGL policy. If a pedestrian tripped over a toolbox left out by one of the contractor's employees and suffered an injury, the pedestrian's bodily injury damages would generally be covered under the contractor's CGL policy.

(2) Umbrella Liability Coverage

An umbrella policy is typically most useful to a larger contractor who operates large construction sites. This type of policy is often a supplement to a CGL policy because the CGL policy has maximum policy limits that may not cover all of the contractor's liability. In that case, an umbrella policy provides coverage for any amounts above the CGL policy's limits.

(3) Professional Liability Insurance

Professional liability insurance provides coverage for those providing a professional service and, in the case of a construction project, protects design professional services against liability incurred as a result of their errors and omissions. Professional liability insurance should be required of all design professionals working on a project.

Professional liability insurance is a separate policy from CGL or other liability insurance products. The characteristics of a professional liability policy are much different from CGL insurance policies. For example, professional liability policies are written on a claims-made basis, meaning the claim must be asserted during the policy term or during a specific retroactive term specified in the policy. The policy must be in place at the time the claim is made for coverage to be available.

(4) Workers' Compensation Insurance

Workers' compensation coverage provides protection for claims from injured workers on the project site. Workers' compensation insurance pays damages for medical and disability claims for employees who are injured or become ill on the job or for the employee's work-related illness.

(5) Automobile Insurance

Automobile insurance is a standard requirement for contractors to cover motor vehicles driven and operated by their employees during the course of the project. The typical requirement is stated as "owned, non-owned, and hired vehicles used in connection with the Work." The intent is to cover vehicles used by the contractor and its employees that are both owned by the company and/or rented for use during the construction of the project.

(6) Additional Insured

Most construction contracts, either in the standard language or in the supplement, require that the contractor name the employer as an additional insured under the contractor's CGL policy. The contractor may also require that its subcontractors name it as an additional insured under their CGL policies.

Additional insured status must be provided by endorsement. Simply being named as an additional insured on a certificate of insurance provided by the contractor is probably not enough to create a binding change to the underlying insurance policy. Be sure to check with insurance adviser to ensure that the appropriate endorsement is included in the contract insurance requirements and also that additional insured coverage can be provided.

(7) Builder's Risk Insurance

The most common form of property insurance carried on construction projects is builder's risk insurance. Builder's risk insurance covers damage to the project on account of covered perils such as fire, tornado, wind damage, etc… The key aspect of builder's risk insurance is that it covers damage to the construction project itself. You may recall that that CGL policies cover property damage; however, it is only in certain narrowly defined circumstances for which that property damage will include the newly constructed work itself. Builder's risk policies are typically written on an "all-risk" or equivalent policy form with policy limits in the amount of the initial contract sum plus the value of subsequent modifications and change orders.

(8) Contractor's Pollution Coverage

A pollution policy provides coverage for third-party claims for bodily injury and/or property damage along with coverage for remediation costs associated with pollution incidents resulting from the contractor's covered operations. This type of policy may be most useful to contractors involved in paving, infrastructure, maintenance, mechanical, demolition, industrial, excavation, grading, carpentry and pipeline and tank installation.

10.3　Construction insurance checklist

Insurance coverages are complex, and each new construction contract presents its own problems in this regard. The contractor should select a competent insurance agent or broker who is experienced in construction work and familiar with contractor's insurance problems. Without competent advice, the contractor may either incur the needless expense of overlapping protection or expose itself to the danger of vital gaps in insurance coverage. In the long list of possible construction insurance coverages, not every policy is applicable to a given firm's operations. The following checklist is not represented as being complete, but it does include insurance coverages typical of the construction industry.

10.3.1　Property Insurance on Project during Construction

(1) All-risk builder's risk insurance. This insurance protects against all risks of direct physical loss or damage to the project or to associated materials caused by any external effect, with noted exclusions.

(2) Named-peril builder's risk insurance. The basic policy provides protection for the project, including stored materials, against direct loss by fire or lightning. A number of separate endorsements to this policy are available that add coverage for specific losses.

(3) Earthquake insurance. This coverage may be provided by an endorsement to the builder's risk policy in some states. Elsewhere a separate policy must be issued.

(4) Bridge insurance. This insurance is of the inland marine type. It affords protection during construction against damage that may be caused by fire, lightning, flood, ice, collision, explosion, riot, vandalism, wind, tornado, and earthquake.

(5) Steam boiler and machinery insurance. A contractor or employer may purchase this form of insurance when the boiler of a building under construction is being tested and balanced or when being used to heat the structure for plastering, floor laying, or other purposes. This policy covers any injury or damage that may occur to, or be caused by, the boiler during its use by the contractor.

(6) Installation floater policy. Insurance of this type provides named-peril or all-risk protection for property of various kinds, such as project machinery (heating and air-conditioning systems, for example), from the time it leaves the place of shipment until it is installed on the project and tested. Coverage terminates when the insured's interest in the property ceases, when the property is accepted, or when it is taken over by the employer.

10.3.2　Property insurance on contractor's own property

(1) Property insurance on contractor's own buildings. This coverage affords protec-

tion for offices, sheds, warehouses, and contained personal property. Several different forms of this insurance are available.

(2) Contractor's equipment insurance. This type of policy, often termed a "floater," insures a contractor's construction equipment regardless of its location.

(3) Motor truck cargo policy. This insurance covers loss by named hazards to materials or supplies carried on the contractor's own trucks from supplier to warehouse or building site.

(4) Transportation floater. Insurance of this type provides coverage against damage to property belonging to the contractor or others while it is being transported by a public carrier. It may be obtained on a per-trip, project, or annual basis.

(5) Fidelity bond. This surety bond affords the contractor protection against loss caused by dishonesty of its own employees.

(6) Crime insurance. This form of insurance protects the contractor against the loss of money, securities, office equipment, and similar valuables through burglary, theft, robbery, destruction, disappearance, or wrongful abstraction. It insures against loss of valuables caused by safe deposit burglary and forgery.

(7) Valuable papers destruction insurance. This policy protects the contractor against the loss, damage, or destruction of valuable papers such as books, records, maps, drawings, abstracts, deeds, mortgages, contracts, and documents. It does not cover loss by misplacement, unexplained disappearance, wear and tear, deterioration, vermin, or war.

10.3.3 Employee Insurance

(1) Employee benefit insurance. This coverage provides employees with designated fringe-benefit insurance such as medical, hospital, surgical, life, and similar coverages.

(2) Social Security. This insurance plan provides retirement benefits to an insured worker, survivor's benefits to his family when the worker dies, disability benefits, hospitalization benefits, and medical insurance.

(3) Unemployment insurance. This insurance plan provides qualified workers with a weekly income during periods of unemployment between jobs.

(4) Disability insurance. This insurance, required by some country, provides benefits to employees for disabilities caused by not occupational accidents and disease.

10.3.4 Business, Accident, and Life Insurance

(1) Business interruption insurance. This insurance is designed to reimburse the insured for losses suffered because of an interruption of its business.

(2) Sole proprietorship insurance. A policy of this type provides cash to assist heirs in continuing or disposing of the business without sacrifice in the event of death of the employer.

(3) Key person life insurance. This insurance reimburses the business for financial loss resulting from the death of a key person in the business. It also builds up a sinking fund to be available upon retirement.

(4) Corporate continuity insurance. In the event of a stockholder's death, this insurance furnishes cash for the purchase of his corporate stock. This provides liquidity for the decedent's estate and prevents corporate stock from falling into undesirable hands.

10.3.5   Liability Insurance

Liability is an obligation imposed by law. In the course of conducting business, a contractor may incur liability for damages in any one of the following ways:

(1) Direct responsibility for injury to persons (not employees) or damage to property of third parties caused by an act of omission by the contractor.

(2) Contingent liability, which involves the indirect liability of the general contractor for the acts of parties for whom it is responsible, such as subcontractors

(3) Liability that arises out of a project after the work has been completed and the structure has been accepted by the employer

(4) Contractual liability, whereby the contractor has assumed the legal liability of the employer, or other party, by the terms of a contract

(5) Liability that may devolve to the contractor as a result of the operation of its motor vehicles

(6) Liability that arises from design and associated professional services rendered by the contractor to the employer

(7) Liability to injured employees, both those covered and those not covered by worker's compensation laws

Liability insurance, also called defense coverage, serves no purpose other than to protect the contractor against claims brought against it by third parties. Insurance of this type pays the costs of the contractor's legal defense as well as paying judgments for which the contractor becomes legally liable, up to the face value of the policy. In the settlement of liability claims against the contractor, the insurance company has the right to settle as it sees fit without the approval or consent of the contractor. Liability insurance provides no protection to the contractor for loss of, or damage to, its own property. It is important to note that many forms of liability insurance customarily include subrogation clauses that give the insurance company the right to file suit to recover losses.

10.3.6   Automobile insurance

The operation of automobiles exposes the contractor to two broad categories of risk. One form of risk is loss or damage to the contractor's own vehicles caused by collision, fire, theft, vandalism, and similar hazards. The other form of risk is liability for bodily injury to others or damage to the property of others caused in some way by the operation of the contractor's automobiles. Many countries have statutory requirements concerning the purchase of liability insurance by employers of motor vehicles. In an insurance context, automobiles or vehicles are construed to include passenger cars, trucks, truck-type tractors, trailers, semi-trailers, and similar land motor vehicles designed for travel on public roads. The contractor is free to choose which vehicles will be insured for automobile liability and which for physical damage coverage.

Automobile liability insurance provides financial protection when the contractor is legally obligated to pay for bodily injury or property damage arising from the employership, maintenance, or use of a covered vehicle. This includes liability coverage for over-the-road hazards for self-propelled motor vehicles used for the sole purpose of providing mobility to construction equipment such as pumps, power cranes, air compressors, electric generators, welders, and drills. The insurer also provides the contractor with legal defense against liability actions. Automobile liability coverage has several exclusions, such as injury to an employee, property owned or transported by the contractor, and others. The insurance carrier will pay all damages resulting from an accident up to the liability limits specified in the policy. In view of recent large awards in cases of bodily injury and the claims consciousness of the public in general, the contractor must maintain high limits of motor vehicle liability coverage.

10. 4 Subrogation

Contractors often require subrogation clauses for their contract workers. To prevent a building employer's insurance company from taking action against a subcontractor who causes harm to a building, all parties in a construction contract should be named as insureds in a construction insurance policy. Beyond that, a waiver of subrogation should be included in construction contracts. The workings of subrogation may be illustrated by the following example. If the employer of insured property should sustain a loss to this property, the insurance company will pay the insured for the damage suffered, up to the face amount of the policy. However, by the terms of the subrogation clause in the policy, the insurance company acquires the right of the insured to recover from the party whose negligence caused the loss. This process of subrogation gives the insurant company the right to sue the offending party in the insured's name for recovery of its loss in the case where the employer provides builder's risk insurance and the general contractor's operations cause or contribute to project damage, the contractor may be exposed to action by the builder's risk carrier for recovery of its loss under the policy. Alternatively, if a sub-subcontractor causes or contributes to a loss on the project, this party may be subject to suit by the insurance company. If the general contractor buys the builder's risk insurance, subrogation applies to its subcontractors if they cause a loss on the project. It is easy to see that application of the subrogation clause by the insurance company could defeat the entire purpose of the project property insurance.

Subrogation means that one party has the right to "step into the shoes" of another party in bringing a claim for damages. Although not all types of insurance claims can be subrogated, the most common type that can be subrogated is claims for property damage. Including the project employer, the general contractor and all subcontractors in a builder' s risk insurance policy help to prevent the builder's risk insurance firm from trying to recover damages from the general contractor or a subcontractor if a loss is allegedly caused by negligence. However, naming all parties in the insurance policy isn't always enough to keep the insurance company from subrogating. Instead, an agreement is needed in which each party to the contract waives his right of subrogation against the other to the extent that the damage is covered by the insurance policy. These kinds of waivers of subrogation clauses are included in both the Associated General Contractors (AGC) and American Institute of Architects (AIA) standard form agreements.

The AIA's form documents are the ones most commonly used in construction projects. AIA B141-1997, 1, 3, 7, 4 states in part that "the employer or Architect, as appropriate, shall require of the contractors, consultants, agents and employees of any of them similar waivers in favor of the other parties enumerated herein."

☞ **疑难词汇** ☜

Contract indemnity provisions 合同赔偿条款

Insureds 被保险人

Subrogation 代位追偿权

Scaffold 脚手架

evolve to 移交给，转移给

If a pedestrian tripped over a toolbox left out by one of the contractor's employees and suffered an injury 如果一个行人被承包商雇员遗落的工具箱绊倒而受伤

Tornado 龙卷风

Demolition 拆除

Excavation 挖掘

Carpentry 木器

Named-peril 指定险

Vandalism 故意破坏

Contingent liability 或有责任，不确定的责任

Prerogative 特权，权利

The extent and magnitude 大小和范围

Inland marine 内陆运输，内陆运输保险

Fidelity bond 忠诚保险

Fringe-benefit insurance 额外福利保险

Corporate continuity insurance 公司存续保险

Latent 潜在的

Trailers 拖挂车

Over-the-road hazards 长途运输的危险

Self-propelled motor vehicles 机动式的机械车辆

Air compressors 空气压缩机

Electric generators 发电机

☞ **中文综述** ☜

10.1 建 筑 工 程 风 险

10.1.1　工程风险的含义

风险代表一种不确定性，同时也是一种概率事件，它是对潜在的、未来可能发生损害的一种估计和预测。项目风险是一种不确定的事件或条件，一旦发生会对项目的目标产生正面的或负面的影响，如对项目的成本，进度计划，质量等造成严重后果。建设工程项目风险则是指在项目决策和实施过程中，造成实际结果与预期目标的差异性及其发生的损失。建设工程项目可能带来的风险包括人员伤亡、财产损失、投资效益低下、法律纠纷、环境问题等，严重的可能连锁引发更为严重的，难以解决的后果。正因如此，识别风险，防范风险是建筑合同管理一个重要的课题。无论雇主、承包商都应引起充分的重视。

10.1.2　工程合同的风险管理

成功的项目决定于项目参与者如何对项目风险进行管理，这就要求项目决策，合同文件准备，施工管理等等诸多环节都要从风险防范的角度加以考量，项目参与者在施工合同成立阶段对项目风险的合理有效分配是降低工程风险的重要一环。以下是在工程施工合同成立阶段应当重点考虑的几个问题。

（1）将风险分配给最易控制风险的一方

在项目初始阶段，雇主与承包商应预测和评估潜在的项目风险，在制定合同条款时，尽可能将项目风险的管理分配给最有利于防范风险的一方。这样做可以有效地降低风险管理成本，为项目的成功铺平道路。例如，在协议合同条款时，将设计错误的责任分配给有设计义务的一方去防范，例如在 FIDIC 新红皮书中，雇主承担设计义务；在 FIDIC 新黄皮书中，承包商承担设计义务。这样做的目的在于负责设计任务的一方与设计单位有直接的委托设计合同关系，可以直接通过设计委托合同，将设计错误的风险分配给可以从源头控制风险的设计单位来承担。

（2）通过索赔条款分配风险

标准建筑工程合同范本一般要求承包商或分包商或两者共同对履行合同过程中因过失对第三人造成的人身伤害和财产损失承担责任；例如，FIDIC 新红皮书 1.1 条规定："承包商应保障和保护雇主，雇主的人员，以及他们各自的代理人免遭与下述有关的一切索赔、损害、损失和开支（包括法律费用和开支）：（a）由于承包商的设计（如有时），施工、竣工以及任何缺陷的修补导致的任何人员的身体伤害、生病、病疫或死亡，由于雇主、雇主的人员或他们各自的代理人的任何渎职、恶意行为或违反合同而造成的除外，以及……"。而雇主也应对由于现场的危险物质给承包商带来的损害承担责任，如果承包商无法通过自己的努力对危险物质进行控制。

（3）通过购买商业保险解决风险问题

建筑合同条款都包含了保险条款，即通过保险条款约定保险责任的分担。例如，合同条款一般规定承包商对商业综合责任险，机动车责任险，工伤险和雇主责任险承担投保责任。

（4）要求附加被保险人资格和保险证据

雇主或承包商经常会要求分包商或较低层的分包商在对相应的风险进行投保时将雇主或承包商作为附加被保险人。这样做的原因是保险公司对附加被保险人的损害承担赔付责任，减轻雇主或总承包商的责任。例如，阳光财产保险股份有限公司《雇主责任保险附加保险条款（2011 版)》对此进行了规定。

（5）放弃代位追偿权

代位追偿权是指第三者对保险标的的损害而造成保险事故的，保险人自向被保险人赔偿之日起，有权把自己置于被保险人的地位，获得被保险人有关该项损失的一切权利和补偿。就是说保险公司对分包商在施工过程中产生的损失进行赔偿后，即取得分包商的地位，向引起损失的第三人索赔。如果引起损失的第三人是承包商，分包商得到的赔偿并没有真正解决损失问题，因为，在国际工程合同领域，承包商与分包商是一体的，他们对工程的顺利完工具有共同责任。因此，只有保险公司放弃了代位追偿权，分包商的保险才能真正起到作用。

10.2　建　筑　工　程　保　险

10.2.1　建筑工程保险的含义

建筑工程保险是承保以土木建筑为主体的民用、工业用和公共事业用的工程在整个建筑期间因自然灾害和意外事故造成的物质损失，以及被保险人对第三者依法应承担的赔偿责任为保险标的的险种。在确定保险内容，投保险别时，必须识别建筑项目可能承载的风险，风险的大小，填补风险的金额等。

10.2.2　建筑工程保险的特征

建筑工程保险，是随着现代工业和现代科学技术的发展在火灾保险、意外伤害保险及责任保险的基础上逐步演变而成的一种综合性保险。其主要特征为：

（1）承保范围广。传统的财产保险只承保物质标的，而建筑工程保险除承保物质标的，还承保责任标的，并对保险事故发生后的清理费用均予以承保，系综合性保险。

（2）被保险人范围宽。被保险人可以包括：①雇主或工程所有人；②总承包人或分包人；③技术顾问，包括雇主聘任的建筑师、工程师及其他专业顾问。凡对保险标的具有利益的人均可作为被保险人列明在一张保险单上。

（3）保险期限不等。传统保险的保险期限通常为一年，期满可续保；而建筑保险的保险期限一般按工期计算，即自工程开工至工程竣工为止。特别是大型工程，其中有的项目是分期施工并交付使用，因而各个项目的期限有先有后，有长有短。

10.2.3　建筑工程保险的种类

责任险与财产险是建筑工程雇主、承包商、设计师、分包商等投保的两大主要险种。财产险主要保障雇主，承包商或使用者的物质财产损失得到补偿；责任险则是针对被保险人给第三人造成的损失，有保险公司予以赔偿。建筑工程保险的种类一般包括以下几种：

（1）商业一切责任险

商业一切责任险（Commercial General Liability，CGL）由承包商承保，覆盖工程施工期间承包商人员的身体健康和财产损失。期限从工程预计动工之日或首批建筑材料运抵工地之日起，到工程预计竣工验收交付使用之日止。该险种的保险金额包括工程本身的物质损失和对第三者责任赔偿限额两部分。前者以工程完成时的总价值作为保险金额，包括运输、关税及其他各种相关费用等。由于大中型工程项目建设周期较长，在办理保险时难以正确估价竣工时的实际造价，因此，投保时可先按合同造价或工程概算金额作为保险金额并计算保险费，待竣工后再按实际造价调整保额和保费。

（2）伞形责任保险

伞形责任保险是一个综合设计，分层保险，无缝衔接的保险体系，即根据每个风险阶段的特点，以财产险和责任险为主，工程险为辅而形成综合保障计划。伞形责任保险提供的保障超越了一般责任险的保险范围。

（3）职业责任险

职业责任险主要是针对为项目工程提供专业服务的设计单位，咨询师等设立的保险服务。

（4）工伤保险

工伤保险分为社保和商业保险两种情况。社会保险意义下的工伤保险是指劳动者在工作中或在规定的特殊情况下，遭受意外伤害或患职业病导致暂时或永久丧失劳动能力以及死亡时，劳动者或其遗属从国家和社会获得物质帮助的一种社会保险制度。而商业工伤保险是雇主或承包商或分包商为劳动者购买的保险。劳动者在劳动时遭受意外伤害或患职业病导致暂时或永久丧失劳动能力以及死亡时，劳动者或其遗属从商业保险公司和国家获得物质帮助的一种社会保险制度。

（5）机动车保险

机动车保险是承包商在施工过程中为施工目的而使用的车辆购买的保险，不论机动车是承包商所有或者租赁的，只要为工程目的所使用，就应当购买保险。

（6）附加被保险人

绝大多数建筑工程合同，或者在标准合同条款里，或者在补充条款里都会在商业一切责任险要求承包商将雇主作为附加被保险人，而总承包商对分包商也会有同样的要求。附加被保险人保险应有背书确认，仅仅将附加被保险人的名字印在保险单上是不够的。

（7）承包商风险保险

承包商风险保险是专为保护正在开发、翻新或建造的建筑物以及在建设工程中使用的设备而设计的保险。承包商的风险覆盖范围包括建筑材料的保护、供暖和空调设备、人工成本和费用，以及临时搭建的建筑，如井框支架、临时支架、围栏、脚手架、建筑标志、甚至树木和其他植物。除了材料、劳动力和费用的覆盖范围外，承包商的风险保险包含了弥补碎片清除和工艺缺陷的费用。

（8）承包商环境污染保险

承包商购买的环境污染保险主要是针对工程施工期间或完工以后，由于工程引起的环境变化给工程项目周围个人或组织造成的身体伤害或财产损失赔偿为目的的保险。

CGL 保单有两个附加的污染责任保险条款：一个为指定地点有限污染责任条款，承保污染事故引起的身体伤害和财产损失责任，一般仅限于被保险人污染环境而造成的突然发生的损害事故；另一个为指定地点污染责任条款，除了承保身体伤害和财产损失外，还承担清除被保险人处所内污染所产生的费用。目前的环境责任保险主要分为两类：环境损害责任保险和场地治理责任保险。

10.3   建 筑 保 险 清 单

保险责任范围是复杂的和专业的，承包商应该根据建设项目的实际情况，风险范围选择了解和熟悉建筑工程的保险代理人提供保险服务。在令人眼花缭乱的保险险种中，不是每个险种都适合某个特定的工程。承包商应该全面了解风险种类，倾听经验保险代理人的保险意见，选择最适合工程项目的保险种类。

10.3.1   项目施工阶段的财产保险

（1）建筑商一切险。建筑商一切险是指建筑商对项目物质损失和损毁，以及相关的材料损毁为承保范围的，以直接损失赔偿为目的的财产责任险种。

（2）承包商风险指定险。主要指对特定或特殊事项的保险。

1）扩展保险条款。这个险种覆盖所有由于暴风、冰雹、爆炸，暴乱，民众骚乱、航空器，车辆和烟雾引起的财产直接损失。

2）故意破坏和损坏他人财产。

3）水责任保险。水责任保险针对意外排放，泄露，水或蒸汽的外溢等造成的财产损失提供保险赔偿。这个险种也包括有缺欠的管道，屋顶和水箱，但是不包括喷水器泄漏，洪水等引起的财产损失。

4）喷水器泄漏险。这个险种对由于泄漏、凝固和喷水器安装问题造成项目直接损失进行保护。

（3）地震险。地震给人类造成的经济损失难以估量，动辄数亿、数十亿甚至数百亿元。由于地震造成损失的巨大性，商业保险公司多将地震损失列为除外责任。缺乏政府的推动和支持，地震保险难以建立。为解决地震所带来的问题，一些发达市场经济国家和地区建立了地震保险制度，目的是积累地震赔偿基金，为灾后复建提供资金，保障国民在遭遇巨大灾害后能迅速重建家园恢复正常生活，增强防灾意识、防预能力和安全保障水平，提高社会文明程度。

（4）蒸汽锅炉和机械设备保险。承包商或雇主对建设中的锅炉的试验、调试或当被用来为墙面和地面工程加热时购买该类保险。与其他财产保险不同，这类保险包含了责任保险，即对承包商使用锅炉过程中造成的伤害和损害提供保障。

（5）安装保险。这个险种是针对指定险和一切险设立，例如项目机械（加热和空调系统）从离开运输的船体到安装在项目上并调试完毕。这类保险在被保险人的保险利益终止，或项目被雇主接受而终止。

10.3.2   承包商自有财产的保险

（1）承包商对工程项目中属于自己的财产进行保险。这个险种对承包商办公室，工棚，仓库和其中的承包商个人财产进行保险。

（2）承包商设备保险。这个险种也通常称为流动保险，对承包商建筑设备，无论位于什么位置，进行保险。

（3）货运卡车货物保险。这个险种涵盖了承包商自己货车承运的从供应商到仓库或施工现场材料和物资的指定风险的损失。

（4）运输流动险。这个险种涵盖了属于承包商的财产或者其他人的财产在被公共运输公司运输时产生的风险。

（5）忠诚保险。这个险种为承包商提供由于其雇员不忠诚给承包商带来损失的填补。

（6）犯罪保险。这个保险险种用于保护承包商金钱、办公设备、证券和其他贵重物品因盗窃、抢劫、毁灭、消失等产生的损失。它也保护贵重物品因保险箱失窃或伪造产生的损失。

（7）贵重文件损毁保险。这个保险险种用于保护承包商贵重文件遗失、损毁，这些文件包括账簿、记录、地图、图纸、契约、抵押文件、合同和其他文件。但是这个险种不保护误放、不能解释的消失、磨损、变质、虫蛀或战争引起的文件损失。

10.3.3　从业人员保险

（1）雇员利益保险。雇员利益保险为雇员提供了指定的额外利益的保险，包括医疗保险，住院保险，手术保险和生命保险等。

（2）社会保险。在我国，社会保险是用人单位给在职职工提供的福利，一般包括五险一金。但是对于建筑承包商临时聘用的临时工或农民工则没有这项福利。2006 年，《国务院关于解决农民工问题的若干意见》（国发［2006］5 号），对农民工特别是建筑行业农民工参加工伤保险提出了明确要求。同时我国《建筑法》也规定，为施工现场从事危险作业的农民工办理意外伤害保险。

（3）失业保险。在我国，失业保险属于社会保险五大险种之一。

（4）伤残保险。在我国，伤残保险属于社会保险项目，但商业保险险种中，很多涉及对伤残者的赔偿。

10.3.4　责任保险

（1）承包商的公共责任和财产损毁保险。这个保险险种用于保护承包商伤害他人的行为，即承包商对第三人的责任或者损毁他人财产的责任。

（2）承包商保护公共财产损失责任险。这个保险险种适用于法律规定的由于分包商行为，不作为而造成的损失的保护。

（3）完工后的责任险。这个保险险种用于已经完成或已经移交给雇主的工程项目，由于承包商原因带来的项目瑕疵而可能给承包商带来损失的保险。雇主一般要求承包商承担此类责任，因为，通常情况下，一般保险通常在完工前对承包商的工程建设设定保障，而很少在完工后对工程瑕疵提供商业保险。

（4）合同责任保险。这个保险险种用于合同一方当事人，根据合同条款，向另一方当事人承诺法律责任，未履行该责任，而进行的保险。一般保险条款并不覆盖这个领域。

（5）职业责任保险。这个保险险种用于承包商对雇主承诺的设计或其他职业服务的责任。

（6）雇员赔偿保险。这个保险险种用于承包商对因公死亡或伤害的雇员赔偿的保险。

（7）雇主责任保险。这个保险种类通常包含在雇员赔偿责任保险里。它提供承包商的雇员在雇佣期间伤害和死亡时更广泛的保障，但是这个保险不同于雇员赔偿法律的相关规定。

（8）雇主保护责任险。这个保险险种保护雇主免受主承包商和分包商行为引起的损失。

10.4　代位求偿权

保险代位求偿权（Right of Subrogation）是指保险人享有的代位行使被保险人对造成保险标的损害负有责任的第三人之索赔求偿的权利。严格来说，保险代位求偿权包括两个方面，权利代位和物上代位。保险代位求偿权仅指其中的权利代位。工程合同是个复杂的合同体系，工程合同的保险事项主要是雇主与承包商之间就建筑工程施工项目涵盖的财产，责任等与保险公司进行的约定。在财产责任险方面，保险公司一般会要求投保人或被保险人用保险公司的赔偿换取其对加害第三人的代位求偿权。这种权利要求，在一般民事保险中没有给当事人带来不便或利益损失，但是在工程保险中，由于分包商与承包商对雇主的连带责任关系，使得由于分包商原因给雇主带来的损失由承包商来承担。因此，如果承包商或雇主的损失是由分包商造成的，在保险公司为雇主或承包商赔偿之后，通过代位权向分包商追偿，最终分割的还是承包商的利益，因此，在工程项目责任险方面，要求保险公司放弃责任险的代位求偿权是承包商或雇主坚持和主张的。在一些国际工程合同的标准范本中也迎合了承包商或雇主要求，规定了代位求偿权放弃的条款，例如美国 Associated General Contractors（AGC）and American Institute of Architects（AIA）standard form agreements.

Questions

1. What is subrogation and how does it affect builder's risk coverage?
2. Situations in which a contractor may incur liability?
3. How does general liability insurance differ from professional liability insurance?

Chapter 11　Claim and counterclaim

11. 1　Claims and counterclaims

11. 1. 1　Definition

In all construction contracts, claims and the right to claim play a significant role in the contractual relationship between the employer and the contractor. Curiously, for such a fundamental aspect of the contract, no express definition appears in the typical standard form of construction contract and it is rare to find a definition of "a claim" in reference texts or authorities on construction contracts. A claim is defined in *The Oxford Dictionary* as a general term for the assertion of a right to money, property, or to a remedy. Strictly speaking then, whenever for example the contractor applies for his monthly interim payment for the original scope of the works, or whenever for example the employer to the contractor requiring him to remedy defective work, it would be a claim under this definition. In construction contracts, a claim is generally taken in practice to be an assertion for additional monies due to a party or for extension of the Time for Completion. This interpretation of "a claim" is borne out by the wording of the contractual provisions relating to claims. For example, in the 1999 suite of the FIDIC Conditions of Contract, clause 2. 5 of New Red Book states: "If the Employer considers himself to be entitled to any payment under any Clause of these Conditions or otherwise in connection with the Contract, and/or to any extension of the Defects Notification Period, the Employer or the Engineer shall give notice and⋯ The notice shall be given as soon as practicable after the Employer became aware of the event or circumstance giving rise to the claim. '" Clause 20. 1 states: "If the Contractor considers himself to be entitled to any extension of the Time for Completion and/or any additional payment⋯ the Contractor shall give notice to the Engineer, describing the event or circumstance giving rise to the claim. '" It is clear then that these forms of contract seem to ignore claims arising from anything other than the assertion for an entitlement to payment or time.

A counterclaim is defined as an assertion made by a respondent party which can conveniently be examined and disposed of in an action originally initiated by the claimant party. It is not necessarily a defence, but a substantive claim against the claimant. The concept of convenience referred to here signifies that the background of the counterclaim is similar to that of the claim and results from the same set of facts and events.

Counterclaims are often confused with set off.

The set-off is available to defendants in civil lawsuits. Generally, civil actions are brought by plaintiffs seeking an award of damages for injuries caused by the defendant. In customary practice the plaintiff files the suit and the defendant answers it. The defendant may assert a counterclaim against the plaintiff based on an event or transaction other than the event or transaction that forms the basis of the plaintiff's suit. A set-off is a counterclaim with the particular goal of defeating or diminishing the amount the defendant will have to pay if the plaintiff's suit succeeds.

The set-off has two distinctive features. It must be based on an entirely different claim from that of the plaintiff, and it must be a valid legal claim that the defendant could bring as a separate suit. For example, a stereo store sues a customer for $700 due in outstanding payments on a CD player. However, the customer's car was damaged in the store's parking lot when the store's delivery van backed into it, and the repairs cost $500. As the defendant, the customer has the right to assert a counterclaim for damages to the car; if the customer is successful, the set-off reduces the amount owed to the plaintiff store so that the defendant owes the plaintiff only $200.

Counterclaims can be used as tactics in legal cases, to confuse or delay proceedings, or to reduce awards. However, this has risks associated with it, and may simply result in higher costs.

11. 1. 2　Categories of the Claims

For the purposes of this chapter, both claims and counterclaims will be referred to as claims. Despite the complexity of attempting to categorize claims, it is useful to have an overview of the subject of claims in construction contracts. Essentially, claims in construction contracts may be based on any one of four legal concepts and one non-legal concept. Therefore, if a claim is required to be categorized, and it is suggested that it should be, the categorization could be done in accordance with the following categories:

(1) A claim under the contract. The first category relates to a claim under the contract between the parties based on the grounds that should a certain event occur, then a claimant would be entitled to a remedy that is specified under a particular provision of the contract, subject to the effect of the applicable law.

(2) A claim arising out of or in connection with the contract. The second category relates to a claim arising not under, but out of or in connection with, the contract, where the remedy is not designated in the contract and the claimant needs to invoke a provision of the applicable law to obtain a remedy. Therefore, if the claim is valid, the remedy lies under the provisions of the applicable law of the contract, for example a claim for a breach of contract. Furthermore, if the employer terminates the contract, the contractor might have a lien over the works, depending on the terms of the contract, which would act as security for the payment of any money owed to it arising from the work performed pursuant to the contract.

(3) A claim under the principles of the applicable law. The third category relates to a

claim arising under the application of the principles of the applicable law, either by the parties to the contract or against third parties. This could lead to a claim under the law of tort, or delict as it is referred to in some jurisdictions. The law applicable to a claim in tort/delict is not necessarily the same as the governing law of the contract. If the claim is successful, the remedy would typically be an award of general damages, the amount being dependent upon the particular circumstances of the case.

(4) A claim arising out of the principle of quantum meruit. The fourth category comprises claims where no contract exists between the parties, or if one existed, it is deemed to be void. It is based on the principle that an individual has the right to be paid a reasonable remuneration for work done. This is referred to in some legal systems as quantum meruit or as much as one has earned and has been often equated to a claim for undue enrichment. The principles of quantum meruit have also been applied to cases where there is a contract in existence but the price is not stipulated; instead the contract expressly provides that the amount to be paid will be based on a reasonable sum or the price will be agreed from time to time.

Generally, the remedy for all the four categories of claims set out above would be sought through an action in arbitration or litigation unless the claim is settled amicably. Such action would usually necessitate the employment of lawyers and the outlay of large expenditure.

11.2   Contractor's claims under the FIDIC

Essentially, a Contractor may assert two types of claims under or relating to a FIDIC contract: First, there are "contractual" claims, that is, claims which the Contractor is entitled to assert by virtue of the specific provisions of the contract and, second, there are "legal" claims, that is, claims which the Contractor may be entitled to assert under the law governing the contract, the most obvious one being breach of contract.

11.2.1   Contractual Claims

Since the first edition of the FIDIC Red Book was published in 1957, the FIDIC contracts have contained provisions entitling the Contractor to claim additional money or time (or both) from the Employer when the Contractor encounters specifically defined unforeseeable conditions. The 1999 edition of the Red and Yellow Books each contain about 30 sub-clauses specifying events which, should they occur, will entitle the Contractor to claim from the Employer. The sub-clauses in the new Red and Yellow Books which entitle the Contractor to claim additional money or time are listed below (when a sub-clause applies to only one of these two Books, this is specified, and when a Sub-Clause is marked with an asterisk, this indicates that it is also contained in the Silver Book):

(1) 1.9 [Red Book only] Delayed Drawings or Instructions

Contractor may claim extension of time, Cost and reasonable profit if Engineer fails to issue a notified instruction or drawing within a reasonable time.

(2) 1. 9 [Yellow Book only] Errors in the Employer's Requirements

Contractor may claim extension of time, Cost and reasonable profit for error in Employer's Requirements which was not previously discoverable.

(3) 2. 1 Right to Access to the Site

Contractor may claim extension of time, Cost and reasonable profit if Employer fails to give right of access to Site within time stated in the Contract.

(4) 4. 7 Setting Out

Contractor may claim extension of time, Cost and reasonable profit for errors in original setting-out points and levels of reference.

(5) 4. 12 Unforeseeable Physical Conditions

Contractor may claim extension of time and Cost if he encounters physical conditions which are Unforeseeable.

(6) 4. 24 Fossils

Contractor may claim extension of time and Cost attributable to an instruction to Contractor to deal with an encountered archaeological finding.

(7) 7. 4 Testing

Contractor may claim extension of time, Cost and reasonable profit if testing is delayed by (or on behalf of) the Employer.

(8) 8. 4 Extension of Time for Completion

Contractor may claim extension of time if completion (see Sub-Clauses 8. 2 & 10. 1) is or will be delayed by a listed cause.

(9) 8. 5 Delays Caused by Authorities

Contractor may claim extension of time if Country's public authority causes Unforeseeable delay.

(10) 8. 9 Consequences of Suspension

Contractor may claim extension of time and cost if Engineer instructs a suspension of progress.

(11) 10. 2 Taking Over of Parts of the Works

Contractor may claim Cost and reasonable profit attributable to the taking over of a part of the Works.

(12) 10. 3 Interference with Tests on Completion

Contractor may claim extension of time, Cost and reasonable profit if Employer delays a Test on Completion.

(13) 11. 8 Contractor to Search

Contractor may claim Cost and reasonable profit if instructed to search for cause of a defect for which he is not responsible.

(14) 12. 2 [Yellow Book only] Delayed Tests

Contractor may claim Cost and reasonable profit if Employer delays a Test after Completion.

(15) 12. 3 [Red Book only] Evaluation

Contractor's entitlement to new rates or prices for work whose quantity has been changed or which is varied.

(16) 12. 4 [Red Book only] Omissions

Contractor may claim a Cost which, although it had been included in a Bill of Quantity item, he would not recover because the item was for work which has been omitted by Variation.

(17) 12. 4 [Yellow Book only] Failure to Pass Tests after Completion

Contractor may claim Cost and reasonable profit if Employer delays access to the Works or Plant.

(18) 13. 2 [Red Book only] Value Engineering

Contractor may claim half of the saving in contract value of his redesigned post-contract alternative proposal, which was approved without prior agreement of such contract value and of how saving would be shared.

(19) 13. 3 Variation Procedure

The Contract Price shall be adjusted as a result of Variations.

(20) 13. 7 Adjustments for Changes in Legislation

Contractor may claim extension of time and Cost attributable to a change in the Laws of the Country.

(21) 14. 4 Schedule of Payments

If interim payment instalments were not defined by reference to actual progress, and actual progress is less than that on which the schedule of payments was originally based, these instalments may be revised.

(22) 14. 8 Delayed Payment

Contractor may claim financing changes if he does not receive payment in accordance with Sub-Clause 14. 7.

(23) 16. 1 Contractor's Entitlement to Suspend Work

Contractor may claim extension of time, Cost and reasonable profit if Engineer fails to certify or if Employer fails to pay amount certified or fails to evidence his financial arrangements, and Contractor suspends work.

(24) 16. 4 Payment on Termination

Contractor may claim losses and damages after terminating Contract.

(25) 17. 1 Indemnities

Contractor may claim cost attributable to a matter against which he is indemnified by Employer.

(26) 17. 4 Consequences of Employer's Risks

Contractor may claim extension of time, Cost and (in some cases) reasonable profit if Works, Goods or Contractor's Documents are damaged by an Employer's risk as listed in

Sub-Clause 17. 3.

(27) 18. 1 General Requirements for Insurances

Contractor may claim cost of premiums if Employer fails to effect insurance for which he is the "insuring party".

(28) 19. 4 Consequences of Force Majeure

Contractor may claim extension of time and (in some cases) Cost if Force Majeure prevents him from performing obligations.

(29) 19. 6 Optional Termination, Payment and Release

Contractor's work and other Costs are valued and paid after progress is prevented by a prolonged period of Force Majeure and either Party then gives notice of termination.

(30) 19. 7 Release from Performance

If it becomes impossible or unlawful to perform contractual obligations, Contractor may be released and can claim as in 19. 6.

11. 2. 2　Standard Format of Claims Clause

To illustrate how these clauses operate, let us take as an example Sub-Clause 2. 1 [Right of Access to the Site] which is contained, subject to minor modifications, in all three Books for major works (the Red, Yellow and Silver Books) . Sub-Clause 2. 1 provides that if the Contractor suffers delay and/or incurs costs as a result of failure by the Employer to give access to, or possession of, the site within the time agreed, the Contractor shall give notice to the Engineer and shall be entitled subject to Sub-Clause 20. 1 to an extension of time and its additional cost inclusive of reasonable profit. After receiving this notice, the Engineer (or the Employer, in the case of the Silver Book) is then required to proceed in accordance with Sub-Clause 3. 5. Like Sub-Clause 2. 1, each of the sub-clauses in each of the FIDIC contracts typically states that, having given a notice to the Engineer (or to the Employer, in the case of the Silver Book) under the relevant Sub-Clause: ① the Contractor is entitled "subject to Sub-Clause 20. 1 [Contractor's Claims]" to an extension of time and additional payment and that ② after receiving the notice, the Engineer "shall proceed in accordance with Sub-Clause 3. 5 [Determinations] to agree or determine these matters" . Accordingly, it is appropriate to examine the general claims procedure provided for in Sub-Clause 20. 1 and then to see how the Engineer (or the Employer, in the case of the Silver Book) is expected to address the claim under Sub-Clause 3. 5.

11. 3　The contractor's claim procedure

FIDIC sets out the requirements a Contractor must follow to institute a claim against an Employer for additional time and/or money. Compliance with Sub-Clause 20. 1 is essential to the protection of any potential claim a Contractor may have against the Employer.

11. 3. 1　Main Elements

Sub-Clause 20. 1 requires:

(1) an "event or circumstance" to occur;

(2) the Contractor to submit a notice by no later than 28 days after it "became aware, or should have become aware, of the event or circumstance";

(3) the Contractor to submit a "fully detailed claim" with "full supporting particulars" submitted 42 days after the "event or circumstance";

(4) the Contractor to maintain "contemporary records"

(5) the Contractor to submit monthly updates if a Claim has a continuing effect;

(6) compliance with other provisions in the Contract;

(7) a response from the Engineer within 42 days of receiving a Claim.

11.3.2   Event or Circumstance

An "event or circumstance" which gives rise to a Claim refers to something in existence rather than merely theorized or foreseeable – it is not an early warning notice but, in our view, something which will cause a delay and/or result in the Contractor incurring costs.

Sub-Clause 20.1 requires a Contractor to not only have actual knowledge of an "event or circumstance" but also applies an objective standard of when he "should have being aware" of the "event or circumstance". In practice, this is often a cause for dispute as it results in difficult questions of fact. For example, when should a Contractor have known of its Subcontractors' claims? The actual date or the date of a Contractor's imputed knowledge also impacts on the date on which the Contractor should have submitted its notice-another reason why this aspect of Sub-Clause 20.1 is often disputed by the parties.

11.3.3   Notice

The Contractor must:

(1) submit the notice in writing, to the Engineer, at the address provided for in the Appendix to Tender;

(2) submit the notice within 28 days after he "became aware, or should have become aware, of the event or circumstance";

(3) state that the notice is given under Sub-Clause 20.1;

(4) describe the "event or circumstance" giving rise to a Claim.

The Contractor does not have to provide details of the extension of time it is claiming nor the amount of additional payment. The timing of a notice is critical and a failure to submit a notice within the stipulated time period is fatal to a Contractor's claim. Under the FIDIC Red Book, once a Contractor is 'time barred' from making claim, he will have no right to make a claim.

11.3.4   Fully Detailed Claim

The Contractor must submit a detailed claim within 42 days of the "event or circumstance". In practice, it may be difficult for a Contractor to comply with this time period if the claim is complex or if the Contractor's resources are limited in the context of the Contract programme. Sub-Clause 20.1 does make provision for the Contractor to propose and the Engineer to approve an extended time period for the Contractor to submit a detailed claim.

This must include "full supporting particulars of the basis of the claim and of the extension of time and/or additional payment claimed". In our view, the detailed claim should include:

(1) details of the "event or circumstance";

(2) a summary of those Red Book clauses on which the Contractor is relying;

(3) the legal basis of the claim;

(4) a clear and rational explanation as to why the claim gives rise to the monetary amount and/or extension of time;

(5) all supporting documents (including contemporary records).

11.3.5　Contemporary Records

Sub-Clause 20.1 imposes a broad obligation on the Contractor, without any specific instruction from the Engineer, to keep those contemporary records which may be necessary to substantiate his claim. The contemporary records must be:

(1) kept on Site or any other location acceptable to the Engineer;

(2) available for inspection by the Engineer;

(3) original documents created at or around the time of the "event or circumstance".

The Engineer can ask for additional records to be kept and may inspect the contemporary records. In determining what types of contemporary records are necessary, the Contractor must consider what he will require to prove his claim.

11.3.6　Monthly Updates

If the "event or circumstance" giving rise to a Claim has a "continuing effect" then the "fully detailed claim" is regarded as interim. The Contractor will have a further obligation to submit monthly, updated particulars to the Engineer. These monthly updates, in our view, only need to contain details on any change to the extension of time required and/or additional payment.

11.3.7　Response to a Claim

An Engineer is obliged to respond within 42 days of Contractor's submission of its detailed claim with: approval; or disapproval with detailed comments.

The Engineer is entitled to request "any necessary further particulars", from the Contractor, but his response must still be given within the stipulated time frame. The Engineer may propose and the Contractor may approve an extension allowing the Engineer more time to give a response.

The purpose of these provisions is to prevent an Engineer unreasonably delaying a response to a Claim or requesting unnecessary further particulars. There is, however, no express sanction for the Engineer's failure to provide a timely response and, in practice, this is often a contentious issue.

11. 4　Employer's Claim under FIDIC

Employer's claims are governed by sub-clause 2. 5 in the Red, Yellow and Silver Books of FIDIC Contracts (and sub-clause 20. 2 in the Gold Book). If an employer considers itself to be entitled to any payment from the contractor in connection with the contract, the employer is required to follow the procedure set out in this sub-clause, which includes the requirement to give notice to the contractor. But is an employer precluded from claiming payment at any later stage from a contractor if a notice in terms of sub-clause 2. 5 is not given under the FIDIC contract? In answering the question, regard must be had to the relevant provisions of sub-clause 2. 5 which provides as:

"If the Employer considers himself to be entitled to any payment under any Clause under these Conditions, or otherwise in connection with the Contract··· the Employer or the Engineer shall give notice and particulars to the Contractor. A notice shall be given as soon as practicable after the Employer became aware of the event or circumstance giving rise to the claim···".

"The particulars shall specify the clause or other basis of the claim, and shall include substantiation of the amount··· to which the Employer considers himself to be entitled in connection with the Contract. The Engineer shall then proceed in accordance with sub-clause 3. 5 [Determinations] to agree or determine (i) the amount (if any) which the Employer is entitled to be paid by the Contractor···".

"This amount may be included as a deduction in the Contract Price and Payment Certificates. The Employer shall only be entitled to set off against or make any deduction from an amount certified in a Payment Certificate, or to otherwise claim against the Contractor, in accordance with this sub-clause."

The sub-clause makes it clear that an employer is entitled to claim a deduction or set-off from any amount owing to a contractor as set out in a Payment Certificate if the employer has complied with the requirements set out in sub-clause 2. 5. But what if the contract is terminated and no further Payment Certificates are issued? Is an employer entitled to claim payment from a contractor by way of a counterclaim in subsequent proceedings?

This is one of the issues which were recently decided upon by the Privy Council in the matter of *NH International (Caribbean) Limited v National Insurance Property Development Company Limited (Trinidad and Tobago)* (England).

In summary, the relevant facts of the case were as follows:

On 6 March 2003, the contractor and employer entered into a contract based on the FIDIC Red Book for the construction of a hospital in Tobago. The project started during March 2003 and the original completion date of the project was March 2005.

The contractor suspended the works on 23 September 2005 and terminated the contract on 3 November 2006. Various disputes arose between the parties and those were referred to arbitration. The contractor claimed damages arising out of the determination of the contract and the employer submitted various counterclaims in the arbitration proceedings.

The contractor only became aware of the counterclaims during the arbitration proceedings given that the employer had failed to deliver a notice in terms of sub-clause 2. 5 at any stage following the conclusion of the contract. The contractor contended that the employer was precluded from raising any counterclaims in the arbitration proceedings given that the employer had failed to give notice of an employer claim under sub-clause 2. 5. The arbitrator rejected the contractor's contention in this regard and held that "clear words are required to exclude common law rights of set-off and/or abatement of legitimate cross-claims". Given that the words of sub-clause 2. 5 were not clear enough, a notice was not required by the employer to raise counterclaims during the arbitration proceedings.

The contractor appealed against this decision (among other findings) of the arbitrator. The High Court and the Court of Appeal agreed with the decision made by the arbitrator in this regard.

However, the Privy Council overruled this decision. It found that the wording of sub-clause 2. 5 is clear. If an employer wishes to raise claims, whether or not they are intended to be relied on as set-offs or counterclaims, those should not be allowed unless they have been the subject of a notice referred to in sub-clause 2. 5. Moreover, this notice must have been given "as soon as practicable". If the employer could rely on claims which were notified well after that, no purpose would be served by the first two paragraphs of sub-clause 2. 5. The Privy Council stated that "If an Employer's claim is allowed to be made late, there would not appear to be any method by which it could be determined, as the Engineer's function is linked to the particulars, which in turn must be contained in a notice, which in turn has to be served "as soon as practicable".

The Privy Council found that although the final sentence of sub-clause 2. 5 limits the right of the employer to claim by way of set-off or to make any deduction from an amount certified in a Payment Certificate, the words or to otherwise claim against the Contractor extends this limitation beyond the claim against any Payment Certificate. In other words, to have a valid claim for payment against a contractor, the employer must comply with provisions of sub-clause 2. 5 by giving a notice to the contractor if it wishes to make a claim, such notice must be given as soon as practicable and the notice is to contain the particulars referred to this sub-clause.

An employer is therefore well advised to give notice of any claim, which it considers it may be entitled to, in writing to the contractor and as soon as practicable after it has become aware of the event or circumstance given rise to the claim. The notice is to contain sufficient particularity of the claim and shall specify the clause or other basis, including the substantiation of the amount to which the employer considers itself to be entitled to from the contractor. If the employer fails to comply with the notification requirements as set out in sub-clause 2.5, the back door to raising the claim at a later stage is firmly shut. It follows that the employer is not entitled to set-off or counterclaim against any amount owing to the contractor, unless a notice has been given to the contractor as provided for in sub-clause 2.5.

11.5 Claim clause under FIDIC 2017

The claim framework of the FIDIC 1999 Suite remains the same in the FIDIC 2017 Suite, i.e. Notice of Claim; Determination by Engineer/Employer's Representative; Decision by DAB/DAAB. These include:

1. Splitting 'Claims' and 'Disputes'

Clause 20 (Claims, Disputes and Arbitration) of the 1999 Suite has been split in two. Under the 2017 Suite, Clause 20 addresses Claims and Clause 21 addresses Disputes. This change emphasises the FIDIC distinction between Claims and Disputes, i.e. a Claim is an assertion of an entitlement under the terms of the Contract, and a Dispute arises when a Claim is rejected.

2. Employer and Contractor Claims

Under the 1999 Suite, Contractor and Employer Claims were dealt with separately, and had different procedural requirements under Sub-Clauses 2.5 and 20.1 respectively. Clause 20 of the 2017 Suite deals with Contractor Claims and Employer Claims together and the same rules apply to both.

3. Early Warning System

New Sub-Clause 8.4 provides that each Party (and the Engineer, where applicable) shall advise the other in advance of any known or probable events or circumstances which may adversely affect the works, contract price or progress. Here, FIDIC appears to have borrowed from the approach taken in the NEC Suite of Contracts.

4. Notice of Claim

New Sub-Clause 1.3 requires Notices (including Notices of Claim) to be identified as a Notice and refer to the provision of the Contract under which it is issued, which aims at limiting the scope for Disputes relating to the validity of a purported Notice.

5. Claim Time Bars:

(1) Under new Sub-Clause 20.2, both the Contractor and the Employer wishing to make a Claim must provide a Notice of Claim to the Engineer (or the other Party under the Silver Book) within 28 days of the date it became aware or should have become aware of the event or circumstance giving rise to the Claim. Failure to provide a Notice of Claim on time will mean that the Claim is time-barred (i.e. the claiming Party loses any entitlement and the other Party is discharged from all liability in connection with the relevant event or circumstance).

(2) The claiming Party must also provide a "fully detailed Claim" within 84 days (rather than 42 days under the 1999 Suite) of the date it became aware or should have be-

come aware of the event or circumstance giving rise to the Claim. The new Suite prescribes the contents for a fully detailed Claim, whereas the 1999 Suite simply required "full supporting particulars". If the fully detailed Claim is not provided on time, the Notice of Claim lapses.

（3）If the Engineer considers that a Notice of Claim or fully-detailed Claim is out of time, it must notify the Parties within 14 days of receipt of the Notice of Claim or expiry of the fully detailed Claim time limit respectively. If the Engineer or other Party says that a Notice of Claim is time-barred, but the claiming Party disagrees or believes that there are justifying circumstances, it may raise this in the fully-detailed Claim and the Engineer or Employer's Representative then proceeds with the determination taking this into account.

6. DAAB Time Bar Waiver

The onerous nature of the time bar provisions is softened by new Sub-Clause 20. 2. 5, which empowers the Engineer (or the Employer's Representative under the Silver Book) to waive a failure to comply with a time bar requirement in making its agreement or determination of the relevant Claim. Sub-Clause 20. 2. 5 provides that the Engineer / Employer's Representative may find that late submission of a Notice of Claim was justified, taking into account factors including whether the other Party would be prejudiced by the late Notice and whether the other Party had prior knowledge of the event or circumstance giving rise to the Claim. Notably, the Sub-Clause provides that the factors which may be taken into account "shall not be binding". One view put forward at the FIDIC International Users Conference was that this contemporaneous determination by the Engineer / Employer's Representative will provide clarity to parties. This may be so if the description of the factors as non-binding is given full force, however, it would remain open for a party dissatisfied with such agreement or determination to refer the matter to a DAAB under Sub-Clause 21. 4, which may in fact lead to more Disputes being referred to the DAAB.

☞**疑难词汇** ☜

1. Borne out by 被 ... 所证实

2. Set-off 抵消

3. Categorization 分类

4. Delict 侵权行为，不法行为

5. Quantum meruit 按劳计酬，按合理价格支付

6. Complied with 照做，遵守

7. Be precluded from 被排除

8. Abatement 减少，消除

11.1 索赔与反索赔

11.1.1 索赔的含义

索赔和索赔权利的安排与设定是雇主和承包商之间权利义务契合度的综合反应。也是所有国际工程施工合同重中之重的条款。奇怪的是，对于这样一个基本概念，索赔的含义并没有在国际上各著名的组织机构颁发的合同文本中出现过，而且在标准合同文本的参考文献或权威机构文献中很少能找到有关"索赔"的定义。《牛津词典》将索赔定义为对金钱、财产或救济主张权利的总称。严格地说，无论什么时候，当承包商按照工作计划申请他的每月进度款支付，或者当雇主要求承包商纠正有缺陷的工作时，它将是在此意义下的索赔。在施工合同中，索赔通常是在实践中被认为是由于一方违反或更改合同约定而引起的额外款项或时间的主张。这种对"索赔"的解释是由与索赔有关的合同条款的措词所验证的。例如，FIDIC 新红皮书第 2.5 条规定："如果雇主认为按照任何合同条件或其他与合同有关的条款规定他有权获得支付和（或）缺陷通知期的延长，则雇主或工程师应向承包商发出通知并说明细节。"20.1 条规定："如果承包商根据本合同的任何条款或参照合同的其他规定，认为他有权获得任何竣工时间的延长和（或）任何附加款项，他应通知工程师，说明引起索赔的事件或情况。该通知应尽快发出，并应不迟于承包商开始注意到，或应该开始注意到这种事件或情况之后 28 天。如果承包商未能在 28 天内发出索赔通知，竣工时间将不被延长，承包商将无权得到附加款项，并且雇主将被解除有关索赔的一切责任。否则本款以下规定应适用。

反索赔就是被索赔方提出的有利于被索赔方的一种主张，是指一方提出索赔时，反驳、反击或者防止对方提出索赔，不让对方索赔成功或者全部成功。一般认为，索赔是双向的，业主和承包商都可以向对方提出索赔要求，任何一方也都可以就对方提出的索赔要求进行反驳和反击，这种反击和反驳就是反索赔。反索赔有工期延误反索赔、施工缺陷反索赔等多种类型，针对一方的索赔要求，反索赔的一方应以事实为依据，以合同为准绳，反驳和拒绝对方的不合理要求或索赔要求中的不合理部分。

11.1.2 索赔的分类

尽管试图对索赔进行分类是很复杂的事情，但是在建筑合同中对索赔分类进行归纳是很有意义的。实践中，索赔发生可以分为以下几种情况：

（1）根据合同提出的索赔。根据合同提出的索赔是指根据双方协议约定发生的某一事件而提出的索赔，索赔人有权根据合同规定的特定条款获得所规定的救济，索赔受适用法律的影响。

（2）由合同引起或者与合同有关的索赔。这种索赔在合同中没有相应的条款加以规定，索赔人需要援引一项适用的法律来获得救济。所以，如果索赔是有效的，则补救办法是根据合同适用的法律规定，例如对违约的索赔。此外，如果雇主终止合同，承包商可能对所完成的工程有留置权，用于担保根据合同履行的工作而产生的任何款项的支付。

（3）根据适用法原则而产生的索赔。这类索赔是根据适用法律的原则所引起的，无论是针对合同当事人，还是针对第三方。这可能导致在某些司法管辖区，根据侵权法或不法侵害提起索赔。适用于侵权法提起的索赔不一定与合同适用的法律相同。如果索赔是成功的，救济通常是一般损害赔偿，数额取决于案件的具体情况。

（4）因按劳计酬原则引起的索赔。这类索赔的特点是当事人之间不存在，或者即使存在合同关系，但是这种合同关系可能是被认为无效的。这类索赔的基础是个人有权对其付出的劳动获得合理报酬。在一些法律系统中，此种索赔的依据被称为按劳计酬。按劳计酬的原则还适用于，在合同存在的前提下，合同价格约定不明的情况。

11.2　FIDIC（1999 年版）条件下承包商的索赔

根据 FIDIC 合同条款的规定，承包商可以主张两种类型的索赔：第一，根据约定的索赔条款提出索赔，也就是说，承包商可以根据合同的具体规定主张索赔；第二，法定索赔，也就是说，承包商可能根据合同的适用法主张索赔权利，最明显的就是一方违反合同规定，触犯了合同适用法律的规定，另一方可以提出索赔。

1999 年版的《红皮书》和《黄皮书》中包含了大约 30 个条款，规定了如果发生类似事件，承包商有权向雇主索赔。

1.（只红皮书）拖延的图纸或指示

当因必要的图纸或指示不能在一合理的特定时间内颁发给承包商，从而可能引起工程延误或中断时，承包商应通知工程师。如果因工程师未能在一合理的且已在（附有详细证据的）通知中说明的时间内颁发承包商在通知中要求的图纸或指示，而导致承包商延误和（或）招致费用增加时，承包商应向工程师发出进一步的通知，且按照第 20.1 款提出索赔。

2.（只黄皮书）雇主要求或指示错误

承包商可以因雇主要求或指示的错误引起的损失向雇主索赔工期延长，成本和合理的利润。

3. 进入现场的权利

如果由于雇主一方未能在规定时间内给予承包商进入现场和占用现场的权利，致使承包商延误了工期和（或）增加了费用，承包商应向工程师发出通知，并依据第 20.1 款进行索赔。

4. 放线

如果由于这些参照项目的差错而不可避免地对实施工程造成了延误和（或）导致了费用，而且一个有经验的承包商无法合理发现这种差错并避免此类延误和（或）费用，承包商应向工程师发出通知并并依据第 20.1 款进行索赔。

5. 不可预见的外界条件

如果且在一定程度上承包商遇到了不可预见的外界条件，发出了通知，且因此遭到了延误和（或）导致了费用，承包商应有权依据第 20.1 款进行索赔。

6. 化石

一旦发现此类物品，承包商应立即通知工程师，工程师可发出关于处理上述物品的指示。如果承包商由于遵守该指示而引起延误和（或）招致了费用，则应进一步通知工程师并有权依据第 20.1 款进行索赔。

7. 检验

工程师应提前至少 24 小时将其参加检验的意图通知承包商。如果工程师未在商定的时间和地点参加检验，除非工程师另有指示，承包商可着手进行检验，并且此检验应被视为是在工程师在场的情况下进行的。如果由于遵守工程师的指示或因雇主的延误而使承包商遭受了延误和（或）导致了费用，则承包商应通知工程师并有权依据第20.1款进行索赔。

8. 竣工时间的延长

如果由于下述任何原因致使承包商对第10.1款【对工程和区段的接收】中的竣工在一定程度上遭到或将要遭到延误，承包商可依据第20.1款【承包商的索赔】要求延长竣工时间。

9. 由公共当局引起的延误

如果下列条件成立，即：①承包商已努力遵守了工程所在国有关合法公共当局制定的程序；②这些公共当局延误或干扰了承包商的工作；③此延误或干扰是无法预见的，则此类延误或干扰应被视为是属于第8.4款【竣工时间的延长】②段中规定的一种延误原因。

10. 暂停引起的后果

如果承包商在遵守工程师根据第8.8款【工程暂停】所发出的指示以及/或在复工时遭受了延误和/或导致了费用，则承包商应通知工程师并有权依据第20.1款要求索赔。

11. 对部分工程的接收

如果由于雇主接收和（或）使用该部分工程（合同中规定的及承包商同意的使用除外，）而使承包商招致了费用，承包商应通知工程师并有权依据第20.1款【承包商的索赔】获得有关费用以及合理利润的支付，并将之加入合同价格。

12. 对竣工检验的干扰

若延误进行竣工检验致使承包商遭受了延误和（或）导致了费用，则承包商应通知工程师并有权依据第20.1款，要求获得任何延长的工期；以及支付任何有关费用加上合理的利润，并将之加入合同价格。

13. 承包商的检查

如果工程师要求的话，承包商应在其指导下调查产生任何缺陷的原因。除非此类缺陷已依据第11.2款，由承包商支付费用进行了修补，否则调查费用及其合理的利润应由工程师依据第3.5款【决定】，作出商定或决定，并加入合同价格。

14. 延迟测试（只黄皮书）

如果由于雇主原因推迟了完工测试，承包商可以主张相关费用和合理利润。

15. 估价（只红皮书）

如果合同中的价格和费率发生变化，承包商可以进行索赔。

16. 省略

当对任何工作的省略构成部分（或全部）变更且对其价值未达成一致时，工程师应依据第3.5款，对此费用作出商定或决定，并将之加入合同价格。

17. 完工后不能通过测试（只黄皮书）

如果完工后不能通过测试是由于雇主引起的，承包商可以索赔费用和合理利润。

18. 价值工程（只红皮书）

如果承包商提出和设计的价值工程造成该部分工程的合同的价值减少，工程师应依据第3.5款商定或决定一笔费用，并将之加入合同价格。使承包商得到相应的补偿。

19. 变更程序

合同价格应因变更而调整。

20. 法规变化引起的调整

如果承包商由于此类在基准日期后所作的法律或解释上的变更而遭受了延误（或将遭受延误）和/或承担（或将承担）额外费用，承包商应通知工程师并有权依据第20.1款提出索赔。

21. 支付表

如果分期支付额不是参照工程实施所达到的实际进度制定的，且如果实际进度落后于支付表中分期支付所依据的进度状况，则工程师可通过考虑所达到的实际进度落后于分期支付所依据的进度的情况，根据第3.5款【决定】来商定或决定修正分期支付额。

22. 延迟付款

如果由于工程师或雇主原因延迟付款，承包商可以进行索赔，停工或终止合同。

23. 承包商有权暂停工作

如果工程师未能按照第14.6款开具支付证书，或者雇主未能按照第2.4款或第14.7款的规定执行，则承包商可在提前21天以上通知雇主，暂停工作（或降低工作速度），除非并且直到承包商收到了支付证书，合理的证明或支付（视情况而定并且遵守通知的指示）。

24. 合同终止后的付款

在根据第16.2款【承包商提出终止】发出的终止通知生效后，雇主应尽快向承包商支付因终止合同承包商遭受的任何利润的损失或其他损失或损害的款额。

25. 保障

雇主应保障和保护承包商，承包商的人员，以及他们各自的代理人免遭与下述有关的一切索赔、损害、损失和开支（包括法律费用和开支）：①由于雇主、雇主的人员或他们各自的代理人的任何渎职、恶意行为或违反合同而造成的身体伤害、生病、病疫或死亡；②没有承保的责任。

26. 雇主的风险造成的后果

如果上述第17.3款所列的雇主的风险导致了工程、货物或承包商的文件的损失或损害，则承包商应尽快通知工程师，并且应按工程师的要求弥补此类损失或修复此类损害。

27. 有关保险的总体要求

如果雇主未能按合同要求办理保险并使之保持有效，或未能按本款要求提供承包商满意的证明和保险单的副本，则承包商可以（按他自己的决定且不影响任何其他权利或补救的情况下）为此类违约相关的险别办理保险并支付应交的保险费。雇主应向承包商支付此类保险费的款额，同时合同价格应做相应的调整。

28. 不可抗力的后果

如果不可抗力阻碍了承包商履行合同义务，承包商可以要求延长工期或要求费用补偿。

29. 可选择的终止、支付和返回

如果由于不可抗力，导致整个工程的施工无法进行已经持续了84天，且已根据第19.2款【不可抗力的通知】发出了相应的通知，或如果由于同样原因停工时间的总和已经超过了 140 天，则任一方可向另一方发出终止合同的通知。在这种情况下，合同将在通知发出后 7 天终止，同时承包商应按照第 16.3 款【停止工作及承包商的设备的撤离】的规定执行。

30. 根据法律解除履约

除非本条另有规定，如果合同双方无法控制的任何事件或情况（包括，但不限于不可抗力）的发生使任一方（或合同双方）履行他（或他们）的合同义务已变为不可能或非法，或者根据本合同适用的法律，合同双方均被解除进一步的履约。

11.3 承包商的索赔程序

FIDIC 新红皮书规定了承包商向雇主索赔必须遵循的程序，根据相关条款的规定，承包商可以向雇主索赔额外的时间和（或）资金。遵守第 20.1 条的规定对于保护承包商的索赔者来说是至关重要的。

1. FIDIC 新红皮书第 20.1 条主要元素的把握

第 20.1 条要求：

（1）事件或情况的发生。

（2）承包商在其"意识到或应该意识到事件或情况"后，在不迟于 28 天内提交通知。

（3）承包商在意识到或应该意识到"事件或情况"后 42 天内提交"全面有证据支撑的索赔要求"。

（4）承包商应在现场或工程师可接受的另一地点保持用以证明任何索赔可能需要的同期记录。

（5）如果索赔持续进行，承包商应不断更新索赔材料。

（6）遵守合同中其他条款的规定。

（7）工程师在收到索赔后 42 天内的答复。

2. 事件或情况

一个"事件或情况"是引起索赔的关键所在，它是现实存在的，而不是单纯的理论或预测。同时它也不是一个早期的警告通知，"事件或情况"的发生将导致承包商的成本增加或工期的延迟结果。新红皮书第 20.1 条要求承包商不仅要有"事件或情况"的实际知识，而且要在"应该了解事件或情况"的情况下对其应用的客观标准。在实践中，这常常是引起争议的原因，因为它导致了难以回答的事实问题。例如，承包商何时应该知道分包商的索赔要求？

3. 承包商必须：

（1）按照投标函附录中提供的地址以书面形式向工程师提交通知；

（2）在承包商"意识到或应该意识到事件或情况"后 28 天内提交通知；

（3）声明根据第 20.1 条发出通知；

（4）描述引起索赔的"事件或情况"。

承包方在提交工程师关于索赔的通知之前，不需要提供其要求的延长时间的详细信息，也不需要提供索赔多少金额。通知和通知的时间是至关重要的，在规定的时间内没有提交通知对承包商的索赔是致命的。根据南非（South Africa）法律，在 FIDIC 红皮书的背景下，一旦承包商被"禁止"进行索赔，他将无权提出索赔。

4. 全面详细的索赔

承包商必须在"事件或情况"发生的 42 天内提交详细的索赔要求。在实践中，如果索赔事件是复杂的，或者承包商的资源在合同条款的范围内受到限制，承包商可能很难在这个期限完成全面详细的索赔资料准备。因此，FIDIC 制定者注意到了这一点，在第 20.1 条中规定，承包商可以建议工程师批准延长 42 天的时间期限，以便承包商提交详细的索赔要求。

在我们看来，具体的索赔要求应包括：

（1）"事件或情况"的详情；

（2）承包商所依赖的红皮书条款的摘要；

（3）索赔的法律依据；

（4）对索赔要求的金额和/或延长时间的清楚而合理的解释；

（5）所有支持文件（包括现场记录）。

5. 同期纪录

新红皮书第 20.1 条规定了承包商的保持同期纪录的义务，保存同期记录是提起索赔的基本要求。同期纪录必须是：

（1）保持工程师可以接受的现场或其他位置；

（2）工程师可以进行检查；

（3）在"事件"或"情况"期间或前后创建的原始文件。

工程师可以要求保留更多的记录，并可以检查同期记录。在确定哪些类型的同期记录是必要的时，承包商必须考虑那些同期纪录是证明索赔要求的。

6. 每月更新

如果引起索赔的"事件或情况"对索赔有"持续影响"，则所谓"充分详细的索赔"是临时的。承包商将有义务向工程师提交每月更新的详细资料。这些每月更新只需要包含延长所需时间和/或额外支付的任何更改细节。

7. 工程师回应索赔

在承包商提交其详细索赔要求的 42 天内，工程师有义务作出回应，批准；或者带有详细理由的不批准。

工程师有权要求承包商提供"任何必要的进一步细节"，但他的答复仍必须在规定的时间内给出。工程师可以提出建议，承包商可以同意延期，以使工程师有更多的时间作出回应。

这些规定的目的是防止工程师无理地拖延对索赔请求的答复或要求不必要的进一步细节。然而，FIDIC 合同条款中并没有对工程师未能及时作出反应的明确制裁规定，这在现实中往往是一个有争议的问题。

11.4　雇　主　的　索　赔

11.4.1　雇主索赔概述

雇主的索赔在 FIDIC 新红皮书、黄皮书和银皮书中的第 2.5 条（以及金皮书中的第 20.2 条）有所界定。如果雇主认为自己有权向承包商要求支付任何与该合同有关的款项，则雇主必须按照本款规定的程序办理，其中包括向承包商发出通知的要求。但是，如果雇主没有按照第 2.5 条关于通知的规定完成索赔程序，是否会阻止雇主向承包商的索赔要求？这一点在 FIDIC 上体现的不是很明确。

新红皮书 2.5 条款规定如下：

如果雇主认为按照任何合同条件或其他与合同有关的条款规定他有权获得支付和（或）缺陷通知期的延长，则雇主或工程师应向承包商发出通知并说明细节。但对于按照第 4.19 款【电、水、气】、第 4.20 款【雇主的设备及免费提供的材料】的规定，承包商应支付的款额或其他因承包商要求某些服务而应支付的款额，则无须发出通知。当雇主意识到某事件或情况可能导致索赔时应尽快地发出通知。涉及任何延期的通知应在相关缺陷通知期期满前发出。

在细节中应详细说明索赔条款或其他依据，包括雇主按照合同认为他自己有权获得的费用和（或）延期的证明，工程师应依据第 3.5 款【决定】作出商定或决定：①雇主有权获得的由承包商支付的款额（如有时），以及（或）②依据第 11.3 款【缺陷通知期的延长】给予缺陷通知期的延长（如有时）。此笔款额应在合同价格及支付证书中扣除。雇主仅有权从支付证书中确定的款额中抵消或扣除，或依据本款向承包商另外提出索赔。

11.4.2 雇主索赔的实体权利

1. 实际进度延误索赔权

在施工过程中，经常会发生实际进度落后于计划进度的情况。这时工程师会要求承包商修订进度计划，以便能按合同规定的工期完工。在判断实际进度是否拖期而影响到工程按时竣工时，工程师是按照批准的进度计划或上一次修订的进度计划进行判断，依据的竣工时间应以合同原定的竣工时间加上工程师已经批准的竣工延长时间值为准。

2. 竣工时间延误索赔权

在施工过程中，虽然承包商经常修订计划、采取措施，但仍然会出现实际竣工日期超过计划竣工日期的情况，从而影响雇主按计划使用工程，给雇主造成经济损失。竣工时间延误的原因多种多样，如果是由于承包商原因造成的，雇主可依据合同向承包商进行竣工工期的索赔。

3. 施工缺陷索赔权

在施工合同中，一般规定如果承包商的施工质量不符合技术规程的要求，或者使用的材料和设备不符合合同规定，或在责任期未满以前未完成应该修补的缺陷工程，雇主有权向承包商要求赔偿经济损失。

4. 违反合作指示索赔权

在 FIDIC 中规定了承包商负有安全履约、避免干扰、现场保安、保护环境等合作义务，工程师有权根据现场施工情况指示承包商履行此类义务，承包商负有合作的义务。否则工程师有权雇用他人完成这些工作。此时，雇主有权向承包商索赔。

11.4.3 雇主索赔的程序

（1）发出索赔通知。当索赔事项发生时，工程师应及时反应，尽快向承包商发出索赔通知。但在确因工程需要，承包商使用现场雇主水、电、燃气，雇主设备等及应付费用，工程师或雇主不需要发出索赔通知，即可按专用条款中所规定的细节和价值，直接与承包商协商确定价格，从工程款中扣除。

（2）协商处理结果。当发出索赔通知后或发生承包商使用现场可供的水、电、燃气，雇主设备等其他服务后，工程师应当按照合同规定，及时与雇主和承包商协商，如果协商达不成一致意见，工程师可以根据合同和其他可以作为索赔依据的规定，考虑有关事实情况，确定一个公正的解决办法。

（3）通知处理结果。当工程师经与雇主和承包商双方协商，根据协商的一致结果或不一致时做出的确定结论后，应当及时将结果通知雇主和承包商。在通知中，工程师应写明索赔处理时的详细依据。

（4）执行处理结果。如果是雇主有权得到的索赔款额，则直接从合同价格和付款证书中作为扣减额扣除或冲销，或者按照批准的索赔数额以承包商的应付款等方式直接支付给雇主。

11.4.4　雇主索赔程序与承包商索赔程序对比

1. 时效性比较

FIDIC 施工合同中，对承包商索赔有很多时效性规定，FIDIC 合同对承包商索赔明确规定：承包商应在索赔事件发生后的 28 天内，向工程师正式提交索赔意向通知书，并且抄送雇主。在承包商察觉（或应已察觉）引起索赔的事件或情况后 42 天内，承包商应向工程师送交一份充分详细的索赔报告，包括索赔依据、要求延长的时间和（或）追加付款的全部详细资料。

而对于雇主的索赔，FIDIC 合同中没有明确的时效性规定，在 FIDIC 合同文件中只提到"雇主在了解引起索赔的事项或情况后，尽快向承包商发出索赔通知"。在合同履行过程中，雇主什么时间内发通知并没有时效严格规定。

2. 逾期处理比较

FIDIC 合同对承包商索赔明确规定，如果承包商在索赔事件发生后的 28 天内，未向工程师正式提交索赔意向通知书，那么工程竣工时间不得延长，并且承包商无权获得追加付款。同时雇主应免除有关该索赔的全部责任。而在雇主索赔中，由于对于雇主索赔报告的提交没有具体时间限制的规定，因此承包商也就没有权利也谈不上对雇主索赔的逾期处理。

3. 索赔资料及索赔报告比较

FIDIC 合同中规定，如果承包商认为根据合同有权得到竣工时间的任何延长或任何追加付款，承包商应在索赔事件发生后的 28 天之内，向工程师发出索赔通知，说明引起索赔的事件或情况。承包商还应提交所有有关此事件或情况的合同要求的任何其他通知以及支持索赔的详细资料。承包商应在现场或工程师认可的地点，保持用以证明任何索赔可能需要的同期记录。同时，承包商也要向工程师提交中间索赔报告或最终索赔报告。索赔报告要求内容详细，包括索赔的依据、要求延长的时间和（或）追加付款的全部详细资料。FIDIC 合同对雇主索赔只规定向承包商提交索赔通知书，没有雇主保持同期记录以及向承包商提交索赔报告的要求。

11.5　2017 版 FIDIC 索赔条款

FIDIC 2017 版对 1999 版 20 条的索赔条款进行了较大幅度的修改，1999 版的"争端裁决委员会"（Dispute Adjudication Board，DAB）改为"争端避免/裁决委员会"（Dispute Avoidance/ Adjudication Board，DAAB），并强调 DAAB 预警机制的作用。DAAB

协议书模板和程序规则也由 1999 版的 6 页增加至 17 页。与 1999 年合同版本相比较，2017 年合同版本索赔条款有如下特点：

1. 分割索赔争议条款为独立的索赔与争议条款

FIDIC 2017 版将 1999 版的第 20 条索赔争议条款分割"索赔"与"争议"两个条款：第 20 条处理索赔，第 21 条处理争议。这一改变强调了 FIDIC 对索赔和争端的区别，即索赔是对合同条款下权利的主张，当索赔被拒绝时就会产生争端。

2. 雇主与承包商索赔

在 1999 年版合同条款下，雇主与承包商的索赔程序是分开处理的，即根据第 2.5 及 20.1 款的不同程序规定处理。在 1999 年版合同条款下，雇主与承包商在索赔程序上相比，雇主有更优越的条件。2017 年版合同条款第 20 条同时处理承包商或雇主的索赔，雇主与承包商索赔适用程序相同。

3. 早期预警系统

FIDIC 2017 版第 8.4 款规定，合同任何一方（或工程师，如适用）应在任何已知或可能的事件或情况下提前通知另一方，这些事件或情况可能对工程、合同价格或进度产生不利影响。在这里，FIDIC 2017 版似乎借鉴了 NEC 合同条款中的某些规定。

4. 索赔通知

FIDIC 2017 版第 1.3 款要求将通知（包括索赔通知），根据签署的合同条款规定，确定为通知，其目的是限制与所称通知的有效性有关的争议的范围。

5. 索赔时效

（1）根据 FIDIC 2017 版红皮书 20.2 条规定，不论承包商还是雇主，如果决定向对方索赔，必须在意识到或者应当意识到引起索赔的事件或情况的 28 天内向工程师提出索赔通知（或在银皮书条件下向合同另一方提出）。未能按时提供索偿通知书预示着提出索赔的一方丧失任何权利，而另一方则可免除与有关事件或情况有关的一切责任。

（2）索赔方还必须在其知晓或应知晓导致索赔的事件或情况之日起 84 天内（而不是 1999 年版合同条件下的 42 天）提供一份"完整详细的索赔"文件。FIDIC 2017 版合同条款规定了完整详细的索赔内容，而 1999 版只要求"完整的支持证据"。如果未及时提供完整详细的索赔证据，则索赔通知失效。

（3）如果工程师认为索赔通知或详细索赔通知已经过期，则工程师必须在收到索赔通知或在详细索赔期限届满后的 14 天内分别通知双方。如果工程师或他方认为索赔通知过了时效的，但索赔方不同意或认为有正当理由的情况下，索赔方可以在完整详细的索赔中提出这一点，工程师或雇主代表随后将予以考虑并进行裁定。

6. DAAB 时效限制的豁免

2017 版要求在项目开工之后尽快成立 DAAB，且强调 DAAB 是一个常设机构（1999 版红皮书要求 DAB 是常设机构，黄皮书与银皮书都可以不是），还对当事人未能任命 DAAB 成员的情况做了详细规定。DAAB 要定期与各方会面并进行现场考察。2017 版提出并强调 DAAB 非正式的避免纠纷的作用，DAAB 可应合同双方的共同要求，非正式地参与或尝试进行合同双方潜在问题或分歧的处理。FIDIC 希望各方用这种积极主动的态度，尽量避免和减少重大争端的发生。

FIDIC2017 版系列合同条件的争端解决相关规定能否达到预期目标，还有待进一步观察，如：DAAB 常设化、预警机制及非正式沟通将增加争端解决的成本，中小型项目的合同双方是否愿意承受。

Questions

1. Please summarize and discuss the contractor's claim under FIDIC Red Book (1999)

2. How do you understand claim clause 20 of FIDIC Red Book (1999)?

3. What is the employer's procedure to submit a claim?

Chapter 12   Alternative Dispute Resolution

12. 1   Introduction

As we know, the arbitration is one of the most useful method to deal with disputes, the main advantages of arbitration have traditionally been privacy, speed of resolution, cost effectiveness, convenience, finality, certainty and choice of tribunal. However, in recent years, some unhappy experiences in arbitration, especially in the construction field, have diminished the effect of these advantages, or at least some of them, in particular speed of resolution and cost effectiveness. The technical and legal journals contain examples of such experiences which have left some employers and contractors disenchanted with the arbitral process and led them to search for a more attractive method of dispute resolution. This is particularly so in the United States where many large corporations and insurance companies have signed pledges to consider amicable methods of resolution when disputes arise. In the UK, the relatively new standard form of contract developed by the Institution of Civil Engineers (ICE), NEC, went into a second edition with no reference to arbitration as the ultimate method of dispute resolution.

One possible solution to the problem of the diminishing benefits of arbitration which was adopted by FIDIC in the fourth edition of the Red Book, in 1987, was the introduction of the idea of amicable settlement as a prerequisite step to arbitration. Sub-clause 67. 2 of the Fourth Edition of the Red Book provides that arbitration should not be commenced unless an attempt has first been made by the parties to settle the dispute amicably.

Since the publication of the Fourth Edition of the Red Book in 1987, many institutions followed the example of FIDIC. The Institution of Civil Engineers in London introduced conciliation procedures in its Minor Works Contract Form, first published in 1988. Its success prompted the introduction of such procedures in subsequent forms of contract: the sixth edition of the ICE Form and the ICE Design and Construct Contract. The more recent forms of contract published by FIDIC in 1995 and 1999, and that for the sub-contract, also incorporate amicable dispute settlement methods in their conditions.

12. 2   Methods of dispute settlement

Many methods of resolving commercial disputes have evolved over the centuries. The most familiar in civilized societies are: ① negotiation; ② mediation; ③ conciliation;

④ Dispute Boards, Dispute Review Boards or Experts, Claims Review Boards and Dispute Adjudication Boards or Experts; ⑤ Adjudication; ⑥ Mini Trial; ⑦ Pre Arbitral Referee Procedure (ICC); ⑧ The ICC Expertise Procedure; ⑨ Arbitration; and ⑩ Litigation.

The last two of the above methods lead to a solution that is imposed on the parties in dispute, through a court judgment or an arbitral award. The other methods are amicable. They are more popularly known as "alternative dispute resolution" or "amicable dispute resolution" methods, and are usually referred to by the acronym ADR. In this chapter, some methods listed above are discussed in detail.

It should be pointed out that the best time to decide on the mandatory use of an amicable method of dispute resolution and the rules to be used for such method, is at the time of writing the contract agreement. A further advantage of using amicable settlement as a mandatory step before reference to arbitration is the avoidance of any possible blame being attached to the decision maker who proposes amicable settlement of a dispute instead of a more adversarial method. These two reasons were influential in the decision by FIDIC to make amicable dispute settlement an obligatory step to be taken prior to arbitration.

Amicable dispute resolution methods are successful when the parties believe that the good faith and trust still exist between them. On the other hand, these methods are generally less successful when emotions are running high and where the parties have no interest in a prompt settlement. In general, however, the ordinary person is not skilled in the art of negotiation and a third person is usually engaged to facilitate the dispute resolution process.

With the exception of direct negotiation, the above methods of dispute resolution differ from arbitration in that they involve a process whereby a third party is simply called upon to facilitate the process and to assist in reaching a settlement by issuing a non-binding evaluation of the dispute and a recommendation of how it could be resolved, or in the case of a dispute adjudication method a decision that is temporarily binding until and unless it is revised in a subsequent forum.

The advantages of these alternative methods can be summarized as follows:

(1) The parties are in greater control of their own destiny, thus avoiding any of the uncertain consequences of litigation or arbitration.

(2) The procedure tends to preserve business relationships and avoids the possibility of one party being viewed as the loser.

(3) The process is much faster than litigation or arbitration as it could be completed in a few days or a few weeks if the dispute is a complex one requiring the preparation of further documents or investigations.

(4) Arbitration or litigation may be pursued should the amicable method fail to produce the desired result. It is important, however, to remember that a written agreement should be signed by the parties to prevent information disclosed during the process from being used in subsequent litigation or arbitration.

12. 3　Direct negotiation

Conflict may be a conflict of interests, conflict of needs, conflict of opinion or simply a conflict of a desired outcome to a previous agreement. In such circumstances, the simplest and cheapest method to resolve the conflict is by negotiation. Direct negotiation between parties in dispute without the intervention of a third party is perhaps the most readily available method of dispute resolution and the most effective. It is effective because of the speed and economy of procedure with which a dispute may be resolved.

Negotiation may be defined as a process where two or more parties in conflict attempt to reach an agreement to settle their differences and where that agreement is such that all the parties involved are prepared to live with it and accept it. Although the simplest and quickest method of solving disputes is through negotiation, it is not in fact easy, especially if there is a clash of personalities behind the dispute, or if in the parties' opinions there are matters of principle at stake. Furthermore, until any of the other methods of resolution have been invoked, the costs involved are rarely appreciated. In some cases, parties embark on litigation simply because they want to have their day in court; in others the parties are simply badly advised.

Negotiation may mean an element of trading or bargaining leading to a reduction in the parties' expectations to a level which is acceptable to all of them. The reduction in one party's expectation may however be greater than that of the other.

Under the FIDIC forms of contract, negotiation is conducted under the due consultation requirements in the specific form of contract. Under the Fourth Edition of the Red Book, there are many instances where due consultation is required to be conducted by the engineer with the employer and the contractor.

12. 4　Mediation

Should negotiations fail between the parties, then a third party may be called upon to assist in finding common ground for compromise. This process can be either mediation or conciliation in that both mediation and conciliation are voluntary forms of dispute resolution where a "neutral" party is appointed to facilitate negotiations between the parties in dispute and to act as a catalyst for them to reach a resolution. However, the difference between mediation and conciliation lies in the role played by the neutral party. In one, he simply performs the task of persuading the parties in dispute to change their respective positions in the hope of reaching a point where those positions coincide, a form of shuttle diplomacy without actively initiating any ideas as to how the dispute might be settled. In the other method, the neutral party takes a more active role probing the strengths and weaknesses of the parties' case, making suggestions, giving advice, finding persuasive arguments for and against each of the parties' positions, and creating new ideas which might induce them to settle their dispute. In this latter method, however, if the parties fail to reach agreement, the neutral party himself is then required to draw up and propose a solution which represents what, in his view, is a fair and reasonable compromise of the dispute. This is a fundamental difference between mediation and conciliation. ❶

Mediation is only marginally more expensive than direct negotiation, but it has the advantage that it exposes senior management to an independent view, which is extremely valuable whether it be adverse or favourable. In this regard, an adverse viewpoint may enable senior management to separate the people involved in the events which gave rise to the dispute from the dispute itself, and from their method of handling the problems which led to the dispute. The advantages of mediation include informality, speed and economy, but more importantly perhaps, it often leads to an agreed settlement between the parties rather than an imposed award or judgment.

However, mediation has little chance of success unless the parties wish to mediate and have a considerable degree of mutual trust in each other's integrity and willingness to resolve the dispute. Apart from this, the main disadvantage of mediation is that the views of the mediator and any conclusion he may reach are not enforceable. Because of this, the success of the process of mediation depends to a large extent on the skills of the mediator. A definition of a mediator's role has been concisely given by the American Arbitration Association under six headings as follows:

(1) The conciliator, who brings parties together in order to engage in face-to-face discussions; opens channels of communication; and defuses hostility.

(2) The facilitator, who keeps discussions going by providing a neutral ground, arranging meetings, offering to chair them, helping to shape the agenda, simplifying procedures.

(3) The resource expander, who helps to gain access to necessary factual and legal information having an important bearing on the dispute; cuts through bureaucratic red tape.

(4) The interpreter/translator, who makes sure that each party understands what the other is saying; and increases perception and empathy between the parties.

(5) The trainer, who instructs the parties how to negotiate more effectively with each other through probing and questioning.

---

❶   On the looks of it, there seem to be no major differences between conciliation and mediation. However, as the names imply, conciliation is a much more formal mechanism of dispute resolution than mediation. Though, just as in mediation, the opinion of the conciliator makes no difference in the process of conciliation and the warring parties, there seems to be unanimity among the people that a conciliator has more powers than a mediator who is at best, a mediator between warring parties. A conciliator also happens to be an expert in the field in which he tries to adjudicate the matters. On the other hand, a mediator is an expert in the techniques of communication and negotiation as he tries to make the parties arrive at an amicable solution. A conciliator seeks concessions from the parties at dispute whereas a mediator tries to make the parties see their own interests and needs in a better light.

(6) The reality tester, who gets each party to look at how the other side sees the problem; makes each side think through and justify its facts, demands, positions and views; encourages the parties to assess the costs and benefits of either continuing or resolving the conflict; makes each party consider and deal with the other's arguments; raises doubts on rigid positions; and explores alternatives.

It is evident from the above that the mediator is to a large extent filling the position of the negotiator on both sides of the dispute and that a skilled mediator would have to possess the dexterity required in an expert negotiator.

12.5   Conciliation

Similar to mediation, conciliation is a voluntary form of dispute resolution where a neutral party, the conciliator, is appointed to facilitate negotiation between the parties in dispute and to act as a catalyst for them to reach a resolution of their dispute.

Whilst it is generally accepted that conciliation is a non-binding form of dispute resolution, an agreement reached between the parties in dispute following a conciliation process becomes binding and has a better chance of being honoured than an arbitration award. Furthermore, conciliation allows the parties the freedom to explore ways of settling the dispute without commitment until they are ready and are prepared to commit themselves. A party which is unhappy with the conciliation proceedings or with its outcome can opt out and proceed to arbitration or litigation, depending on the terms of the contract.

Conciliation should be used in, or is suited to, any dispute in which any or a combination of the following exist:

(1) a desire for a negotiated settlement which can be approved and sanctioned by those in charge of negotiations;

(2) a desire or a need to maintain an existing relationship;

(3) the need for privacy and confidentiality (this is one of the most attractive qualities of the conciliation process in that private conversations with the conciliator during private meetings are not divulged to the other side and are considered to be privileged and confidential so that the parties can feel free to confide fully in the conciliator);

(4) time is a matter for concern;

(5) the issues are complicated involving highly technical and interlinked problems;

(6) the costs are of concern; and

(7) there are more than two parties.

However, mediation or conciliation are generally not suitable where the following circumstances exist:

(1) there is a need for an authoritative interpretation of the law;

(2) there is a risk of harm to reputation, whether of an individual, a company or a

product;

(3) there is a need to discourage similar future disputes; and

(4) the issues involved are of a criminal, constitutional or civil rights nature.

It is particularly important that the representatives from all parties at a conciliation should be of such calibre that they possess the decision-making authority to accept or reject proposals for settlement of the matters in dispute. They should be in possession of any authorisation required by their company or organisation to sign a document committing that company or organisation to the extent required.

12. 6 Mini-trial procedure

A mini-trial is really not a trial at all. Rather, it is a settlement process in which the parties present highly summarized versions of their respective cases to a panel of officials who represent each party (plus a "neutral" official) and who have authority to settle the dispute. The presentation generally takes place outside of the courtroom, in a private forum. After the parties have presented their best case, the panel convenes and tries to settle the matter.

The 'mini-trial' is designed to resolve disputes arising from matters of fact rather than matters of law and to take no longer than three or four days. The procedure also provides for a neutral advisor who can assist the negotiators in understanding matters of law and assessing the merits of the claim.

The mini-trial procedure was developed by the Zurich Chamber of Commerce to meet the demand for alternative methods of dispute resolution to the traditional methods of litigation and arbitration. At approximately the same time a similar procedure was developed in the United States when in 1984, the US Army Corps of Engineers developed a pilot programme designed to expedite the settlement of claims pending before the Board of Contract Appeals.

As it developed, the mini-trial procedure has the following features:

(1) An independent and impartial adviser is appointed to take control of the proceedings, to act as adviser to the parties in dispute, to ask questions of witnesses, to provide comments if the parties so request, to enforce time limits and to act as chairman to two assistants who may be selected from among the senior corporate officers of both parties and who are expected to make an independent assessment of the issues in dispute.

(2) The mini-trial panel is expected to hear the parties and then to propose or to facilitate a settlement. If no settlement is reached or proposed within a reasonable time, then the panel should submit a recommendation either unanimously or by the chairman.

(3) The procedure is brief with only a few weeks allowed for the parties to prepare their case followed by a 'trial' of a few days' duration.

(4) Lawyers are permitted to represent the parties at the trial.

(5) A memorandum is exchanged between the parties and copied to the adviser two weeks prior to the trial, in which each party outlines its position on the dispute in question as well as all documentary evidence to be presented at the trial.

(6) The presentations are informal with rules of evidence not strictly adhered to. Cross-examination of witnesses is allowed but severely limited in duration.

(7) The proceedings are confidential and no transcript or recording is allowed. None of the material generated by the trial may be used as evidence in pending or future proceedings.

12.7　Dispute Review Board

As explained above, the innovative concept of a Dispute Review Board was to continuously track the progress of a project and assist the parties in resolving any points of contention between them, should they arise. Many felt, and practice confirmed, that in reality the very existence of such a Board during the construction of a project would reduce to a minimum the number of disputes arising. The basic principles, objectives and procedures of the concept of Dispute Review Boards in the international field were summarized as follows:

(1) The Board members visit the site periodically, but at least three times every year, to keep abreast of construction activities and problems and of any developing potential claims. At the end of each visit, the Board provides a report to both parties.

(2) The terms of reference given to the Board provide, as a general rule, that a claim is referred to the Board only after the engineer's decision and when either of the two parties has expressed its non-acceptance of that decision. The first submission to the Board, therefore, should be a written statement of claim by the appellant party, complete with relevant correspondence and other documentation of the appellant's choosing. A copy is provided for each member of the Board and for the other party.

(3) The Board may hold hearings, review the project records and take testimony from the parties and their technical representatives. Upon completing its deliberations, the Board issues a non-binding recommendation to the parties. This review of the dispute and recommendation by the Board is a condition precedent to implementation of the contract's dispute clause. No party is obliged to accept the Board's recommendation, in which case the dispute may proceed to another method of dispute resolution, generally arbitration. Even if there is an intermediate step, if the parties (or one of them) do not accept the Board's recommendation, the ultimate solution is arbitration in accordance with the rules selected under the contract.

(4) If neither party sends a written notice to the other party (copied to the DRB) expressing its dissatisfaction with a recommendation within a certain number of days of receiving it, it is deemed to become a binding decision, the parties are required to comply

with its terms, and they waive any right of recourse they may have against it

12. 8   Dispute Adjudication Board

12. 8. 1   Introduction

FIDIC based Dispute Adjudication Boards (DAB) were introduced into the FIDIC Forms of Contract in 1999, thereby allowing parties to a construction contract the right of having contractual adjudication.

The DAB comprises either one or three people. The one-person Board is chosen by agreement at the start of the project. For the three-person Board each side proposes one person for the other side's agreement and the Chairman is chosen by agreement. Failing agreement, the selection is made by an independent organization, such as FIDIC or The Institution of Civil Engineers, named in the Appendix to Tender.

The DAB procedure described in this section is the procedure from the Conditions of Contract for Construction. This is the preferred procedure, although the Conditions of Contract for Plant and Design-Build include a procedure under which the DAB is only appointed after the dispute has arisen and is only appointed for that dispute. The detailed procedures for the selection of the DAB members are mentioned in a number of different documents. The FIDIC Guidance for the Preparation of Particular Conditions states the important principle which should govern the process as it is essential that candidates for this position are not imposed by either Party on the other Party. Sub-clause 20. 2 and the Appendix to Tender state that the Parties shall jointly appoint the DAB by the date 28 days after the Commencement Date.

The DAB has four main functions:

(1) To visit the site periodically and become familiar with the details of the project

(2) To keep up to date with activities, progress, developments and problems at the site

(3) Encourage the resolution of disputes by the parties

(4) When a dispute is referred to it, hold a hearing, complete its deliberations and prepare a Decision in professional and timely manner

The DAB's role is to settle disputes. Settlement will not have been achieved if a party subsequently refers the dispute on to arbitration.

12. 8. 2   Disputes to DAB

FIDIC clause 20. 2 states that disputes shall be adjudicated by a DAB. The scope of a dispute is made in Clause 20. 4, which is wider than the requirements for a notice under Clause 20. 1.

FIDIC does not define what is meant by the word dispute. The word will therefore have its normal meaning, that is, any statement, complaint, request, allegation or claim which has been rejected and that rejection is not acceptable to the person who made the original statement or complaint. It is clearly not necessary for a complaint to have been considered by the Engineer in order to create a dispute. The wording of Clause 20. 4 states that a dispute of any kind whatsoever may be referred to DAB in connection with or arising out of the contract or the execution of the works including any dispute as to any certificate, determination, instruction, opinion or valuation of the engineer.

A dispute may be said to have arisen when:

(1) A final determination has been rejected

(2) Discussions have been terminated without agreement

(3) When a party declines to participate in discussions to reach agreement

(4) When so little progress is being achieved during protracted discussions that it has become clear that agreement is unlikely to be achieved

12. 8. 3 DAB Constitution

Clause 20. 2 deals with the appointment of the DAB. It requires that the DAB shall be jointly appointed by the parties by the date stated in the appendix. The default date is stated to be 28 days after the Commencement Date. The DAB shall comprise of either one or three suitably qualified persons. The definition of suitably qualified persons will be discussed below.

FIDIC conditions of contract state that that the DAB's decision shall be binding on both parties who shall promptly give effect to it unless and until it shall be revised in an amicable settlement or an arbitration award. Hence the parties empower the DAB to reach decisions with which they undertake to comply. The DAB members must therefore be selected very carefully. In order to maximise the DAB's chances of success in avoiding arbitration members must be trusted and have the confidence of both parties. It is therefore essential that the membership of the dab is mutually agreed upon by the parties and not imposes at the party. This Clause states that in the case of a three person DAB each party shall nominate one member for the approval of the other party. Approvals, as stated elsewhere in the contract, shall not be unreasonably withheld or delayed. Each party should endeavour to nominate a truly independent expert with the ability and freedom to act impartially and develop a team spirit within the DAB and make unanimous decisions. It may therefore be reasonable to withhold approval of a proposed member if it appears unlikely that he will not endeavour to reach a unanimous decision. This reason for disapproval may be based upon reasonable grounds for anticipating that he will decline to discuss matters constructively within the DAB.

Having chosen two members the parties are then required to consult both the members chosen and agree upon the third member, who shall become the chairman of DAB. The agreement on the chairman can sometimes be difficult for numerous reasons. In reality the members may find it easier to agree with each other the nomination of chairman and then propose that person to the parties for their agreement.

The Clause anticipates that the nomination of a one person DAB or the chairman of a three person DAB is mutually agreed. In such cases the Employer normally provides the names of suitable persons for the tenderer to select. A party may be reluctant to choose names from a list of people who have already been contacted by the other party. Experience shows that this process becomes more difficult during the contract when the DAB has not been established at the start of the project.

12. 8. 4   Selection of members

As mentioned above each party nominates one potential member. Often the invitation to tender issued by the Employer contains a schedule with names of potential DAB members. The Tenderer is not obliged to select anyone from this list and may substitute further names which become suggestions and do make the tender conditional. It is preferable that the list of potential names is prepared jointly by the parties. In such cases nominations may be agreed after the submission of tenders but prior to the commencement date.

In the event of failure to agree nominations the provisions of Clause 20. 3 will apply. Clause 20. 3 provides a default appointment procedure in the event that the parties fail to agree nominations by particular dates. The specific "failure" dates are:

(1) Failure to appoint a sole member by the date stated in the appendix to tender

(2) Failure to nominate members by the date stated in the appendix to tender

(3) Failure to agree on the appointment of chairman by the date stated in the appendix to tender

(4) Failure to agree member replacement within 42 days of vacancy

The default appointment procedure allows for the appointing entity to appoint members upon a request by either or both of the parties for such appointment. In the appendix to tender the default appointment entity is the President of FIDIC or a person appointed by him. The Clause allows for due consultation with both parties by the appointing entity on prior to its determination of the appointment. This provision may prove problematic in the case where one party is already resisting the appointment of anyone on to the DAB. The consultation process may be seen as a further opportunity for delay and veto.

12. 9   Arbitration

Arbitration is a private, contractual form of dispute resolution. It provides for the determination of disputes by a third party arbitrator or arbitration panel, selected by the parties to the dispute. Disputes are resolved on the basis of material facts, documents and relevant principles of law.

The arbitration process is administered by an appointed arbitrator subject to any relevant contractual rules and subject to the statutory regulatory framework applied by the domestic courts. There are only limited rights of appeal and legal costs are usually awarded to the successful party.

English law does not insist on any formal requirements for an arbitration agreement (for example it can be verbal)，however if the agreement is not in writing it will be outside the supervisory regime of the courts established by the Arbitration Act.

Arbitration clauses are traditionally found in all standard form contracts used in the UK，often with related adjudication clauses (for example JCT 16，and ICE 7th Edition (now withdrawn in favour of NEC3)). In the last few years there has been a tendency to set the dispute resolution default at litigation rather than arbitration，leaving the parties to specifically agree to arbitration.

Arbitration commences with a notice to concur which provides for agreement on the appointment of an arbitrator，failing which an arbitrator may be appointed by a nominating body (which should be named in the contract). Arbitration is now usually combined with adjudication and mediation in tiered dispute resolution procedures.

☞疑难词汇 ☜

1. Disenchanted with 不再着迷的，不再幻想
2. No reference 无参考
3. Yielded to 屈服，让步
4. Prerequisite 前提，先决条件
5. Extendible 可延伸的
6. be perceived as 被视为
7. Entrenchment 防卫
8. Dictated 口述，口授
9. Embark on litigation 进行诉讼
10. Catalyst 催化剂
11. Shuttle diplomacy 穿梭外交
12. Probe 探索，探查
13. Marginally 少量地，最低限度地
14. Be adverse or favourable 不利的或有利的
15. Defuses hostility 平息敌意
16. Opt out 决定退出，请求免除
17. The ease with which 易用的，方便的
18. Calibre 才干，水准
19. Throw revealing light on 把······暴露在
20. Expedite 加快，促进
21. Deliberations 商议，审议意见

☞ 中文综述 ☜

12.1 概　　述

正如我们所知，仲裁是处理纠纷最有效的方法之一。仲裁的主要优势通常是隐私、迅

速、经济、方便、确定。然而，近年来，在仲裁方面，特别是在国际工程领域的一些不愉快的经历，削弱了仲裁这些优势的作用，或至少是其中的一些优势，特别是在解决速度和成本效益方面。这些优势的丧失，使雇主和承包商对仲裁程序不再抱有更多幻想，并促使他们寻求一种更有吸引力的争端解决方法，这在美国尤其如此。在美国，许多大公司和保险公司在工程合同实践中都已默示的认可了友好解决争端的基本原则。在英国，由土木工程师学会（ICE）和 NEC 发布的最新合同文本并没有提及仲裁作为争议解决的最终方案。

在 1987 年，FIDIC 在《红皮书》第四版中采用了淡化仲裁的规定，即引入友好协商程序作为提交仲裁的先决条件。《红皮书》第四版第 67.2 条规定，除非双方作出了友好解决争端的尝试，否则不应开始仲裁。自从 1987 年 FIDIC 出版了《红皮书》第四版以来，许多机构都以 FIDIC 为例，引入了友好协商的规则。FIDIC 的成功促使后来各国工程合同文本修订引入了这样的程序，主要表现在 ICE 第六版标准文本和 ICE 设计和建造合同中。FIDIC 在 1995 年和 1999 年发布的较新的合同文本，以及 2011 的分包合同文本，也将友好争端解决方法纳入合同条款之中。

12.2　可替代争议解决方法

ADR，即 Alternative Dispute Resolution 的缩写，这一概念源于美国，原来是指 21 世纪逐步发展起来的各种诉讼外纠纷解决方式，现已引申为对世界各国普遍存在着的、民事诉讼制度以外的非诉讼纠纷解决程序或机制的总称。这一概念既可以根据字面意义译为"替代性（或代替性、选择性）纠纷解决方式"，亦可根据其实质意义译为"审判外（诉讼外或判决外）纠纷解决方式"或"非诉讼纠纷解决程序"、"法院外纠纷解决方式"等。由此可见，ADR 机制是一种独立或相对独立于法院诉讼的非诉讼纠纷解决方式，ADR 作为多元化纠纷解决机制中的一种替代性解决方法，与法院诉讼的解决方式形成协调互动的关系，对于社会纠纷的解决起着越来越重要的作用。

几个世纪以来，解决商业纠纷的方法都有了很大的发展。文明社会中最熟悉的商业纠纷解决方法，即可替代争议解决方法主要包括：①谈判；②调解；③调停；④争议委员会、争议审查委员会或者专家组、索赔审查委员会和争议裁决委员会或者专家组；⑤裁定；⑥小型法庭；⑦仲裁前裁判程序（ICC）；⑧国际刑事法院的专家意见程序；⑨仲裁；⑩诉讼。

上述方法的最后两种方法是通过法院判决或仲裁裁决解决纠纷的办法，其他方法是通过协商渠道友好解决纠纷的，它们通常被称为"可选择的争议解决"或"友好争议解决"方法，通常简称为 ADR。本章将讨论这几种方法的应用。

应当指出，决定适用哪一种纠纷解决的方法，并将该方法规定在合同当中的最佳时间是在合同起草或协商阶段。使用友好办法解决问题的好处是在提交仲裁之前避免任何可能的相互指责，以及相互之间关系的伤害。正因如此，FIDIC 将友好解决办法作为提请仲裁之前的强制义务写进条款。当双方认为善意和诚信仍然存在时，友好的争议解决方法是成功的。另一方面，当当事人对迅速解决不感兴趣时，这些方法通常不太成功。一般来说，并不是所有合同当事人都擅长谈判的艺术，这个时候第三人介入的调解方法就成了争议主体选择纠纷解决的第二选项。

可替代的纠纷解决方法有如下优点：

（1）当事人对自己的命运有更大的控制权，从而避免了诉讼或仲裁带来的不确定后果。

（2）程序倾向于维持商业关系，避免一方被视为输家的可能性。

（3）对于复杂的需要准备进一步文件或调查的争议，这个过程比诉讼或仲裁快得多，因为它可以在几天或几周内完成。

（4）如果可替代的纠纷解决方式不能产生预期的结果，当事方可以选择仲裁或者诉讼。

12.3 直 接 洽 商

冲突可能是利益冲突、需求冲突、意见冲突或仅仅是对先前协议的期望结果的冲突。在这种情况下，解决冲突的最简单最方便的做法就是谈判。在没有第三方介入的情况下直接谈判，可能是最容易获得和解的方法和最有效的方法。直接洽商可以被定义为两个或两个以上的冲突方试图达成协议以解决他们之间的分歧的过程，而在该协议中，所有当事各方都准备接受它。虽然解决争议的最简单和最快的方法是通过协商，但实际上这并不容易，特别是在争端背后有个性的冲突，或者在双方的意见中有原则问题。

在 FIDIC 合同条款下，协商在充分咨询的条件下，以具体的合同规定的形式进行协商。在《红皮书》的第四版中，在许多情况下，需要由工程师与雇主和承包商进行适当的协商。

12.4 调　　解

如果双方之间的谈判失败，那么可能会寻求第三方协助达成妥协。这一过程可以是调解，也可以是调停，调解和调停都是自愿解决争端的方式，即"中立"的一方被争议方指定，为争端各方之间的谈判提供便利，充当他们达成决议的催化剂。然而，调解与调停的区别在于中立方所扮演的角色。其中一种方法是，"中立"方只是简单地完成了说服争端各方改变各自立场的任务，以期达到争议各方立场的一致，或者说它是一种穿梭外交，"中立"方并不主动提出任何关于争端如何解决的想法。在另一种方法中，"中立"方更积极地去探究双方争议的优势和弱点，提出建议，为双方的共同立场寻找有说服力的论据，并提出可能促使他们解决争端的新想法。但是，在这后一种方法中，如果双方未能达成协议，则要求中立的一方提出一个在他看来是一个公平合理的争端解决办法。这是调解与调停的根本区别。

调解只是比直接谈判稍微贵一些，但它的优点是能够决定争议解决处理结果的高级调解人员坦诚自己的意见，无论这个意见对争议解决是不利的还是有利的，它都是极其宝贵的。调解的好处包括非正式性、高速和经济，但更重要的是，它往往导致双方达成协议，而不是强加的裁决或判决。

然而，除非当事方愿意调解并彼此间建立了高度的信任与和解的意愿，否则调解成功的机率并不是很大。除此之外，调解的主要缺点是调解者的意见和他可能促成的结论对当事方不具有约束力。因此，调解的成功在很大程度上取决于调解员的技能。美国仲裁协会在以下六个方面简明地给出了调解员角色的定义：

（1）调解人，引领当事各方进行面对面的讨论，开启沟通渠道，消除对立情绪。

（2）促进者，通过提供一个中立的场地，安排会议，并主持会议，帮助制定会议议程，简化程序。

（3）资源扩张者，帮助当事各方获取必要的对争议具有重要影响的事实和法律信息，削减官僚主义繁文缛节。

（4）翻译/翻译员，确保双方理解对方的意思，增加双方之间的感知和同情心。

（5）教练，指导各方如何通过探究和提问更有效地进行谈判。

（6）现实测试员，让每一方都看对方是如何看待问题的；让双方思考并证明其事实、要求、立场和观点；鼓励各方评估持续下去或解决冲突的费用和利益；使各方考虑并处理对方的论点；对僵局提出质疑；并探讨替代解决问题的方法。

从上面可以明显看出，调解员在很大程度上填补了争端双方的谈判者的地位，而且一个熟练的调解人必须具备专家谈判人员所需的灵活性。

12.5   调　　停

与调解类似，调停也是一种自愿解决争端的方式，其中一个中立的调停人被任命，调停争议事项，并充当争议各方达成和解的催化剂，使争议得到解决。

虽然一般认为调停是一种不具约束力的争端解决方式，但在调停过程中达成的协议则具有约束力的，而且比仲裁裁决更加获得争议各方的尊重。此外，调停使双方可以自由地探索解决争端的方法，直到他们准备好作出承诺为止。不满意调停程序或调停结果的当事人可以选择退出，并根据原合同条款或法律的规定进行仲裁或诉讼。

调停应适用于下述任何一种或合并情况下的纠纷解决：

（1）有谈判解决的愿望，同意接受调停的结果；

（2）同意维持现有关系的愿望；

（3）隐私和保密的需要；

（4）时间是一个值得关注的问题；

（5）问题是复杂的，包括高技术和相联的问题；

（6）成本问题；

（7）争议方超过两方。

但是，在下列情况下，调解或调停一般不适用：

（1）争议点的解决有必要对法律进行权威解释；

（2）个人、公司或产品的声誉有损害的风险；

（3）有必要阻止类似的未来纠纷；

（4）问题涉及刑事、宪法或民事权利的性质。

对于调停的参加人，所有当事各方的代表应具有这样的才干：即他们拥有决策权力，接受或拒绝解决争端的建议，持有其公司或机构要求的授权，签署和解文件。

12.6   小型审判程序

小型审判根本就不是一场真正意义上的司法审判。相反，它是一个和解的方法，各方将各自的案情汇总材料呈递给可以代表他们，并可以作出裁决的官员小组。小型审判不是发生在法庭，一般安排在私人会所，在争议各方陈述了他们的情况后，官员小组召集并设法解决争议问题。小型审判旨在解决因事实而非法律问题引起的纠纷，时间较短，不超过三、四天。该程序还规定了一名中立的顾问，他可以协助谈判人员了解法律问题，并评估索赔的是非曲直。

小型审判是由苏黎世商会首创的，以满足对传统诉讼和仲裁方法解决争议问题的不足。与此同时，美国在 1984 年制定了类似的程序，美国陆军工兵部队开发了一项试点计划，旨在加速在合同上诉委员会之前解决索赔问题。

随着小型审判形式的发展，小型审判程序体现以下几个特点：

（1）选任独立和公正的顾问作为调解小组的主席（另两名辅助调解人员从争议公司的高管中选出）。起作用是把控调解程序，为争议各方提供咨询，提问证人，应当事人请求，对争议事项进行评论，把控调解时间。

（2）小型审判小组将听取各方的意见，然后提出问题，并促成问题解决。如果在合理时间内无法达成和解或提出解决方案，则该小组应提交一项小组通过的或主席一人同意的建议。

（3）程序是简短的，案件准备只有几周的时间，案件"审理"也只有几天的时间。

（4）律师可以在案件审理中代表当事人。

（5）双方之间交换备忘录，并在审理前两周将其抄送给顾问，双方在审理过程中陈述其争议的立场，以及在审理中提出所有书面证据。

（6）陈述是非正式的，没有严格遵守的证据规则。对证人的提问是允许的，但在提问时间受到严格限制。

（7）争议审理会议记录是保密的，不允许录音或录像。审理所产生的材料中不允许作为未决诉讼或未来诉讼的证据。

12.7　争议评审委员会

争议评审制度起源于美国，其概念在 20 世纪 60 年代美国华盛顿州大坝工程中首次应用，当时的联合技术咨询组针对一些争议问题提出了建议。但这还不是真正意义上的争议评审。建设工程争议评审委员会（Dispute Review Board，现称 Dispute Resolution Board，简称 DRB）制度最早在 1975 年美国科罗拉多州艾森豪威尔隧道工程中采用，取得了成功。这条隧道的土建、电气和装修三个合同共计 1.28 亿美元，都采用了争议评审的方式解决争议。在 4 年时期内有 28 次不同的争议听证和评审，而 DRB 的意见都得到了双方的尊重而未发生仲裁或诉讼，在美国赢得了较大的正面效应。由 14 个建筑业有关机构和代表组成的美国建筑业争议解决委员会，协助美国仲裁协会（AAA）制定了几种可供建筑业选择使用的非诉讼纠纷解决程序（Alternative Dispute Resolution），简称争议评审委员会（ADR）。

世界银行关注到美国的实践，逐渐在其贷款项目中试用。1980 年至 1986 年由世界银行和泛美开发银行贷款的洪都拉斯 ElCajon 大坝项目，首次在国际工程项目中采用争议评审委员会。金额高达 2030 万美元的 5 次争议均由 DRB 调解成功并为争议双方所接受，工程按期完工，DRB 费用仅为 30 万美元。至 2006 年，有超过 2000 宗国际性项目使用或计划使用争议评审为纠纷解决机制，项目建设总值超过 1000 亿美元。

争议评审委员会与其他争议解决机制相比的优势是：专业性、快速反应、现场解决问题、创造良好气氛、争议双方不需要律师的介入，以及双方最终仍保留诉讼或仲裁的救济途径。

12.8　DAB争端解决机制

12.8.1　DAB 的产生与发展

在 1999 年红皮书出现以前，FIDIC 用来解决工程中的争端的方式是工程师决定。该决定在工程实践中确实起到了一定的作用，但随着该决定运用的广泛深入，其缺点也逐渐显现出来。这主要表现在工程师与雇主的关系问题上。由于工程师是由雇主确定并支付其所有的费用，所以其在工程中的中立性受到了普遍的质疑。自 20 世纪 80 年代以来，在国际承包工程合同中。产生了一种新的解决争议的方式，即采用"争议评审团"（Dispute Review Board）的方式，简称 DRB。DRB 即是 DAB 的前身。该方式改变了过去由工程师在工程合同争端中作为中间人的局面，开始由工程师以外的第三人对工程争议进行独立的评判。随着世界银行 1995 年 1 月将 DRB 纳入了世界银行的招标文件范本，DRB 开始全面进入国际工程项目领域。FIDIC 敏锐地观察到了这一点，顺应了历史的潮流，果断地放弃了工程师作为争端裁判人的模式，将 DRB 引入了其新版的合同中，建立了 FIDIC 合同下的全新的"争端裁决委员会"（Dispute Adjudication Board，简称 DAB）争端解决机制。该机制是 FIDIC 借鉴并吸收了 DRB 方式，并适当加以改造，使之适用于国际工程实施的成功改革。

12.8.2　DAB 组成

DAB 的组成成员通常有三名，一般来自国际知名组织的专家库，一名由雇主推荐，经承包商同意；另一名由承包商推荐，经雇主同意；第三名由已选定的两名成员提名推荐，经雇主和承包商同意，并任命为主席。在实践中，由于聘请此类专家比较昂贵，对于小型项目此类委员会可以由一名专家组成，无论世界银行，还是 FIDIC 都对此有规定。

在挑选 DAB 委员时，除了职业素质外，还要考虑以下几点限制条件：

（1）任何成员不得与争议的任何一方有从属关系；

（2）任何成员不曾受雇于合同的任何一方，没有与任何一方发生过经济关系；

（3）任何成员在担任 DAB 工作以前，不曾介入过此工程项目的重要事务，以免妨碍其独立公正地进行调解工作。

DAB 成员的任命时间既可以是合同签订后的某一时间，也可以是在争议发生后。FIDIC 的不同合同版本，对聘用此类专家成员也有不同规定。一般来说，在实践中，若工程复杂，合同额度大，则最好在合同签订工程开工后，就任命此类成员，目的是使这些专家成员早日介入项目，熟悉项目的进程以及争议产生的背景，这样就能更好地公平解决合同双方的争议。反之，若项目规模小，工期短、技术简单，发生争议的可能性小，即使发生，后果影响也小的话，就没有必要在合同开始时就聘请此类专家成员。

对于 DAB 人选的来源，可以由承包商或雇主选择自己了解的相关专家，也可以寻求国际上一些相关组织提供推荐人选。如 FIDIC 就有自己的争议评判员（Adjudicator）专家库，中国国际经济贸易仲裁委员会（CIETAC）也正在积极筹建自己的此类专家库。在实践中，对于彼此不同意对方提供的专家人选，FIDIC 合同规定：在双方对评判员人选不能达成一致意见时，由 FIDIC 主席来指定。

12.9　仲　裁

12.9.1　仲裁含义

仲裁是双方当事人在自愿基础上达成的书面仲裁协议，将所约定的争议提交约定的仲裁机构进行审理，并由该机构做出具有约束力的仲裁裁决的一种争议解决方式。如果国际工程合同规定采取司法程序解决争议，或者在合同中未提及争议解决的方式，那么，此类争议就有可能通过司法程序，即国际工程诉讼的方式来解决。争议的任何一方都有权向有管辖权的法院起诉。

12.9.2　仲裁协议条款

国际工程合同中，大都包括仲裁协议条款，主要覆盖以下内容：

1. 仲裁事件

约定的仲裁事件决定了仲裁庭的管辖权范围，即合同双方提交仲裁解决的争议内容。合同双方请求仲裁的事件只限于仲裁协议中规定的争议内容。

2. 仲裁机构

各国法律和实践都要求仲裁协议中对仲裁机构或仲裁庭的约定具有确定性。合同双方在进行选择时，如果是机构仲裁，应采用规范性的约定方法。国际上知名的仲裁机构包括：国际商会仲裁院（The International Court of Arbitration of International Chamber of Commerce ICCCA），斯德哥尔摩商会仲裁院（The Arbitration Institute of the Stock-holm Chamber of Commerce，SCCCA），中国国际经济贸易仲裁委员会（China International EconomIc and Trade Arbitration Commission，CIETAC，又称中国国际商会仲裁院），伦敦国际仲裁院（LCIA），等。

3. 仲裁地点

当事人具有约定仲裁地点的权利。在没有特殊约定时，通常将被选定的常设仲裁机构所在地作为仲裁地点。国际工程仲裁中，仲裁地点是一个至关重要的因素。除合同双方另有约定外，仲裁协议效力的准据法，仲裁程序法，仲裁实体法的国际私法规则等都将适用仲裁地点的法律。不同国家的法律对合同双方的利弊程度有很大区别。雇主一般要求在项目所在国的仲裁机构仲裁，而承包商则希望在承包商总部所在国的仲裁机构仲裁，常见的妥协方案是在第三国或被申请人的国家仲裁。

4. 仲裁规则

仲裁规则是合同双方和仲裁庭在整个仲裁过程中所必需遵守的程序规则，主要规范仲裁机构的管辖权、仲裁申请的提出与答辩、仲裁员的选定和仲裁庭的组成、案件审理及裁决的做出与效力等内容。它直接涉及合同双方实体权利和仲裁程序权利的保护，参与方在订立仲裁协议时，应当明确约定仲裁所使用的程序规则。通常选择"按该仲裁机构的仲裁规则进行仲裁"，也有一些常设仲裁机构允许双方自行选择本机构外合适的仲裁规则。

5. 仲裁语言

双方可以约定仲裁语言，一般采用的语言与合同执行所用语言一致。

6. 仲裁裁决的效力

一裁终局是仲裁制度的一种重要的法律特性和优势。绝大多数国家的仲裁立法和司法实践以及仲裁实务都认可，仲裁机构做出的裁决具有终局效力，对合同双方具有法律约束力，任何一方不得上诉或申诉。但少部分国家立法并未确立此终局性，因而在仲裁协议中对裁决的效力加以约定，可以避免当事人就已定案的问题重新提交法院审理的风险，多数国家的立法、司法以及仲裁实践都承认这种约定的效力。

对于国际仲裁裁决，1958年的纽约公约"承认及执行国外仲裁裁决公约"对此做出了明确规定。截止到2007年9月，该公约目前的签字国有142个，我国于1987年参加了该公约。这一公约保证了国际仲裁裁决的可执行性。

12.9.3　仲裁程序

仲裁程序是指从合同一方将争议提交仲裁，直至最终做出仲裁裁决并执行的全过程中，仲裁活动应采取的步骤和方式的总和。各国法律对仲裁程序都作了规定，包含的内容也基本相同。具体包括下面几部分：

1. 仲裁当事人

仲裁当事人指在协商一致的基础上以自己的名义独立提起或参加仲裁，并接受仲裁裁决约束的地位平等的自然人、法人或其他组织，通常指仲裁程序的申请人和被申请人。在国际工程索赔争议中多为雇主或承包商。当事人双方具有平等的法律地位，订立有效的仲裁协议，且将提交的争议必须在仲裁协议规定的范围内。

2. 申请和受理阶段

申请是当事人根据仲裁协议将争议提交仲裁委员会进行仲裁的行为。申请以具有仲裁协议为前提，当事人应当提交仲裁申请书，载明当事人的基本状况，列明具体的仲裁请求及所依据的事实、理由、证据和相关信息，并且必须符合仲裁委员会的受理范围。仲裁委员会收到当事人的申请后，进行表面审查，对于符合条件的予以受理，仲裁活动由此开始进入审理阶段。

3. 审理阶段

（1）答辩与反请求

答辩是仲裁争议的被申请人为了维护自己的权益，对申请人提出的仲裁请求和所依据的事实和理由进行答复和辩解的行为，是被申请人一项十分重要的权利。反请求是针对原申请书中的请求提出来的，目的在于抵消或吞并申请人的仲裁请求，使其失去意义，从而维护自己的合法权益。

（2）审理和裁决

仲裁审理包括开庭原则、不公开原则等，审理中要严格遵守仲裁法和仲裁规则中规定的庭审程序，并做好开庭笔录。审理由仲裁庭进行，但审理过程中，财产保全、证据保全等强制措施需要法院的协助。审理终结后，根据已查明的事实和认定的证据对当事人提出的仲裁请求、反请求或与之有关的其他事件做出书面决定。根据各国仲裁制度的惯例，裁决一般应按多数仲裁员的意见做出。裁决书自做出之日或通知当事人之日起生效。

（3）和解与调解

和解是当事人通过协商对已经提交仲裁的争议自行达成解决方案，体现了当事人对该事件具有完全的处分权。调解方式包括仲裁庭与各方当事人共同磋商，当事人自己磋商并将一致意见告知仲裁庭，仲裁庭与合同双方当事人分别磋商三种。调解必须是在双方自愿的基础上，在仲裁庭主持下进行，调解协议必须是双方协商达成的一致意见。

（4）仲裁裁决的执行

执行仲裁裁决，通常需要当事人在法定期限内向享有管辖权的法院申请执行，某些法律规定的特定情形下，法院可以应当事人的请求，甚至是主动裁定撤销裁决或者不予执行。《纽约公约》规定，外国仲裁裁决具有以下情形之一的，可拒绝承认及执行：

1）仲裁协议的当事人根据对他们适用的法律，订立仲裁协议时有某种无行为能力情形者，或根据双方当事人选择适用的法律，或者在没有这种选择时，根据裁决做出地国家的法律，仲裁协议无效；

2）作为裁决执行对象的当事人，未曾被给予指定仲裁员或者进行仲裁程序的适当通知，或者由于其他情况未能提出申辩的；

3）裁决涉及仲裁协议不曾提到的，或者不包括在仲裁协议规定之内的争议；或者裁决内含有仲裁协议范围以外事件的决定；但对于仲裁协议范围以内事件的决定，如果可以和对于仲裁协议范围以外的事件的决定分开，则该部分的决定仍然可以承认和执行；

4）仲裁庭的组成或仲裁程序同当事人间的协议不符，或者当事人间此种协议和进行仲裁的国家的法律不符；

5）裁决对当事人尚未发生约束力，或者裁决已经由做出裁决的国家或者裁决所依据法律的国家的主管机关撤销或停止执行；

6）依被请求国法律，争议事件不可以用仲裁方式解决；

7）承认或执行裁决违反请求国的公共秩序。

另外，很多国家的法律规定，若仲裁庭的审理不符合仲裁程序、双方签订仲裁协议的效力有问题、仲裁过程中仲裁员出现"行为不当"等情况，则一方当事人可以向有关法院申请撤销裁决或宣布裁决无效。从上面的内容看出，仲裁裁决，尤其是国际仲裁裁决，即使仲裁获胜之后，若另一方不愿意主动执行，也可能面临仲裁裁决被承认和执行方面的困难。

Questions

1. How do you understand the difference between mediation and conciliation lies in the role played by the neutral party?

2. Discuss and compare the different methods of Alternative disputes resolution?

3. How is the DAB worked?

4. How will contract related disputes be resolved?

参 考 文 献

[1] 韦嘉. 国际工程合同管理(双语)[M]. 北京：中国建筑工业出版社，2010.

[2] 崔军. FIDIC 分包合同原理与实务[M]. 北京：机械工业出版社，2009

[3] 吕文学. 国际工程合同管理[M]. 北京：化学工业出版社，2015.

[4] 何伯森. 国际工程合同与合同管理[M]. 北京：中国建筑工业出版社，2010.

[5] 李启明. 土木工程合同管理实务[M]. 南京：东南大学出版社，2009.

[6] 李德智. 公司法新论[M]. 沈阳：辽宁大学出版社，2007.

[7] 冯果. 公司法要论[M]. 武汉：武汉大学出版社，2003.

[8] 本书编委会. 建设工程施工合同(示范文本)(GF-2017-0201)使用指南[M]. 北京：中国建筑工业出版社，2017.

[9] 国际咨询工程师联合会、中国工程咨询协会编译. 周可荣、刘雯、万彩芸、王健翻译. 设计采购施工(EPC)/交钥匙工程合同条件[M]. 北京：机械工业出版社，2017.

[10] 国际咨询工程师联合会、中国工程咨询协会编译. 王川翻译. "生产设备和设计-施工合同条件" [M]. 北京：机械工业出版社，2017.

[11] 田威. FIDIC 合同条款应用实务[M]. 北京：中国建筑工业出版社，2009.

[12] 朱中华. 最新招标投标法律实务操作[M]. 北京：中国法制出版社，2014.

[13] 李德智，刘亚臣. FIDIC 合同条款概论(双语)[M]. 北京：中国建筑工业出版社，2017.

[14] 李德智，赵世忠. 国际工程管理承包商标准信函[M]. 北京：中国建筑工业出版社，2017.

[15] Property Law Act 2008, New Zealand.

[16] Burrows, Finn and Todd on the Law of Contract in New Zealand，6th edition [M]，Lexis Nexis，2018.

[17] FIDIC. Conditions of Contract for Construction for Building and Engineering Works Designed by the Employer[M]. First Edition 1999.

[18] FIDIC. Conditions of Subcontract for Construction. For building and engineering works designed by the Employer[M]. First Edition，2011.

[19] Aspen Publishers. Legal Guide to AIA Documents 2007 Supplement fourth Edition[M]. January 1，2007.

[20] Michael Rowlinson. "Practical Guide to the NEC3 Engineering and Construction Contract" 2nd Edition[M]. Wiley-Blackwell. December 14，2015.

[21] UKEssays . Com. http：//www. ukessays. com/essays/construction/nominated-and-domestic-subcontractor-construction-essay. php.

[22] John J. P. KROL. Construction ContractLaw[M]. John Wiley&Sons Inc. 1993.

[23] Routledge. Construction Contracts：Law and Management (5 edition) [M]. April 23，2015.

[24] Peter Hibberd. Paul Newman. ADR and Adjudication in Construction Disputes[M]. Wiley-Blackwell，1999.

[25] Michael Robinson. A Contractor's Guide to the FIDIC and Conditions of Contract [M]. Wiley，2011.

［26］ Kit Werremeyer. Understanding & Negotiating Construction Contracts: A Contractor's and subcontractor's Guide to Protecting Company Assets[M]. John Wiley & Sons Inc. 2007 .

［27］ Richard H. Clough. Construction Contracting. a Practical Guide to Company Management(Seven Edition) [M]. John Wiley & Sons Inc. 2004.

［28］ Andy Hewitt. Construction Claims & Responses(Effective Writing & Presentation) [M]. Wiley-Blackwell. 2011.

［29］ American Institute of Architects. The American Institute of Architects Official Guide to the 2007 AIA Contract Documents 1st Edition[M]. Wiley. March 23, 2009.

［30］ Dimitar Kondev. Multi-Party and Multi-Contract Arbitration in the Construction Industry[M]. Wiley-Blackwell. April 17, 2017.

［31］ AIA. General Conditions of Contract for Construction. 2007.

［32］ ICE. the Engineering and Construction Contract. 2005.

［33］ JCT. Design and Build Contract. 2005.